Political Crime and the Memory of Loss

New Anthropologies of Europe
Daphne Berdahl, Matti Bunzl, and Michael Herzfeld, founding editors

Political Crime and the Memory of Loss

John Borneman

Indiana University Press
Bloomington and Indianapolis

This book is a publication of

Indiana University Press
601 North Morton Street
Bloomington, Indiana 47404-3797 USA

iupress.indiana.edu

Telephone orders	800-842-6796
Fax orders	812-855-7931
Orders by e-mail	iuporder@indiana.edu

Manufactured in the United States of America

Library of Congress Cataloging-in-Publication Data

Borneman, John, [date]
  Political crime and the memory of loss / John Borneman.
      p. cm.—(New anthropologies of Europe)
  Includes bibliographical references and index.
  ISBN 978-0-253-35689-5 (cloth : alk. paper) — ISBN 978-0-253-22351-7 (pbk. : alk. paper)
1. Political anthropology—Case studies.   2. Political crimes—Case studies.
3. Democratization—Case studies.   4. Loss (Psychology)—Case studies.   5. Government accountability—Case studies.   I. Title.
  GN492.B673 2011
  306.2—dc23
                                                                              2011016620

1 2 3 4 5 16 15 14 13 12 11

Contents

Preface

Loss is a fundamental human condition, simultaneously a process and a structure, a psychological state and a form of accounting, as well as a euphemism for death. It is also the condition of a specifically human consciousness, beginning with an emergence from the womb—physical separation from what becomes defined as a mother—and the learning of a cultural code for cognition and the channeling of emotion, as the loss of an original unity deepens through a cumbersome reckoning. All subsequent losses—of love, life, material objects, and even memory itself—enrich this initial separation, accumulating in a labyrinth of experiences that are then refigured in ways partially inaccessible to our consciousness. In sport and politics loss is interpreted as defeat, often a collective defeat for the team or party, accompanied by a hope that the future might bring its reversal. For the individual, however, loss cannot be simply overcome or reversed. When it is most acute, individual loss is experienced as singular grief, a volatile process of emotional reckoning and ambivalent engagement with a memory. Defeat and grief assume widely variable cultural forms and at the same time resist the closure that these specific forms offer, often leading to the violence of collective and individual revenge. These essays take up the memory of loss and its refiguring in a variety of cases, moving back and forth between the individual's grief and collective defeat, though my concentration is on the refiguring of losses that result from political crime.

By political crime, I mean the wrongful infliction of injury on individuals or collectives by actors or institutions in circumstances they designate as specifically political. In this I follow a tradition of political anthropology that takes as its point of departure how the actors themselves define injuries, the cultural forms of redress these injuries assume, and the social contexts in which they are open to refiguring. I also follow a tradition, shared by structuralism and systems-theory alike, which assumes that "the political" in modern societies with states is not in and of itself a discrete field but is defined in a process of differentiating itself from other domains of life. These two traditions, political anthropology and structuralism, are especially germane to a study of the people in Europe and the Middle East, the two culture-areas in which I have engaged in ethnographic fieldwork. In both areas, state actors and institutions are omnipresent in everyday life, at times causing massive injury and at other times themselves victimized and appealed to for remedies. In theory, then, it is important to remain agnostic about the state's actual location in political crime and not to presuppose that it acts as either protector or wrongdoer.

Accordingly, political crime includes actions that are often intended as threats to states (e.g., rebellions, dissidence, resistance), as well as actions of states themselves that intend harm (e.g., war crimes, massacres, torture, wrongful imprisonment, and other unjust restrictions on individual liberty). Conventional contemporary political theory often distinguishes between "state crime" and "political crime," the latter being individuals or groups who prejudice the interests of the state or challenge its survival. To frame relations as the "state against society" or against "the individual" is usually misleading, however, because such categories considerably overlap and are fundamentally ambiguous. From the perspective of political anthropology, this distinction is not useful to understand the social life of loss. The agents of political crime often alternate between positions within and outside the state and experience life as the oscillation between perpetration and victimization. Moreover, consciousness of one's experience of political crime as well as of other significant experience, is always deferred, *nach-träglich*. Injuries from the past are carried into the present and changed through retroactive comprehension and the assignment of meaning, most specifically through their proposed remedies or modes of redress, through attempts to attenuate losses, to reduce the amplitude of their resonances, and to blunt the inner messages of violation.

It is therefore difficult, but analytically relevant, to ask about the sequence of victimization and wrongdoing in any experience of loss of life or of material objects to which one is attached. This sequence may be represented by the actors involved as causal and linear, but it is more likely experienced as alternating, disjunctive, or cyclical. In this temporal sequence of experience in highly varied social contexts, loss and political crime become invested in objects—persons, places, and things—that make them meaningful in new ways. These patterns of meaning may suggest a compulsive repetition and attempt to return to the original loss or, alternatively, ways to depart from such repetitions.

Ethnographies of Countries and Theorizing National Loss

One mode of anthropological theorizing is to generalize from specific ethnographic cases. The essays that follow rely largely on the two cases in which I have done conventional ethnographic fieldwork: in Germany and Central Europe over twenty years and in Lebanon and Syria over eight years. There is also much comparison with the United States. Although most of my ethnographic data is intersubjective and encounter-based, each of my interlocutors belongs to collectives that both preceded them in time and yet were quite labile in the relatively short course of my fieldwork. The collective to which I most often refer is "country," a term that implies nationals, the states that circumscribe them (or try to) in a territory with a set of binding legal norms, and some meaningful patterns of life which we usually refer to as distinctive cultures. Country is a collective unit of inter-national order, a social fact in the Durkheimian sense—enduring, coercive, and external—with an existence dependent on other similarly constituted countries. Ethnographically, what is distinctive about belonging to a country is that it refers to an imaginary place, a cultural landscape with a strong phantasmagoric component that both informs and shapes concepts of group belonging such as nation, nationality, and ethnicity (Anderson 1998, 46–57).

Of my two primary cases, Germany is the more extreme. It is neither typical (representing the average) nor paradigmatic (exemplary of more general patterns), nor is it necessarily critical (of strategic importance). Because of the radicality of its political crime and the long time span in which Germans have consciously reflected upon and reckoned with problems of loss, it reveals a greater depth of causes and consequences and more attempts to address them than most other cases. Hence its centrality for theorizing loss and its refiguring across time in a particular space.

Lebanon is also an extreme case of a country that has had to confront political crime. Like Germany, it has in the recent past disintegrated—been destroyed, defeated, divided—and then, in some fashion, been put back together again. These two countries are not alone in this fate, of course, but in juxtaposition they present an important comparative opportunity. As countries, they have much in common: both have been particularly volatile and unstable in the internal composition of the social; both have suffered major loss of life and property in protracted wars; both have enjoyed little sovereignty and were recently occupied by foreign powers. They are, however, dissimilar in the geopolitical contexts (an occupied and "liberated" Europe, on the one hand, and a "postcolonial" Middle East, on the other) that have contributed to very different and uneven trajectories in response to the pressures of group fusion or fission.

In 1989, two unrelated events of historical significance formally ended two conflicts: the opening of the Berlin Wall signaled the end of German division and the Cold War between the American and Soviet superpowers; and the signing of the Ta'if Agreement signaled the end of the Lebanese Civil War. I had just completed a study of the construction of Cold War differences in the two Berlins, and I followed this with one of retribution—legal accountability—for crimes of and during the previous regimes in East Germany and East-Central

Europe. By 1999, my ethnographic research in Germany had been ongoing for seventeen years, and I thought a comparative focus outside of the European context would sharpen my understanding of Germany and perhaps lead to different theoretical insights than would comparisons within Europe. Thus, in the summer of 1999 I began ethnographic fieldwork in Lebanon. A civil war had raged there off and on since 1975, for which the Ta'if Agreement of 1989 (also called "Document of National Accord" or "National Reconciliation Accord") provided the basis for a peace. This Agreement was supposed to do three things: (1) restructure the sectarian political system, transferring some of the power away from the formerly dominant Maronite Christian to the Shi'ite community, the economically poorest and largest disenfranchised group (much as after 1945, the power of Germany was restructured—ceding territory to its victims and shifting its borders to the West); (2) legitimate Syrian occupation to enforce the peace between warring tribes and sects (much as the Allied Forces were brought into a defeated Germany in 1945); and (3) reassert Lebanese state authority in South Lebanon, which had been occupied by Israel since its invasion in 1982.

In the European events of 1989 that formally ended the Cold War divisions, Central European governments pursued extensive though uneven legal accountability and, along with other social groups, experimented with different forms of redress for political crimes during the prior regime; also, the Allied occupiers left soon thereafter, restoring Germany and other Central European countries to "full" sovereignty. In the Lebanese event of 1989, by contrast, the perpetrators of political crime nearly all escaped accountability (many even assumed positions of political leadership in parliament), leaving most victims to stew in their losses; moreover, the new occupation, by the Syrians, was legitimated by American, European, and (at the time) Soviet powers, while the new government was altogether unable to wrest control of the South from Israel. This situation did change during the course of my research: Israel ended its occupation there in 2000; Syria ended its in 2005. However, the end of these occupations did not result, as they did in the German or East-Central European cases, in the restoration of national sovereignty. On the contrary, as of this writing Lebanon remains in a political crisis whose resolution is contingent, again, in the same way as it was for Germany in the European case, on an international geopolitical solution.

Although each case deserves explication and analysis in its own temporal and geopolitical contexts, in most of these essays I shall instead move out of the longer-duration German to the unresolved, shorter-duration Lebanese case. To be sure, this way of comparison does an injustice to the Lebanon, which might look significantly different if afforded the same extensive attention I give to Germany and if compared to its neighbors (for example, Jordan, Egypt, and Israel) rather than to a country from an entirely different cultural context. In short, the relative advanced nature of accounting in the German-European event may cast an unduly bright light on the absences in the Lebanese-Middle Eastern context. Yet all comparisons have their limitations while at the same time remaining analytically indispensible—if only as background noise—to help delineate the distinctive processes peculiar to any single place in time. Comparisons with Lebanon have helped me appreciate Germany's singularity.

On the other hand, the ways in which loss and memory have been refigured in Germany, and the relative social peace (internal and external) that has followed, might point us not only to central absences in Lebanon but to the specific conditions that contribute to the intractability of its liminal political situation. In neither setting is a narrow focus on legal accountability, or what is often called "transitional justice," alone sufficient to understand the social life of loss following political crime. Rather, one must consider a wider array of remedies and forms of redress, which nonetheless remain in articulation with the promise or threat of law. In the interests of brevity, I sacrifice a great deal of ethnographic and historical depth, and I apologize for omitting reference to much relevant and important work on these topics. Moreover, it is clear that some of the processes delineated here are relatively foreign to some parts of the world and that the insights to be drawn cannot be applied directly elsewhere. In any case, despite our efforts at clarity and rigor, units of analysis are themselves ambiguous and never totally comparable, and theory can never be applied but only brought to bear or used as a set of initial questions to think more carefully about a particular time and place.

This book is divided into three parts, each of which takes up a specific relation of political crime to the memory of loss. The first part theorizes modes of accountability; the second, the meaning of "regime change" and the American occupation of Iraq; and the third, the mechanisms and operation of democratic authority in Europe and North America.

Acknowledgments

The author gratefully acknowledges previous publication of the following essays, most of which are slightly revised:

"On Money and the Memory of Loss." *Etnográfica* 6 (2) (Fall 2002): 281–302 (Portuguese Journal of Social Anthropology).

"Public Apologies, Dignity, and Performative Redress." Published as "Public Apologies as Performative Redress," Johns Hopkins *SAIS Review of International Affairs* 25 (2) (2005): 53–66, special issue "Pride and Guilt in International Relations."

"Reconciliation after Ethnic Cleansing: Listening, Retribution, Affiliation." *Public Culture* 14 (2) (2002): 281–304. Commentary and Response to Laura Nader, Richard Falk, Richard Wilson, and Seven Sampson in *Public Culture* 15 (1): 197–206.

"The State of War Crimes following the Israeli-Hezbollah War." *Windsor Yearbook of Access to Justice* 25 (2) (2007): 274–89.

"Terror, Compassion, and the Limits of Identification: Counter-Transference and Rites of Commemoration in Lebanon." Published as "Terror, Compassion, and the Limits of Identification," in *Violence: Anthropological Encounters,* ed. Parvis Ghassem-Fachandi, 119–34. London: Berg Publishers, 2009.

"Responsibility after Military Intervention: What is Regime Change? What is Occupation?" Published as "Responsibility after Military Intervention: What is Regime Change?" in *POLAR: Political and Legal Anthropological Review* 26 (1) (2003): 28–48. Response by Kunal Parker, my "Rejoinder," *POLAR* 26 (1): 49–54.

"Politics without a Head: Is the Love Parade a New Form of Political Identification?" Published as "Politics without a Head: Is the Love Parade a New Form of Political Identification?" (co-author Stefan Senders) in *Cultural Anthropology* 15 (2) (2000): 294–317.

"Is the United States Europe's Other?" *American Ethnologist* 30 (4) (2003): 487–92.

PART 1 Accountability

This book is divided into three parts, each of which focuses on a specific relation of political crime to the memory of loss. Part 1 takes up, in turn, the four modes of accountability: compensation/restitution, performative redress, reconciliation, and the issue of retribution and war crimes. What are the symbolic forms of redress? What is their relation to individual grief and collective mourning? What kind of work do they intend to accomplish? Chapter 1, specifically, theorizes these different modes of accountability as events of closure and rites of repetition.

1 Modes of Accountability: Events of Closure, Rites of Repetition

Refiguring Loss and Modes of Accountability

Whether balancing financial transactions or constructing a memorial for the dead after a massacre, individuals and groups resort to various modes of accountability to refigure their losses. In other words, loss is always accountability's object. And while accountability tries to settle accounts, over time it speaks, not to the actual loss, but increasingly to its memory. In modern societies with states, accountability is used in two completely entangled senses: one refers to calculability and explanation the other to a narrative of responsibility and being answerable or liable. In both senses, of calculability and of answerability, particular modes of accounting redress social relationships and refigure loss at single points in time, though the process of reckoning usually unfolds in much longer time frames. Before taking up these modes in the particular cases of the countries of Germany and Lebanon, let us first delineate them theoretically.

We can identify four ideal typical modes of accountability—ways to calculate an accounting and/or to make answerable or responsible: (1) retribution, (2) restitution/compensation, (3) performative redress, and (4) rites of commemoration. Although these modes assume distinct cultural forms, they are available in all social settings to respond to wrongs and losses, and their efficacy seems partly dependent on the particular sequence in which they are used or on their timing. The first three of these modes are *events*, which intend to be single happenings or intend closure; the last mode, *rites*, intends repetitions.

The place of law, and therefore the state, is integral to understanding the distinction between events and rites in the modern world. When accountability takes form in events, it is often (though not always) driven by legal process, whereas accountability within rites tends to unfold with minimal reference to law. For example, *retribution*—the punishment of wrongdoing, rewarding of good—usually frames the issue of redress for injury in legal terms. And *restitution/compensation*—the return or restoration of a prior condition, ordinarily transvalues a loss through substitution of money for the injury, and frequently involves legal mediation in obtaining a settlement. On the other hand, *performative redress*—events of cultural accountability such as apologies, commissions of inquiry, historical and "truth" commissions—though it also makes minimal reference to legal conventions, consists nonetheless of an event, like the first two modes, and therefore performs an accounting that intends to occur only once. The staging of all three of these events—retribution, restitution/compensation, and performative redress—signals a break or end, a putative departure from a particular sequence of actions considered wrongful retrospectively if not at the time of the injury. By contrast, the fourth mode, *rites of commemoration,* initiates a repetition by institutionalizing days of mourning or constructing commemorative sites such as monuments or museums to be visited ritually with no foreseeable end.

Any mode of accountability responds to the tension between answerability and quantification. *Webster's* lists fourteen definitions of accountability, eight of which refer to money, debit, enumerating, or computation—all forms of either restitution or compensation. The emphasis on money is eerily presupposed even in the first definition, which it refers to as "archaic": "to give or receive a financial account, to settle an account." So both etymologically and in its root ('to count'), we are directed to the issue of commensurability and monetary exchange, what *Webster's* calls the ability "to determine or establish by comparison with a fixed point," or simply "calculation."[1] That is to say, legal liability and a narrative of responsibility are in a supplementary relation to counting, remuneration, and computation, or vice versa. A narrative of responsibility may in fact be the "repressed" aspect of calculation, or vice versa. Our central question is how the two aspects—calculation and responsibility—react to and change each other over time.

Early twentieth-century anthropological research in so-called primitive societies frequently took up the narrative sense of accountability in studies of witchcraft as stories of ascribing collective fault and responsibility, of making sense of wrongdoing and attributing causality, but such studies largely ignored accountability as calculation and quantification (Evans-Pritchard 1976). This may have been largely because in those types of society—kinship-based, pre-state or not fully integrated into the state, pre-industrial—the money economy seemed nonexistent or of marginal importance to daily life. Most anthropologists of that time were not studying societies invested in bureaucracies and the rationalization of procedures; aspects of quantification were peripheral to their research.

This avoidance of quantification also accorded with evolutionary assumptions about the place of law, individualism, and modern bureaucracy in society, which

Moore (1978: 82–134) critically analyzes in a 1972 essay on legal liability—to my knowledge, the only anthropological essay to address this topic directly. In that essay, she argues that it is wrong and misleading to assume analytical distinctions between "public" and "private" law, civil and criminal law, or between a general movement from collective to individual responsibility. First, public and private or civil and criminal law are not mutually exclusive categories because elements of both are found in the same individual cases; second, notions of individual liability coexist with notions of collective liability in both pre-industrial and industrial societies—neither concept is prior in time nor logically more advanced. Consequently, she concludes, we are left with the task of understanding in each social formation the specific articulations between civil and criminal domains as well as those between individual and collective liability.

If I am correctly following the gist of Moore's pioneering essay, we should ask, in the spirit of Durkheim (1965), about the relation between different modes of accountability in events and rites, their specific effects and potential substitutability, and about the relation between individual and collective responsibility. And we should focus, in the spirit of Weber (1958; Gerth and Mills 1946), not on accountability's evolutionary development in law or elsewhere—it would indeed be difficult to substantiate progress or regress in this field—but on the particular modes of its employment and the sequence of its enactment over time. In other words, modes of accountability are used most frequently in sequence and not simultaneously. Each mode does particular and limited kinds of redress for loss, yet there exists a restricted range of possibilities for substitution of one mode for another that is contingent on cultural context and timing.

With these distinctions in mind, let us examine, in the German case, each mode of accountability in turn as the basis for a more general theoretical orientation about the refiguring of loss and accountability. Because of the depth, intensity, and length of time in which Germans have been dealing with contemporary issues of accountability, what is often called *die Aufarbeitung der Geschichte* (the working-through of history), Germany presents an extreme case from which to theorize political crime and the refiguring of loss over time.

Retribution and Compensation in Germany

My own ethnographic fieldwork in Germany began in the 1983 in the divided Berlin during the last decade of the Cold War division of Europe. Seven years later, in 1990, the German Democratic Republic (GDR) was dissolved and the two Germanys were reunited. The forms of refiguring loss then changed, for mourning for the disappearance of the GDR and all it had symbolized and losses from the Cold War division were added to the political crimes of the

Holocaust, World War II, and World War I. These postwar experiences of loss drew on the reservoir of experience with reckonings with the first half of the twentieth century.

The standard of evil to which philosophers continually turn as metric for modern political crime at its most excessive and therefore most clearly intelligible is Nazi Germany's crime of the century, the "Final Solution," the attempt to systematically exterminate European Jewry.[2] This most deadly phase of the Holocaust, fully implemented from 1942 to 1945, precipitated and provided the international legitimation for founding the state of Israel in British-ruled Palestine in 1948, an event directly relevant to the discussion of political crime in Lebanon at the end of this essay. It is the history of this set of relations today—between Germany and Israel, Germany and the Holocaust, and among Germans, Jews, Muslims, and Arabs—that continue to refigure the relation of the living to the dead in Germany, and to various degrees in other parts of Europe. There is always, in some sense, an infinite regression of losses: the occupation and division of Germany for some forty years can be attributed directly to its "unconditional defeat" in World War II, and that loss can be traced directly back to Germany's refusal to accept defeat in World War I.

Yet by the time of my initial research, this infinite regress of prior losses had come to be filtered through what is called *Vergangenheitsbewältigung:* the ongoing redress of Germany and Germans for the individual and institutional survivors of the Holocaust and their descendants. This perspective is in large part due to the shock of a historical reckoning with what Dan Diner (1988) has called a *Zivilisationsbruch* ("civilizational break"): the particularly barbarous crime of genocide (state-organized and bureaucratically administered) and its relation to German and European self-expectations. By the time of our current millennium, however, the political crimes of the first half of the twentieth century have become understood as a rupture in German history, radically discontinuous with its own present self-conception, discontinuous with its sense of collective responsibility and with its own sense of the directionality of social change. This transformation in collective self-understanding took place through a series of events of redress, revision, and rectification.[3]

The use of compensation and retribution were the first modes of accountability to which Germans turned. In the last century, Germany and the people who live in that country have been positioned, not primarily to receive money as compensation for injuries suffered or for death, but to pay money to compensate for injuries inflicted. One should undoubtedly begin, not with 1945, but with 1918 and the "war guilt clause" of the Versailles Treaty that Germans were forced to sign and with the crippling reparations—calculated at $33 billion in gold-based exchange in 1921—they were obligated to pay. That Germans have come to see themselves as the aggressors in World War I is a remarkable outcome of memory work, especially since the reason they had to pay reparations was not because of the singularity of their crimes but because they lost the war. My interest is precisely in how this initial "loss" has been incorporated into a new narrative of "memory of loss" that is relativized by the Holocaust and other events having to do with World War II. It was not initially the French losses in World War I that Germans assigned weight in memory, but rather the neglect of German suffering. Germans widely interpreted these reparations as *Vergeltung* (revenge/retribution), and in subsequent decades the accusation of having been "stabbed in the back" was leveled against internally identified traitors—Jews, Jewish capitalists, communists and the like. By the Nazi era, and as Germany pursued victory in World War II, the resentment at reparations paid to foreign powers contributed to a discourse of German innocence, or blamelessness, with respect to others.

Nationally, after World War II, the issue of German suffering was primarily symbolized by the large number of refugees and expellees from the Eastern territories—*die Vertreibung*, or forced exile—as the borders of Europe shifted and Germany lost its territories in the East. These experiences created within Germany a memory of German suffering, of the losses inflicted on Germans, that frequently irrupted in public discourse and served as a challenge both to international powers who either occupied or wanted to punish Germans and to the growing international narrative that the crime of the Holocaust and the fate of European Jewry eclipsed German suffering. However, for the community of nations outside Germany—and a nation makes sense only as part of such a community—Germany and Germans were decidedly situated on the perpetrator and not the victim side of the question of *Schuld*: guilty and in debt to the memory of loss.

The narrative of national *ressentiment* following World War I contrasts starkly with the narrative of coming to terms with defeat following World War II. Two difficult-to-translate and awkward concepts were widely circulated for this new kind of memory work: *Aufarbeitung der Geschichte* (working-through of history) and *Bewältigung der Vergangenheit* (reckoning with history). Within two decades of World War II, Germans had largely internalized the narrative of the victors (which also became a global narrative): that Germans collectively were responsible for the harm they had inflicted, which required active redress, and that Germany itself required an external presence (Western Allies) to intervene, orient, and stabilize internal divisions.

During the lengthy Allied occupation, Germans—and here I speak about the citizens of the two German states—were constantly reminded of how others saw them; and in response they attempted to change both their own vision of who they were to themselves (through changes in textbooks, critical journalism, and alternative perspectives on radio and television) as well as the perspective of non-Germans through cultural programs for foreigners. The Goethe Institute, for example, in its export of language training and self-critical cultural products throughout the world, was instrumental in effecting this change. In the field of journalism, perhaps the best example of this self-consciousness was *Der Internationale Frühschoppen,* a widely popular Sunday morning television news program that featured foreign journalists commenting on Germany and the world.

These activities led to an acute sensitivity to, and unusual range of identifications with, forms of victimization elsewhere. And because other Europeans and Americans came to emplot the Holocaust as the ultimate historical crime, German self-consciousness about responsibility for political crimes led to degrees of internalization of many of the most critical representations of Germans by significant outsiders. The circulation of these representations internationally had to do not with fairness or objectivity but with the extremity of the crimes and the impossibility of public secrets due to Germany's importance in postwar geopolitics.

Already in 1944, the Allied military authorities in Germany asserted the legal right to seize and control property and the assets of the Nazis, and they restored confiscated property to its original owners. After German leaders agreed to the unconditional defeat, the Allies also began to assess individual responsibility, disqualifying Nazi Party members from civil service jobs (Vollnhals 1991, 227–36).[4] In this, they deployed a *sign of collective liability*—Nazi Party affiliation—to assess individual fault, independent of the individual's direct engagement in crime.[5] In 1947, the Allies passed a law mandating restitution or compensation of property acquired under duress (Feldman 2001). The focus on restitution for property losses soon shifted to individual restitution for non-material losses, taking the form of social assistance on a local level for victims of National Socialist persecution. This collective retribution and restitution was redress not primarily for the Holocaust but for damage inflicted during the war.

Simultaneously, between 1945 and 1949 the Allies began prosecuting and punishing war criminals, most famously in the Nuremberg Trials. These trials were restricted to war crimes and crimes against humanity; genocide was not yet defined as a crime.[6] Because the prosecution was of only one side of the war, with many of the charges first defined as crimes during the trials, many Germans thought initially of Nuremberg as a form of victor's justice. With the founding of the two German states in 1949, trials of individuals continued in both Germanys, with many individuals tried and executed or sentenced to long prison terms in both, although many other individuals, including high-ranking politicians, escaped prosecution (Müller 1991). From 1953–1956 in the Frankfurt Auschwitz Trials in West Germany, major figures involved in specifically Holocaust-related crimes were prosecuted together for the first time, and this event has since come to rival Nuremberg in West German memory. Nonetheless, scholars tend to be critical of the relatively few prosecutions of middle- and lower-level Nazi perpetrators and accomplices—judges and doctors, for example—in the 1950s, with even fewer in West than in East Germany. The number of prosecutions for state crimes picked up again in 1957–58, and after the 1961 Eichmann Trial in Jerusalem (which found little public support in Germany), public interest in and debate about the question of responsibility grew, and support for investigations and prosecutions increased. This increase was paralleled by calls for amnesties, leading to debate about the statute of limitations for Nazi-related crimes. In 1969 a general amnesty coincided with a ten-year extension of the statute of limitations for murder (Miquel 2006; Rückerl 1982).

A more active, German-initiated reckoning with the Holocaust began, not with retribution in 1945, however, but with compensation in 1952, when the West German state, in the search for its own international recognition and legitimation, signed the Luxembourg Agreement with the state of Israel, agreeing to pay DM 3.45 billion to the state of Israel and various Jewish organizations, most of which went to resettling Jewish victims of Nazi persecution. What has subsequently become known as *Wiedergutmachung*, this "making-good-again" was a reiteration of the assumption of collective responsibility, and it functioned initially and primarily by transforming claims of symbolic debt into *Entschädigung* (monetary compensation), *Schuld* (guilt/fault/debt) into *Schulden* (monetary debt). Many Jewish groups in Israel vehemently opposed the transvaluation of loss into a numerical figure, calling it "blood money," "sacrilege," and "betrayal [of] the memory of six million Jews who had perished in the Holocaust by negotiating the forgiveness of their blood" (Barkan 2000, 24). This payment from national collective to national collective was followed by other forms of redress (e.g., initially from state to harmed groups such as Jewish organizations, and subsequently from state to harmed individuals), most of which similarly turned moral rectification into monetary remuneration (Lillteicher 2006, 79–95; Pross 1998; Vollnhalls 1991).[7]

Initial retribution and restitution, irrespective of the various intentions of redress, provoked further debate among Germans about the "burden of history" (*Last der Vergangenheit*) or the "burden of responsibility" (*Last der Verantwortung*). Since there is in fact no way to calculate the costs of a genocide, many scholars, following Arendt and Adorno, have maintained that the Holocaust itself was an ungraspable event that continually points to all limits of possibility (Friedlander 1992, 1–21; Giordano 1987).[8] Any proposed remedy or understanding, accordingly, would always be too little, a point many German authorities themselves reiterate today.

The symbolic excess from the Holocaust, that which escapes all calculations of injury and remedy, is framed by what Karl Jaspers in 1946 (1947) aptly called the *"Schuldfrage."* Jaspers assumed the possibility of collective liability for crimes committed during the Nazi era, but he attributed all four kinds of guilt (criminal, political, moral, and metaphysical) to individuals and further restricted guilt in a temporal sense to individuals who were living at the time of the genocide.[9]

Many questions of legal liability and guilt were revisited after 1989 as both an extension of the pre-unification restitution policies regarding the Holocaust and World War II of the Federal Republic and a new reckoning with the political crimes in and often initiated by the authoritarian East German regime. By early 1998, Germany had provided more than DM 100 billion ($120 billion) in restitution and compensation for its political crime of a half-century earlier, with additional payments off DM 10–13 to German-speaking Eastern European Jewish victims of National Socialist persecution. In 1999 German industry, working with the government, began a new effort to compensate the victims of Nazi forced labor still living, mostly Slavs residing in Central Europe (Niethammer 2007; Spiliotis 2006).

Although there were major differences in intent and in the scale of criminality between the fascist Nazi regime and the communist regime of the German Democratic Republic (GDR), the attempt to deal with the political crime of the GDR inevitably drew upon the similarities between these two experiences (for a fuller analysis of retribution after 1989, see Borneman 1997). The most widely publicized attempt at retribution were the trials in the federal courts of politicians, high-ranking officers, and soldiers involved in shoot-to-kill orders on the German-German border, known as the *Mauerschützen-Prozesse.* In 1996, the German Constitutional Court affirmed federal court rulings assessing responsibility for killings, including convictions for 120 border guards. In 1997, former Politbüro members Egon Krenz, Günter Schabowski, and Günther Kleiber were convicted for the shoot-to-kill order and each sentenced to several years in prison. Regarding the behavior of border guards, the Constitutional Court reasoned that even common soldiers, who could have chosen to work on the border or not, should have recognized that the GDR ordinances governing behavior on the Wall were fundamentally in conflict with the International Covenant on Civil and Political Rights, which the GDR had signed and ratified. Hence, these GDR ordinances were not law but a kind of "formalized injustice," and the soldiers ought to have disobeyed their commanding officers (Meier 1991).

For many of the injuries suffered during the Cold War, retributive justice proved politically or practically impossible to pursue. Indeed, monetary compensation appeared as a more appropriate mode of redress for certain categories of political crime such as loss of reputation and status due to denunciation or expropriation of real estate in a prior generation. In chapter 2, I discuss this type of case, where the original condition before the loss could not be restored. Of most importance is timing, for compensation that is seen as inadequate immediately following an injury may be embraced as liberating years later. The point is that only loss to which money speaks directly can be calculated; other kinds of loss, such as trauma, that are by their nature difficult to assimilate into structures of meaning, resist transvaluation and therefore cannot be sufficiently redressed by compensation. That is, the initial empirical loss in trauma cannot be transvalued, but the *memory of these losses* can be. In most experiences of loss, money is indeed able do some of the work of redress, but only when monetary remuneration is supplementary to other forms of redress and when sufficient time passes after the injury.

One question that grows out of this line of inquiry is how money or "calculation" assumes agency in this form of justice in which case the narrative of responsibility that the injured party and the perpetrator might jointly construct is wholly repressed or wholly instrumentalized for purposes having little to do with the original injury. That is, what does calculation do when it is used to redress crime independent of the work of refiguring the story of culpability and its relation to the past and future? Of interest here is the unusual role of international publics, third or peripheral parties to conflicts, whose singular ability to focus attention on and intensify the issues—through access to media, monetary pressures, or lobbying groups that rely on shaming. Such publics are often key to mobilizing redress, as has been the case with Holocaust related injuries; they are often steered by international legal firms who specialize in such injuries; and they appear to favor restitution/compensation as the mode of accountability for harmed individuals or groups. Nader (1985) argues that in international disputes verdicts tend invariably to favor the most powerful actors, such as corporations. In the case of redress for the German Holocaust, however, such corporations have been successful only at delaying a reckoning. Nonetheless, large corporations have had an influence on making popular a particular mode of accountability in that, in the few cases where they are convicted of harm, they tend to favor converting issues of responsibility into monetary damages. In many of these cases, however, monetary redress is no longer a substitute (compensation) for restitution or admissions of guilt but becomes in itself—driven in part by international legal firms—the major goal of efforts at redress.

In the last several decades, especially in Europe and North America, repression of the narrative of responsibility and prioritization of calculation in redress have become a common first step and precondition to the reformulation of the relation between harm, compensation, and collective liability. This corresponds to a growing cultural elaboration in the last half-century in the West, though not only there, of the notion of collective liability, which is increasingly employed as if such liability could be converted into monetary compensation to resolve existential questions concerning the relation between groups and between corporate entities and individuals. Two such elaborations of collective liability are the "socialized management of risk" and the extension of the concept of "no fault." Both are used as principles of redress in a wide variety of cases, for example, race discrimination, worker compensation for on-the-job injury, environmental harm (toxic tort cases), divorce, and personal accidents. In these cases, the assessment of responsibility is conceptualized primarily as collective and not individual liability, and this assessment is made without imputing the responsibility for an action to any particular agent. It is sufficient in itself to establish that someone was harmed in a particular place.

Responsibility, then, is assessed on risk factors or proof of injury alone, without attaching fault to an individual. It is assumed that the individual or collective harmed receives monetary remuneration in lieu of any punishment of the wrongdoer (such as legal trials and imprisonment) or other form of redress for the victim (such as changing the conditions that produced the injury). We might question whether the principle of substitution (money for punishment) contributes to any progressive or "civilizing" process in the making of justice, or whether it is merely the prioritization of a different mode of accountability (from retribution to compensation) that does little to redress the actual relations that caused the injury. On the one hand, although it usually is the case that particular individuals and not the entire corporate body were responsible, monetary remuneration tends to be a transfer of wealth from collective to individual or collective, allowing the culpable individuals to escape answerability for their wrongdoing. On the other hand, by leaving the conditions of the crime untouched, compensation may introduce a new, repetitive cycle into refiguring loss: the creation of loss in order to obtain monetary redress, or the rational infliction of injury where the rewards outweigh the possible penalties. Without having to substantiate that a specific person perpetrated a wrong, individuals or "corporate individuals" can, if wealthy enough, insure themselves for risk against harm (hence enabling them to continue harming without risk to themselves); alternately, victims may sue in court for compensation without having to prove individual intent, hoping for an out-of-court settlement that ultimately leaves the question of answerability unaddressed.

This tendency to acknowledge harm without a consideration of individual fault also poses some peculiar problems for the *ascription of collective liability over time:* with the exception of cases where there is a statute of limitations for specific crimes, collective liability can be invoked ad infinitum. Consider the most extreme case of collective liability for human rights atrocities: genocide, war crimes, and crimes against humanity such as slavery and forced labor, torture, forced disappearances, and racial discrimination. The assessment of collective responsibility for such crimes differs from individual responsibility in that there is usually no empirical end to the corporate body. Whereas individual liability becomes moot after all of the victims, perpetrators, and witnesses have passed away, collective liability continues—theoretically, at least—as long as the name of the collective is still claimed by nature of descent. Since there is no statute of limitations, no chronologically fixed endpoint for human rights violations, liability can be traced through some notion of group descent, members of which inherit the liability in perpetuity. German responsibility for the Holocaust is a case in point, and I return to this issue below.

The theoretical question, then, is what might constitute sufficient redress that would justify release from such a strict notion of collective liability in perpetuity? Insistence on a notion of collective debt, fault, and guilt with no temporal or generational limit functions in a way analogous to the Christian doctrine of original sin. If one is born guilty and fault is assessed as collective liability, then the idea of imputing agency to an individual for having chosen to harm or injure is unnecessary. As Ricoeur concludes in an essay on responsibility, the idea of evaluating "the subjective link between an action and its author [is obliterated]. From this is born the idea of responsibility without fault" (2000, 25). This new conjuncture of relations between insuring against risk so as not to have to impute fault, the assumption of collective responsibility long after the individual perpetrators and victims are dead, and the turn to monetary compensation as a "universal" form of redress simultaneously removes the agent from relations of accountability, meaning answerability, while constructing harm or injury as an objective social fact capable of quantification.

Performative Redress in Germany

Initial responses to crimes of the Nazi regime and period focused collectively on material forms of redress, first for property loss, and shortly thereafter on retribution for persecution based on race, religion, or political beliefs. Increasingly, however, the work of compensation and retribution for refiguring the losses of this period appeared inadequate to victims and perpetrators alike. The more temporal distance from the injuries, the greater resonance of this "*Schuldfrage*"— the question of fault, guilt, and debt. The point is that only after addressing issues of compensation and punishment through the criminal courts and federal government did the demands for more varied responses grow louder within and outside Germany. What remained of the *Schuldfrage* after individual criminal liability and collective compensation had been addressed was not individual fault or a numerically calculable debt but collective guilt. The question seemed to be, much as Jaspers initially asked, to what extent were Germans individually and collectively responsible for "political" and "metaphysical" guilt, which could not be addressed monetarily or in criminal courts?

Subsequently, in the 1960s, many Germans, incited by a generation of post-war children dissatisfied with the responses of their parents and grandparents, began addressing this guilt in the cultural domain by performative redress and rites of commemoration.[10] By performative redress, I mean public apologies, investigatory or "truth" commissions, support for historiography, and local initiatives for return and revisits (or even repatriation) of the formerly persecuted. By rites of commemoration, I mean the setting aside of days of mourning, constructing memorials, and the use of museums for presenting the past—sites of memory intended primarily as provocations to further thought (*Denkmale*) or as admonitions (*Mahnmale*).[11]

During the Cold War, there was a continuous demand for Germans to apologize for the many kinds of injustice perpetrated by individuals, corporations, political parties, and the state. Unlike a confession, or giving witness to a new truth as in a trial or hearing, an apology is a symbolic purification rite that when effective entails, first, a form of self-punishment, an obligation to relive the sorrowful events, and, second, a willingness on the part of the victim to receive the apology. It is a form of paying tribute for the damage done to the other as a condition of one's own future constitution in a reconciled relationship, and in this respect, the apology is an act of care that reverses roles of perpetrator and victim.

Along with apologies, truth commissions captured the public imagination in the period after the end of the Cold War.[12] Employed in several continents, and often modeled on the South African commission conducted by Sir Desmond Tutu, they are a kind of accounting that do work similar to apologies, commissions of inquiry, or historical commissions. That is, first, they attempt to redress past harm through spoken or written narratives of responsibility, and second, they perform a symbolic purification whereby the perpetrator and victim are brought into a relation in which they potentially reverse roles. Some of the disappointment over such modes of redress stems from an expectation that they can substitute for all other modes of accountability, such as legal retribution or monetary restitution. But the mode of performative redress is usually supplementary; rarely could it alone provide sufficient redress to accomplish a reconciliation between the injured person or group and the perpetrators.

For example, truth commissions are often understood to operate as an exchange: in return for narrative disclosure—the true story—perpetrators are often promised kinds of immunity from legal prosecution. But such commissions might in some circumstances do their own work (of revealing the truly culpable, constructing a narrative of responsibility) while becoming an obstacle to punishment or legal retribution. With no enforcement power, they cannot compel witnesses to testify; they have no established procedures to verify or falsify testimony; and the way in which they often gather information might make it unusable as legal evidence. Moreover, nowhere are they funded or equipped to intervene in the lives of the victims whose stories they seek to uncover, which makes them equally incapable of compensating individuals for their material or nonmaterial losses.

On the other hand, acts of performative redress might, in some contexts, lead to individual redress by creating narratives of legal liability. But such acts, including the testimony of truth commissions, are usually possible only in situations where the issue of individual legal or monetary redress is foreclosed. Nonetheless, all forms of performative redress do in fact rewrite official narratives about collective injustice, responsibility, and political agency, and thus have the potential to destabilize existing power dynamics between groups. This more limited contribution is not negligible, for any departure from violence between groups within a society requires such narratives in order to initiate long-term processes of reconciliation.

Although intended as single events that will provide a sense of an end, acts of performative redress can also be given institutional form as admonishments for the future. In such cases, a rite of closure can become an ongoing ritual such as a rite of commemoration.

Rites of Commemoration in Germany

Rites of commemoration, our fourth mode of accountability, include the construction of memorials or museums with permanent themes or displays and the setting aside of ritual days for mourning or celebration. These rites usually follow the employment of one or more of the other modes discussed above, and they are distinctive in one respect: their aim is to establish an ongoing ritualized dialectic between past and present. By contrast, *events of accountability*—retribution, restitution/compensation, and performative redress—set up a dialectic between future and past, thereby seeking to liberate the present from the past so as to prevent a repetition.

The German case speaks directly to three relatively neglected aspects of commemorative rites. First, they are to operate ad infinitum, after the perpetrators are dead and the question of individual fault and debt, of collective remuneration and individual redress, are no longer relevant. Hence, even though in their formative stages commemorative rites may merely arise to mark individual or collective loss at a particular time, they tend to become issues of the inheritance of collective accountability across generations.

Second, such rites may at any point in time provoke a new search for retribution, restitution/compensation, or performative redress, negating prior events of closure and leading to demands for additional rites of commemoration or even additional events. In other words, they can initiate a repetition.

Third, commemorative rites, while usually categorized as about mourning, are analytically quite the opposite in that they reverse the direction of the relation to the past and therefore differ fundamentally in ways of addressing the dead. In a short and remarkably perceptive passage on time in "The Savage Mind," Levi-Strauss draws our attention to the fact that rites of mourning transport the present into the past. By contrast, commemorative rites "transport the past into the present. [They] recreate the sacred and beneficent atmosphere of mythical times—a 'dream' age . . . and mirror their protagonists and their high deeds" (Levi-Strauss 1966, 314). The purpose of commemoration in transporting the past into the present is clearly to secure a seamless repetition of that past (albeit in a transformed state and context); the revisit is a phantasy of unregistered loss and unbroken unity with ancestors in a mythical time. By contrast, mourning, he argues, goes in the opposite direction, seeking to return to the past rather than to bring the past into the present. Mourning rites "guarantee that men who are no longer among the living will be converted into ancestors" (314).

The implication is that, whereas commemoration keeps the past alive by incorporating the dead into a myth in the tragic mode, mourning rites— conversion of the dead into ancestors—constitute an efficacious overcoming of the dead's hold on us by taking us back to a past that is acknowledged as separate from our own time. From this perspective, the dead are an irrevocable loss that, if converted into ancestors in this mourning rite, promise us a type of closure. Mourning, therefore, is not a commemorative rite that secures a repetition of the past in the analytic sense discussed above but consists of events that enable a departure from it.

This difference between mourning as events of accountability and commemoration as rites of repetition recalls the Freudian distinction between mourning and melancholy (Freud 1917). Mourning, as he defined it, is the "reaction to the loss of a loved person, or to the loss of some abstraction which as taken the place of one" (1917, 243). It entails letting go of the lost person, object, or event, to allow for the development of a self worthy of life and new attachments. Melancholy, which grows out of the same loss, is a reaction of self-reproach that keeps the dead alive, entailing a refusal to acknowledge the loss as irrevocable and therefore foreclosing new attachments. While this distinction has proven immensely productive theoretically, there are, as many scholars have maintained, different degrees of letting go and holding on and therefore a large range of grieving practices partaking of both of these two poles. Much subsequent research has questioned Freud's assumption of the health of a narcissistic ego that needs to overcome loss and has therefore questioned the very possibility and desirability of exchanging one loved object for another. Moreover, the presence of ghosts, djinns, and spirits across cultures makes it doubtful that the conversion of the dead into ancestors is ever complete or permanent and suggests that mourning work involves a third subject. It requires the mediation of another relationship, even one with a phantasmatic figure. Along these lines, mourning rites could be seen as Sisyphean: stalling devices that attempt to prevent the fairly inevitable return of a mythical past in the future. If mourning rites in fact intend to release us from the past, so the argument goes, they most frequently fail to effect this transformation. Commemorative rites take into account this failure in advance, displacing the struggle from *whether* to commemorate to one over the *form* commemoration should take, that is, the form in which the past returns.

Nonetheless, it is worth asking what more or less efficacious conversions of the dead into ancestors might look like, and if some forms of revisiting the past are more transformative and more open to futures than others. For one, an effective conversion of the dead into ancestors does not mean that the attachments to the dead and lost objects leave no traces, a point that Freud addressed and clarified in his later work. In *The Ego and the Id* (1923, 29), for example, Freud explicitly insisted on the permanent traces left by losses, a point Laplanche (1999) has made central to his work on Otherness. Freud (1923, 29) conceptualized the healthy ego not merely as an autonomous object free to love but as always "a precipitate of abandoned object-cathexes." In short, our losses remain with us as internal objects, which, in the case of melancholy, leads to an identification with the dead. The lost person is then "transformed into an ego-loss" (Freud 1917, 249), which leads either to a reaction of reproach directed at oneself (depression) or, alternatively, to mania, assertions of victory over the loss without adequately understanding what it is one has lost.

The question, therefore, always turns around the kinds of attachments to lost objects once grieving begins. In an effective mourning, the spirit of the dead— the affect of our past attachment—is incorporated into our ego in a way that does not attack it but nonetheless changes the understanding of our own temporal existence; the dead in this vision occupy a lost world in which we no longer live and which we have abandoned. The presence of the dead would be remembered as ancestral, prior in time, and not invoked as a living fetish—creating illusions of a determinative presence inherent in the lost objects of our attachment. We would not, then, attribute causality to the dead as specters outside ourselves, but we would nonetheless admit their power over us, which arises solely from our internal reckoning with the experience of loss and the feelings of powerlessness and abandonment that accompany it.

Because of the private nature of grief and its significance for the individual's outlook on the future, events of mourning and commemorative rites take on special importance among the modes of accountability discussed above. Germans necessarily turned to these events and rites as part of a relatively delayed reckoning with individual responsibility for World War II and the Holocaust. The initial reckoning, as I have argued above, was imposed from without—collective defeat, occupation, division of Germany into zones, and denial of national sovereignty. These measures nonetheless found resonance among many Germans, from politicians to journalists to intellectuals to private citizens. Externally imposed measures of accountability functioned as a stimulus to citizens to debate the meaning of a narrative of responsibility for political crime and also undoubtedly mitigated for some Germans extreme forms of internally imposed punishments. That is, although the legal retribution, restitution, and monetary reparations in the early postwar period followed the Allied leads, Germans themselves initiated events of performative redress and rites of commemoration. If the former events were largely the response, often reluctant, of a generation of actual participants and witnesses of the war and the Holocaust, performative redress and commemorative rites were largely the response of a generation who were either children at the time of the crimes or were born after the events. For both generations, the experience of collective defeat contributed to a consciousness of collective accountability, which in turn led to the insistence on a break with the past and the necessity of a self-transformation at the group level concerning the nature of *Deutschsein* (Borneman 2002a, 173–94).

This self-transformation was highly ambivalent and conflictual and was accompanied by individual and collective resistance, but as each mode of accountability was tried, the forms of addressing the past kept refiguring initial losses—both those suffered and those inflicted on others—and therefore what it means to be a subject of Germany. Over time, the emphasis of accountability shifted from one of calculation of debt to a narrative of responsibility—and that at the level of collective guilt. Early retribution, compensation, as well as Chancellor Willy Brandt's apology in 1970 and much critical historiography reframed this narrative, often radically. Brandt's act of performative redress was eventually transformed into a commemorative practice; it now plays continuously in a looped video recording inside the German Historical Museum in Berlin, alongside recordings of other famous events in twentieth-century German history such as scenes of Nazi death camps and both the building and the opening of the Berlin Wall. Moreover, the apology is repeatedly invoked in other milieu, in books and TV talk shows, and now all German heads of state acknowledge at some point in their careers that crimes were committed *"im Namen Deutschlands"* for which the collective is responsible. Even Chancellor of Unity Helmut Kohl, who had coined the clever phrase *"Gnade der späten Geburt"* (lucky to have been born late) to indicate his lack of individual fault by having been born too late to be complicitous with the Nazis, reiterated the phrase *"im Namen Deutschlands"* in a visit to Yad Vashem in Jerusalem in the late 1980s.

Distinctive about this kind of performative redress-cum-commemoration is that it involves a critique of one's own group's relation to others, a radical demythologization of the tragic mode of history. In principle, it is a commemoration that is anti-commemorative in spirit. It intends a radical break with the past by converting those one unjustly killed into one's own ancestors. In this, Brandt set up a dialectic between present and past that was oriented to a refiguring of the future relations between the countries Poland and Germany.

Yet this is only part of the story. Elsewhere I have amended the well-known argument put forward by Alexander and Margarete Mitscherlich (1975) that after the war Germans were unable to mourn—meaning, in their terms, unable to begin an emotional accounting of their losses. I argued that its seems as if this thesis applies less to private than to public mourning or collective displays of grief, which were indeed absent from most German life (Borneman 2004b). This initial absence of public mourning and therefore truncated nature of the grieving process is significant for understanding the relatively delayed and extensive response of public commemoration in the present. This extensive response can be seen as a manic defense to what Melanie Klein (1940) has called the "depressive position." The anxiety over loss and the collapse of the inner world that accompanied German defeat was in some sense repressed in the 1950s and, as the Mitscherlichs argued, was compensated for by an investment in work and the material rebuilding that initiated the "economic miracle." Economic recovery and growth was surely experienced as a triumph over the shame for the Nazi period—particularly for the self-mobilization for eugenics projects, internal cleansings, and the destruction of war. Yet, as Klein would put it, the fear of the unchecked growth of and persecution by the "bad" internal objects (threatening, frustrating, punitive, persecutory) of the recent past continued, driven both by the importance of judgments of external authorities (e.g., the Allied occupiers) and by an internal struggle between remembering and repressing. The fear of being overwhelmed by this darkness was accompanied by a pining for the lost "good" objects (nurturing, loving, caring, comforting), and the relative absence of these "good" objects—of unadulterated feelings of love, security, comfort, and ties to a positive history—led to an idealization of the losses and the manic defense expressed in the multiplication of public commemoration.

Indeed, Germany in the early twenty-first century has become a country full of commemorative sites of the Holocaust and the Nazi period of varied purposes and effects, a point James Young (1994) made in a pioneering survey of such sites. The capital city of Berlin, called "capital of remorse" (*Hauptstadt der Reue*) by Germany's newspaper of record (Schuller 1996), is particularly dense with such sites—they are everywhere, in every district of the city, on streets, in front of many private homes and public buildings—and they take many forms.[13] Their creation began in the 1970s, expanded in the 1980s, and proliferated in the 1990s as the capital was moved from the provincial town of Bonn to the cosmopolitan city of Berlin (Borneman 1998a; Borneman and Bude 1999). The most unusual of the sites are those that deal with injuries that resist redress through the first three modes of accountability (retribution, retribution/compensation, and performative redress). They intend to go beyond rational understanding and to make representable events that resist comprehension. Among the most unique responses is the permanent memorialization of the Nazi death camps—Birkenau, Auschwitz, Bergen-Belsen, Dachau, Treblinka, Sachsenhausen, and others—all envisioned by their planners as temporary constructions, as labor camps and/or places to eliminate the Jews and other persecuted groups. After the war, however, these camps were eventually, without plan or foresight, turned into what Pierre Nora (1997) famously calls *lieux de mémoire,* sites of collective memory and identification to which one continually returns and which one transforms. Their permanence is now largely assumed by both Germans and the international community (Ryback 1993). Their intended effect is not to restrict the damage of loss, however, but to generalize its memory and make it permanent through collective identification.

Yet even if it were possible and desirable to guarantee the permanence of a memory, memorialization has certain predictable but unintended perlocutionary effects, temporal consequences outside the purview of those initiating this mode of accounting. For one, since no particular cultural form can enclose or contain or even adequately represent memory of loss (given the multiplicity of perspectives and interests), there is a dynamic of proliferating memorials and commemorative events, each intended to give another expression to those inassimilable memory traces that speak the language of the memory of loss. This dynamic coincides with and is inseparable from a social process of generational differentiation and the transmission of generational accounting, from memory of a direct experience of events to an increasingly distanced, socially mediated one.

Suffice it to say here that Nora's analysis of sites or realms of memory contains a very underdeveloped theory of mourning over time, of exactly how one can revisit the dead or lost relationships and objects in a way that also opens one to new objects of attachment. To be sure, *lieux de mémoire,* predicated on the rupture of modernity itself in memory work, has a different intent: it seeks to recover and protect national memory through a critical historiography that reconstructs its sites and controversies. This reconstruction of national memory may facilitate a critical refiguring of the relation of past to present, but it does little mourning work in the conventional sense of the term: orienting the dialectic of past and present to an openness to future attachments.

Nora's commemorative approach might be usefully contrasted with the mourning work accomplished in the writing of W. G. Sebald (2000), a German of the second postwar generation who decided to live abroad. We might call his form of memory work "associative temporalities." Unlike Nora's critical concern for a chronological, objectifiable, empirically locatable memory that historicizes collective national-cultural sites, Sebald instead sees the tracking of memory across cultural groups as a moral imperative for each individual. For him, memory work is always individual, always in some kind of oppositional relation to institutionalized collective memory; it is a painful, elusive, and very personal search for the collective elisions in memory, a search for a *Zeitheimat,* an imagined temporal home that is neither fixed nor perhaps possible to find.

This temporal home Sebald finds in unplanned encounters with various lost worlds—of Jews, immigrants, victims of violence, the dead and their objects. These encounters are of an unspecifiable duration, and it is uncertain what actual objects, persons, or histories will be found. Personal engagement is not with historically constructed genealogies of social conflict and tension, as in Nora's project, but with an admittedly flawed collective memory. Experience is narrated through and about an Other and never merely a reflection on one's own past. Often it is experience itself that is "lost"—more specifically, an experience that is felt to have been withheld. His approach to memory offers not the personal or collective redemption of a "site of memory" but responsibility for the past in the unsettling process of a highly individual encounter with a collective liability.

While Sebald's project in memory may produce a more nuanced personal reckoning with loss, associative temporalities do not offer redemption or social unity of a sort that Nora's project does. Neither astute and planned commemoration nor intensive mourning has released members of the second generation of postwar Germans from the responsibility for political crime that preceded them in time. Collective guilt, apparently, cannot be discharged through any empirical practice, for some part of the symbolic excess of political crime remains to speak a language of memory of loss from a seemingly inaccessible and secure position.

But *Schuld* is also unstable, and subject to a history of transvaluation. My final question here is, after more than a half-century of deployment of modes of accountability, by what metric do we assess the effect of the proliferation of commemorative sites on this collective debt? The most frequent argument made is that monuments keep debate, and hence consciousness of the loss, in the public sphere; they prevent forgetting. Stated succinctly most recently by Peter Carrier (2005, 228) in a consideration of Holocaust monuments in Germany and France: "The real monument is not the stone object but the debate itself." This monument and "the debate itself," or "complex dialogue," as he concludes (230), operates in many registers—aesthetic, political, cultural, and historical; it is significant as a "non-prescriptive heuristic stimuli that enable individuals to encounter and understand both the past and their relation to the past via representations of it." But the question of commemorative sites such as this is not only about our relation to the past but also about how that past relates to our future. Commemoration, in this sense, is not about fixing memory but about contemporizing it to prevent a repetition though a continual *Auseinandersetzung* (taking apart/putting back together, debate/dialogue) with the crime and the loss perpetrated and incurred. To honor the dead and preserve their memory serves also to admonish us about the future. This explains the importance of the paroles "Never again" and "Never forget."

The question of the meaning of debate presented itself in an exemplary fashion in the planning, building, and use of the Holocaust Monument in Berlin, which I followed closely from the time of its initial proposal in 1988 through its completion in 2004 (see Young 2002). Today, hardly any visitor to Berlin misses this monument: an undulating labyrinth of stone plinths. Officially called the "Monument for the Murdered Jews of Europe," it was built on a piece of ground the size of a football field (204,440 sq. ft.), adjacent to the Brandenburger Tor on Unter den Linden, the gate rich with political significance that most recently comprised part of the Wall that divided East and West. It is a three-minute walk to the Reichstag, the seat of parliament, and it sits above Josef Goebbel's former bunker very close to the discretely marked "Hitlerbunker" where Hitler committed suicide. In other words, this memorial is not just in any place but is on symbolically condensed ground, a prototypical *lieux de mémoire*.

The history of debate around the memorial has been well documented and publicized (Carrier 2005: 99–153). It began in 1988 with a citizen initiative headed by a German journalist and activist, Lea Rosh, whose mimetic identification with Jews led her to change her name (from Edith to the more Jewish-sounding Lea) and to cultivate a Semitic profile so convincing that people in Berlin have often asked me, assuming I should know such things, if she is Jewish (she is not). After several architecture competitions and a ten-year delay, a jury chose the New York architect Peter Eisenman's mega-design of a field full of uniformly placed giant concrete columns, each one a unique shape and size.

During the competition on its design and in parliamentary debate, discussion focused primarily on whether the monument should be mammoth in size or

more modest in scale and whether it should commemorate only Jews or all victims of the Holocaust. Among my very diverse acquaintances over two decades
of fieldwork in Berlin, many commented critically about the monument, but
no one dared to make such comments in public for fear of being accused of
anti-Semitism. Nonetheless, the idea of the monument periodically erupted in
debates in the televisual and print media.

Today the Holocaust Monument, along with the "Topography of Terror"
and Daniel Liebeskind's highly praised Jewish Museum, is considered part of a
trilogy of Berlin sites marking the special significance of Nazi terror.[14] Each site
is said to complete and complement the others: the Holocaust Monument is to
Jewish victims alone; the "Topography" is about the German perpetrators; the
Jewish Museum is about Jewish history in Germany from the ancient past to the
present. We might ask of each of these memorials how they bring the past into
a relation with the present: do they restage the past in mythical terms, thereby
assuring a melancholic permanence to mourning process, or do they convert the
dead into ancestors, thereby creating a sense of closure that opens one to new
attachments in the future?

No monument can determine its own reception, and the final design of the
Holocaust Monument remains controversial in part because its very abstractness
seems open to different re-stagings of the past. There are no inscriptions on the
stones; nothing mars their smooth surfaces, which were also treated (against
the express wishes of the architect) with an anti-graffiti agent to prevent the
public (especially neo-Nazi sympathizers) from leaving marks on them that
might suggest a particular interpretation. Nonetheless, public attempts to mark
and attribute specific contemporary meanings to the monument are inevitable.

In October 2003, nearly two years before the monument's completion, a scan-
dal erupted when it was discovered that the supplier of the anti-graffiti agent, a
daughter company of Degussa, had produced the Zyklon B poison used in Nazi
gas death camps. Construction was halted for one month but then resumed, with
Degussa still participating. Since its official dedication on May 10, 2005, the
monument has been kept remarkably graffiti-free. Inexplicable hairline cracks
of up to 4.7 meters (15.4 feet) began appearing in some of the concrete slabs in
2007, letting in rain and causing a hard lime deposit to appear and ooze out
of the concrete slabs. This immediately led to accusations that mediocre material was used and fears that the monument might not survive as a testament
for centuries. Over time, the range of reactions has narrowed, with most being
extremely positive. For now, it appears that the monument serves simultaneously as a tourist site of attraction to the city, as a scene of contemplation and
reflection about the relation of Germany to Jewish victims of the Holocaust,
as a quiet place to meet friends and have lunch, and as a site to threaten with

defacement. In other words, the monument does keep the past and debate about the past alive. But what does it say about the future?

By singling out Jewish victimhood among all groups that suffered from German aggression, the Holocaust Monument provides an inviting platform for the continuous re-stagings of anti-Semitism in its contemporary forms. In particular, it is an inviting stage, a *Kinderspielplatz,* for various rightwing, anti-immigrant, or neo-Nazi groups to desecrate "art"—what better art for this purpose than a memorial specifically to the murdered Jews—which then enables other Germans a facile identification of themselves as "anti-fascist." Its location in the center of Berlin and its popularity, with more than seven million visitors a year, make it the primary site for this sort of staging to international audiences. In this way, the monument serves multiple purposes: to grieve the dead and to act out in distorted and changing form the initial relationship between representatives of the victims and perpetrators.

What the memorial means will only be revealed in actual practice over time as different generations appropriate it for their own purposes. From the theoretical perspective advanced here, the least desirable outcome of the Holocaust Monument would be an invocation to commemorate and keep the memory of these particular dead alive, forestalling conversion of the dead into ancestors with the consequence that the lost world is mistakenly identified with the current one. In his analysis of memorials for the dead after World War I, Winter argues that they facilitated conventional grieving practices that "enabled the bereaved to live with their losses, and perhaps to leave them behind" (1995, 5). Given the relative speed in which these same European countries jumped into World War II, the memorials would seem to have had the opposite effect: of motivating people to act in the name of the dead. In that case, transformations of loss and therefore of this world, including acknowledgment of forms of redress since the commission of crimes, were not adequately contemporized. The collapse of the lost world into the present seems to have filtered out the thought of ongoing repetitions of political crime in the future; thus, the purpose of preventing repetition was repressed.

Beyond the debate about any single site, the memorialization wave in Berlin and Germany might itself be understood as a symptom of and manic reaction to this repression. The pluralization of sites of collective atonement appears as a defense from the accusation of not remembering the past and feeds on itself like an obsessional neurosis. Repetitive self-admonishment of this extent no longer resembles a working-through of the trauma of failed collective responsibility but appears a form of pleasure through guilt, like the wearing of a hair shirt in the Middle Ages to atone for sin. Here, the hair shirt is collectively worn in the site of the memorial, making visually permanent and material a fixation on a past event and a particular kind of guilt.

Admittedly, the opposite interpretation is also plausible: that the call for new museums and commemorative practices seeks to reinforce a narrative of responsibility and that the desire for a multiplicity of sites is merely supplementary to this more fundamental assertion. The major question here is whether these practices and sites create *contemporary* narratives of responsibility, ones that make the old narratives about present and past speak to new and emergent events. Key for these new events is to ask how the commemorative practices marking German responsibility for the Holocaust, and indirectly for the establishment of a Jewish state, affect Germany's relation to Israel and to the half-century of Israeli-Jewish victimization of Palestinians (Silberstein 1999). At stake is the relation of answerability for pre-1945 Jewish victimization to a present in which the victim group looks markedly different (Morris 2001, Rose 2007, Segev 2000).

There is no easy response to this question other than to acknowledge that the struggle to redress the relations of Germans to Jews is increasingly inflected by those between Jews and Arabs and Muslims. We might follow several lines of critical inquiry about whether new demands for commemoration of Jewish victimization in Germany are rites of mourning that intend repetition or events that intend closure: (1) What is the relation between the search for new narratives that might disturb or contemporize the understandings of Nazi-era crimes to a recurring monetization of some of the established liabilities, to which a form of calculation is applied that demands instead new memorials? (2) What is the status of new attachments resulting from the assumption of responsibility for the past in the face of conscious attempts to freeze the current narrative about Holocaust responsibility and make the debt of future generations of Germans permanent?

The very intimate and nuanced relations between Germany and Israel offer strong evidence that the history of accountability sketched above has indeed had major transformative effects on Germany and its citizens. This relationship is continually tested by contemporary relations of Israel and Jews to Palestinian victimization, but that testing has not to date led to a shirking by Germans of issues of accountability. Especially in the media but also in foreign policy, Germany has in fact shown an increased willingness to engage in debates concerning Israeli-Palestinian conflicts, although as of this writing these engagements have had no consequential effects on Israeli settlements or occupations. In 2006, for example, Germany was reluctant to station its soldiers as part of a NATO or UN force on the Israeli-Lebanese border for fear they would have to shoot at Jews and Holocaust victims or their children; ultimately, they were stationed on the border, but the word among the Lebanese was that they were authorized to shoot only at Arab transgressors.

In sum, then, the sequence of modes of accountability as they have been invoked and practiced since 1945 in Germany—retribution, monetary compensation, performative redress, memorialization—suggests not only alternative forms of redress but a maturation in the use of accountability mechanisms, from calculation to responsibility, from material to symbolic wounds. The ability to make reparations, in the widest sense of the word, has lessened considerably the sense of debt/guilt among a third generation of postwar Germans and may provide the basis for their reengagement with the world that is quite different than that which existed for the generations more directly involved in World War II and the Holocaust. This sequence of actions also suggests that to reckon with an "unmasterable past," in the memorable phrase of Charles Maier (1988), is an elusive and reversible process of redressing a relationship to an event or series of events. That past has its own weight, but this comes to include the modes in which it has been addressed and redressed over the years. Since every generation offers its own interpretation of the memory of loss and therefore views rectification in a different light, demands for redress may reappear at any time and be invoked for purposes other than the original accounting.

Political Crime and the Memory of Loss in Lebanon

In November 1989, representatives of the different conflicting factions in Lebanon signed the Arab League-sponsored Ta'if Accords, ending the civil wars that had engulfed the country for some fifteen years (1975–1990). Unlike East-Central European states and Germany after 1989, the Lebanese state issued a general amnesty assuring that some of the major culprits in acts of forced displacements, ethnic cleansing, and massacre could be elected to and seated in parliament—which in fact they were. Although the wars had ended, this integrative act compromised the authority of the democratic Lebanese state, which, much as during the wars, operated with a weak executive in a moral vacuum, making it easy for internal groups to do what they had been doing for a long time: appeal to various external authorities (e.g., other states, international agencies, the United Nations) for remedies and solutions to their problems. This case raises the question of the limited availability and efficacy of modes of accountability in a cultural context where, unlike in the German case, the external factors *militate against any internal reckoning* with loss (Khalaf 2004; Mallat 2007; Young 2010). That is, here a theory of modes of redress of loss within the country also requires a theory of international relations. The history of these relations in Lebanon is dizzying.

Lebanon's present territorial form dates to 1926. It has always been less a nation than a society-in-the-making—an amalgam of tribes, religious sects, and groups who shared representation in a weak political structure that is continually asked to respond to (incorporate, appropriate, expel) extra-Lebanese forces, especially Syria (to which it, arguably, formerly belonged) to its north-east and Israel to its south (Havemann 2002; Salibi 1990). In the last several decades, Iranian influence and pressure has also increased. In October 1990, a joint Lebanese-Syrian military operation forced the interim prime minister, General Michel Aoun, and his Christian militia to capitulate; Aoun took refuge in the French embassy in East Beirut. Despite widespread international recognition of the Muslim-led government (which included Christian ministers and deputies) in West Beirut, Aoun, from East Beirut, had refused to recognize its authority. Not until August 27, 1991, was General Aoun issued a special pardon and allowed to leave the French embassy and take up residence in exile in France. Meanwhile, the Lebanese state, under Syrian hegemony, began to assert control over its territory, disarming and dissolving the various militias in May 1991—with the important exception of Hezbollah, founded in 1982 to organize resistance to the Israeli occupied south—and disarming Palestinian refugee factions (the first 180,000 refugees had arrived from Israel in 1948–49) in Sidon in July 1991 (on these refugees, see Peteet 2009). The last of the western hostages taken during the mid-1980s by Islamic extremists was released in May 1992. For many of the participants, however, the losses incurred in the Lebanese wars remained unaddressed, as did their causes.

When the wars exactly began is as disputed as when they stopped. Certainly, following the Arab-Israeli War of Attrition in 1968–1970, two formally external factors aggravated the social and economic cleavages internal to Lebanese society and led to the collapse of the formal political system in 1975: the Palestinian Liberation Organization established its principal base in Beirut; and Saudi Arabia, a distinctly Islamic oil-producing state, became more powerful through the accumulation of petrodollars and began to assert its influence in other Arab and Muslim countries (Rabinovich 1984). The civil wars that began in 1975, then, further undermined the sovereignty of the Lebanese state, a weakness preyed upon by Israel in an occupation of the South that had begun in 1982 (an event to which I return below), and by Syria, whose hegemony in the northern two-thirds of Lebanon became stronger after 1990.

In short, the conditions for the Lebanese state to establish political and territorial sovereignty were still less than optimal in 1992, more than two years after the signing of the National Reconciliation Accord. At the experiential level, there have been few events of accountability but many rites of commemoration, nearly all local and sectarian rather than national. The amnesty had tied the state's hands with regard to legal retribution—hence, there have been few trials. Only two men were put in jail for crimes related to the war, and there has been little civil redress for the approximately 100,000 victims and their families. Some individuals and groups have actively called for and even engaged in various modes of redress: public demonstrations, creation of commemorative sites, demands for apologies, compensation schemes for displaced persons, and provocative art exhibitions questioning the culpability of various actors (Irani 1997). At local levels there was, in fact, a great deal of swapping of territory to accord with new patterns of population displacement and concentration, sometimes facilitated by the state, and the new state itself supported limited restitution and compensation for lost property. Most importantly, however, the state lacked the authority to engage extensively in redress. On the contrary, its legitimacy was captive to the reintegration of former militia leaders into the dominant political and economic structures, which ensured group representation by those very leaders who at various times lived off of the impasses of the civil war. In other words, the violence inherent in the social relations between groups, a lucrative source of material and symbolic power, was frozen, and the state became a mere arbiter, at best, among a set of mobilized and self-conscious hierarchies (Gilsenan 2003; Traboulsi 2007).

My own ethnographic work in Lebanon began in 1999 and coincided with the first of the two great withdrawals: of Israel in 2000 and Syria in 2005. In my first evening in Beirut in the summer of 1999, I was kept awake by very loud noises that punctuated the late night. Part of a new building boom, I thought. Before I arrived I had been assured that Lebanon was no longer at war, so I did not know how to interpret these sounds. In the morning I was told that Israel had been bombing power plants around Beirut. Everyday travel in Lebanon at that time included many Syrian checkpoints, mostly on major roads between cities or villages—stops ostensibly to control for the movement of weapons but often also used to extort better-off Lebanese citizens. The following year as I visited in the summer, Israel suddenly and without warning withdrew from the South, admittedly for reasons internal to Israel politics. That ended 18 years of occupation and was followed by the immediate disbanding of its proxy force, the Southern Lebanese Army (some of whose members found refuge in Germany). UN troops moved in to monitor the border with Israel, and the central government of Lebanon officially reincorporated the South but with a tacit agreement that Hezbollah take over policing there (Norton 2007). Hezbollah promptly turned several important places into commemorative sites and museums, including the former center for Israeli detainment and torture of Lebanese suspects in Khiam.

In between these two withdrawals of external colonizing powers, an important attempt at legal retribution grew out of Lebanese civil society: employment of international justice—the doctrine of universal jurisdiction—to achieve local justice. The original attempt was for the most disturbing of the slaughters during the civil wars: the 1982 massacre at the Sabra and Shatila refugee camps in

Beirut, most of whose victims were stateless Palestinians (see Fisk 2002; Mallat 2004).[15] On June 18, 2001, a criminal complaint, brought by legal scholars Chibli Mallat of Lebanon, Luc Walleyn of Belgium, and students working with Paul Kahn of Yale, among others, was lodged on behalf of 28 witnesses and survivors and brought before a Belgian court. After a long trial and several appeals, the Belgian Supreme Court agreed with the plaintiffs and the prosecution that they indeed had legal recourse in Belgium, and it confirmed the principle of universal jurisdiction encoded in the Fourth Geneva Conventions, customary international law, and the 1984 Convention on Torture, which assumes that all signatories to the convention have not only the right but also the duty either to prosecute or to extradite individuals guilty of war crimes, crimes against humanity, or genocide. According to this doctrine, any particular group's claim of suffering that falls under the rubric of these crimes has the right to a hearing before a local magistrate, irrespective of where the plaintiff or defendant reside or where the crime took place.

Much as the internal Lebanese conflicts are inextricably bound up with external alliances, so also some resolution of issues of justice appear possible only through international participation. Over the course of two-and-a-half years, Belgian courts repeatedly affirmed the rights of the survivors of the massacre. But on August 5, 2003, a political solution was reached that nullified the Supreme Court's decision. Under tremendous pressure from the U.S. and Israeli governments, the Belgium parliament substantially changed its victim-friendly national law, severely restricting the ability of foreigners to lodge complaints in Belgian courts regarding heinous crimes. For the longer term, however, the case alerts us to some theoretical possibilities in the use of the doctrine of universal jurisdiction to redress group victimization where national courts are incapable of considering claims. By unlinking the issue of justice from citizenship (peoplehood and territory), the doctrine of universal jurisdiction bypassed the international economy of victimization and promised redress to those whose suffering would ordinarily be forgotten. Moreover, the novelty of offering an extra-national legal remedy to a problem—the massacre of refugees—that had thus far been dealt with only militarily, did not go unnoticed in the Middle East and elsewhere and constitutes a particular site of memory as a warning to future perpetrators and for the hope of future legal accountability.[16]

The Syrian withdrawal from Lebanon in 2005, ending 29 years of what many Lebanese prefer to call hegemony instead of occupation, was quite dissimilar from the Israeli withdrawal of 2001. It was neither sudden nor surprising and was more a response to the organized movement called the "Cedar Revolution"—a direct reaction to the suspected Syrian role in the assassination of the former prime minister of Lebanon, Rafik Hariri, in February of 2005—than to an internal political dynamic in Syria. This movement addressed Lebanese losses in two ways: first, in demanding the withdrawal of Syrian troops from Lebanon, it addressed some civil war losses by trying to reinstate Lebanese political and territorial sovereignty; second, it pressured the United Nations into sending a fact-finding team to Lebanon, which resulted in a unanimous UN Security Council vote, in April of 2005, to authorize an international investigation Special Tribunal for Lebanon) into Hariri's assassination. The tribunal convened four years later, in March 2009, and despite skilled independent and primarily external (European) prosecutors, all its actions have become mired in the politics of the region. In fact, the investigations have spawned tragi-comic plots, including the targeted assassination of possible witnesses or supporters of the tribunal resulting in more than one hundred deaths, four generals imprisoned and then released after the admission of fabricated evidence, and Syrian arrest warrants for some of the Lebanese and German prosecutors in the case. As of this writing, arrest warrants are expected, but the tribunal's prosecutions are unlikely to result in any redress soon. Independent of this issue, the tribunal ultimately represents, together with the unsuccessful Sabra and Shatila prosecution, a site of memory for hope, but also of stalled justice.

The Cedar Revolution coincided, and was in part inspired by, political opportunities created by the American occupation of Iraq, which itself increasingly turned sour and, because of its illegitimacy, tainted the democracy movement within Lebanese that it officially encouraged. The euphoria of the movement and the experience of collective effervescence that usually accompanies a radical democratic opening nonetheless lasted for little more than a year (Young 2010; Mallat 2007). For the first time since the time before the civil wars, there was the possibility that the Lebanon state would assume formal sovereignty over its territory. Citizens made creative interventions in many areas of social life. New and ironic art proliferated, as did mixed-sect public gatherings. There even appeared limited openings for competition among rival candidates for public office. Whatever social unity was created quickly dissipated, however, as forces led by Hezbollah (supported by Syria and Iran) occupied downtown Beirut and held the political system hostage. The Hezbollah demand of wresting more power and representation for the majority Shi'a of the South was an initial condition of the Ta'if Accords of 1989, to recalibrate representation more in line with population, effectively increasing the number of Shi'a representatives, had never been met (on the Shi'a community, see Deeb 2006b). By July 2010 this demand had been met, with a new power-sharing arrangement that granted Hezbollah veto power in Lebanon's parliament. This new conflict revived old religious and territorial loyalties within Lebanon along with the memories of the civil war; and, in the short term, at least, it effectively advanced the fragmented exercise of power (sectarianism) independent of any democratic processes of control, and strengthened the influence of the Syrian Ba'ath Party in Lebanon through its support of Hezbollah.

Formally, this democratic experiment ended with collective punishment, and that by an American ally: the massive Israeli bombing of the South and of southern Beirut in the summer of 2006, which was justified as a response to the kidnapping of two soldiers and as necessary to eliminate Hezbollah. The bombing campaign was premised on a logic that, if Israel could neither realistically annihilate Hezbollah militias nor the Shi'ite community in South Lebanon, then at least it could punish the Lebanese citizens for its own unsuccessful occupation and perhaps thereby incite violence and instability within the Lebanese polity. That punishment, it was hoped, would split Hezbollah (and Shi'ite support for it) from the interests of other social groups and sects (e.g., Christian and Sunni communities), and a weakened Lebanese state would be unable to intervene and stop the internal cycles of violence between different sects. A weak neighbor economically and politically would buy time for Israel to deal with its Palestinian problem on its terms. The bombing did indeed fragment the democratic movement (was Hezbollah or Israel to blame?). It also inflicted severe damage on Lebanese infrastructure and on its environment, and it had the perverse consequence (from the Israeli perspective) of buttressing Hezbollah's claims—that it represented the only effective resistance to the Israeli aggression against Arabs. Hezbollah leader Hassan Nasrallah, largely responsible for provoking—or, minimally, providing an excuse for—the 2006 Israeli attack, thus increased his standing not only within Lebanon but among Arabs generally, obtaining thereby a near-veto on internal government policies (including the end to disarming independent militias).

With this event, the Lebanese state's attempt to establish itself as an authority that could not only represent all the people but also protect them was halted. Apart from the perspective of Hezbollah, which heralded the war as a victory, surely this bombing signaled a defeat for both "Lebanon" and Israel, as even Israelis themselves have subsequently acknowledged. A UNIFIL peace-keeping force of 15,000 troops was subsequently stationed on the border to Israel, and the Germans, with the strong urging of Israel, contributed 3,000 troops to this effort, assuming that, in the case of armed conflict, German soldiers would have problems firing on Israeli Jews.

In sum, the losses from the civil war violence in Lebanon continue to speak loudly to contemporary Lebanese largely because they have been so inadequately addressed, if at all. Whatever legal redress might accomplish in the form of retribution for the injuries its citizens suffered during the civil war, the Lebanese state has never been able to establish the executive or judicial authority to engage in this redress by means of symbolic retribution. To be sure, Iran and Syria, with their support of a Hezbollah militia largely independent of the Lebanese state, have substantially contributed to weakening the state. But it also appears that Israel has thought that a divided Lebanon is better, for now, than a united one. Following Syrian withdrawal in 2005, several of the old and disgraced militia leaders from the civil wars were reincarnated as public leaders: General Aoun returned from exile in France to lead a coalition with Syrians (his former opponent), and former Lebanese Forces leader Samir Geagea (the one militia leader who actually served time) was released from prison and also promptly reentered politics. Both leaders, along with the new dominance of Hezbollah, represent the real threat to regress the Lebanese society into sectarian division. The brief period of peace following the end of the civil war therefore seems to mark a pause and not a break in a pattern of rebounding violence in Lebanon. The democratically unifying revolutions in the Arab world that began in Tunisia and Egypt are, as of this writing, in 2011, sparking revolts against similar authoritarian rule in other Arab countries. They are unlikely to be repeated in Lebanon, however, which not only lacks the strong state and leader against whom to rebel but also is, of all Arab states, most dependent on a regional geopolitical solution to settle its internal schisms. The country continues to wait for a more decisive and most likely violent resolution to this impasse.

2 On Money and the Memory of Loss

How do we explain the uncanny intransigence—individually and collectively—of memory, especially the inability to settle accounts following severe losses of life and property? Contrary to a popular wisdom, time does not heal all wounds. In fact, only with the passing of time is it possible to register some losses and to recognize the language of a wound. Healing the wound or the memory of loss is a process about which we know little. Such memory appears to act like gravity, pulling us, indebted and guilty, toward an inescapable fault. We appear to have an obligation or duty to address the memory of loss and to seek redress. But while memory can often speak eloquently, it rarely listens well. Memory's instability and inflexibility makes it difficult to address directly. Hence we need interlocutors—imagined and real spirits, ghosts, djinns, therapists, even anthropologists—who might provide access to memory's speech, a speech about our duty to address loss. We expect these mediators to talk with memory and absolve us of our individual and collective fault, debt, guilt—what is bundled together in the German concept *Schuld*. Even in those rare cases where legal remedy exists, where the apparatus of the state (or states) offers a fair legal accounting and an indemnity for the loss, the wound resists final closure and continues to speak from a seemingly inaccessible and secure position.

It is this insoluble problem of addressing and redressing memory of loss that I want to examine, specifically in its relation to money as a form of redress. Under what conditions does money contribute to the transvaluation of the memory of loss? My argument follows in three parts: a theoretical discussion checked against cases of acceptance and rejection of monetary compensation for loss; a brief summary of arguments from chapter 1 on the collective level of fault, guilt, and debt as it relates to money in Germany; and a comparison of the relation of money and memory in the lives of two German individuals.

Memory, Money, and Compensation for Loss

The offer of money to compensate for a loss, wound, or injury is widely practiced, but it is not always accepted. Because of its liquidity, money distinguishes itself as a form of indemnification from restitution of material goods such as land. Often property called "land" is given a special value. Land that is stolen or lost cannot be replaced by a substitute object; it cannot be transvalued. Like an eye for an eye, so to speak, only land can replace land. This form of restitution is similar to what in anthropology is called "restricted exchange," a theory developed out of a consideration of wife exchange between two groups where only a woman can replace another woman. Valued goods of another order—such as pigs or cowry shells or even money—are never adequate recompense for giving up a wife.

Restricted exchange is in fact rare, as is actual restitution. The more common form of recompense is called "generalized exchange," and the use of money as compensation or reparation, as a substitute for loss, is of this type. Most lost or stolen or confiscated objects change over time and therefore can never be returned in their original form; one must propose and accept a substitute, that is, compensation. Today, most transvaluation of loss involves the substitute of money. When is money an appropriate or adequate substitute for severe loss?

The possibility of restricted exchange was posed following the collapse of Communist governments in 1989–90. Should the successor states return property expropriated and redistributed after 1945, or should they compensate former owners? Only in Germany, with the policy of *"Rückgabe vor Entschädigung"* (return/restitution before monetary compensation), did the state make restricted exchange official policy in the former German Democratic Republic (GDR). Other East-Central European states practiced generalized exchange: returning property only on a case-by-case basis, favoring compensation and taking into consideration the experiences and needs of present owners and users. In Germany, the guiding principle was that the original land and the original real estate should be returned to prior owners as if there had been no subsequent history of other occupations and ownerships since 1933. This did not of course prove workable, for practical and political reasons, and in most cases monetary compensation was paid instead as recompense in a generalized exchange. In what way did money "talk" to this prior injury? Let us examine more closely exactly how and from where money speaks.

Two of the most recent highly public refusals to accept a monetary transvaluation of loss have been the case of the "comfort girls" who were coerced into working as sex slaves for the Japanese in World War II and that of the Argentinian "Mothers of the Plaza de Mayo" whose children and relatives were "disappeared" during the government's "dirty war" against its civilians suspected of opposition between 1976 and 1983. In both cases, the wounded refuse to let go of their memories of having been harmed. And they refuse to accept the monetary (in legal jargon, "punitive") damages from the perpetrators (represented by successor governments)—unless those damages are accompanied by other forms of rectification such as punishment, acts of atonement, apology, or memorialization. Sometimes victims may accept money only if it is camouflaged or hidden and not seen as a direct substitute for the loss. At other times victims desire to see the "punitive" aspect of damages, where the perpetrator is punished in some way, and where the source of the money is seen as coming directly from the perpetrator.

When money, as a substance, is offered to address the memory of injury or when additional conditions are stipulated before agreeing to accept money as remedy for an injury, we often say that money "cheapens memory," and we disparage money's value even as we accept it by calling it "bitter money," "poison money," or "blood money." In this sense, money never really compensates adequately for loss but may instead devalue or trivialize the harm and actually increase the sense of injury. When confronted with this situation, we often say, "It's like adding insult to injury." In both cases of the refusal to accept money, of Japanese sex slaves and Argentinian "mothers" of the approximately 30,000 "disappeared," there is no possibility of restricted exchange or substitute redress. The losses are permanent and irrecoverable.[1] May it not be, then, that the money offered is not to compensate for the loss, but for the *memory* of the loss?

One of the major reasons why injured parties reject this monetary compensation is that they demand other, nonmaterial forms of redress of memory before accepting money. The memory of the loss seems to have a direct hold on the actual injured parties making the demands for redress that money cannot address. Money appears inadequate to the task of absolution from guilt and release from debt. Memory's grip is too strong. Money cannot speak to this memory of loss directly or it would in fact "cheapen memory."

Alternatively, money often seems to possess curative powers that enable it to act as compensation and to transform one's past harm or loss into future opportunity. Here, it seems as if no demands are placed on the wrongdoer other than payment, and payment appears to substitute for the memory of the injury. There is the sense that loss can be adequately quantified and that memory itself can be redressed by money. Two of the most recent highly public "acceptances," both still not fully completed, are the $5 billion German reparations fund set up in 2001 to compensate the million or more people who were forced to work in concentration camps, ghettos, and German businesses in the Nazi era; and a settlement reached on April 12 of 2001 by New York Life, one of the largest life insurance companies in the United States, to pay up to $10 million to heirs of the victims of the Armenian genocide in Ottoman Turkey. Both of these "acceptances"—of money for Nazi forced labor and of life insurance payments to Armenians victims of the Ottoman massacre—appear to be monetary substitutes for the injury or death. They appear to be examples of a monetization of the memory of loss. Let us examine this transvaluation more closely.

Many factors enter into explaining why the German government and industry settled the case of slave laborers under the Nazis so long after the injury. Above all, the end of the Cold War made it possible to unify victims across borders, and in the face of reunification the German state had to re-legitimate itself internationally. Also, two recent precedents were decisive with regard to government restitution, leading also to a change in the private sector's sense of responsibility for past human rights violations: the Swiss government initiative establishing a five-billion-dollar Holocaust fund (Barkan 2000), and the willing and continuous intervention of U.S. American courts in hearing restitution claims against foreign governments and companies (Bazyler 2001).

Here I want to focus theoretically rather than historically on three factors that make a monetary substitute for loss acceptable, the conditions under which money can, or is made to, speak to memory. There were many previous efforts by the German state to rectify losses inflicted under the Nazi regime. These include historiographical work, apologies, memorials, commemorative events, treaties, and, most prominently, the policy of *Wiedergutmachung* (a direct exchange of money for loss), which initially addressed Jews and the state of Israel but later was extended to other victim groups.[2] In short, more than a half-century after the war, most of the Nazi-era claims had already in fact been addressed, if not adequately settled. Money, then, has not been asked to speak alone, but always as a supplement to other means of addressing memory of injury or loss, which allows the payment of money to appear as a direct and restricted exchange.[3] And this is the first factor: Money is acceptable as a supplement to other remedies.

For former slave laborers, the critical element missing in the initial constitution of loss was in fact money: if the workers had been paid at the time of their labor, there would be at most a demand for nonmaterial indemnification for coerced labor as a foreign national under the conditions of war (a demand unlikely to be heard on a world stage). A second factor is temporal: the advanced age of those injured makes the monetization of loss more acceptable. The surviving forced laborers were nearing the end of their lives, meaning they had little to gain from holding out, and the delay in compensation has made the payments more affordable for German industry and government. A third factor is the growth and prominence of a primarily American legal industry, itself driven by profits, active in a type of indemnification called "class action" lawsuits, where the remedy tends to be money for loss. Some U.S. American law firms, for example, have entire departments engaged in investigating "war crimes practices," involving primarily restitution claims in countries wealthy enough to present the possibility of a monetization of loss (Bazyler 2001). I'll return to these factors later.

My second example, life insurance to be paid to Armenian survivors of the Ottoman genocide, is an extreme case of the association of money with the ultimate loss, death. Life insurance establishes equivalence between death and its monetary value. The insurance payment is a reimbursement to pre-specified survivors, which, according to the insurance industry's "indemnity principle," is "limited to losses actually sustained by the policyholder." The benefits must be "no larger than the loss sustained (though it may be smaller)" (Heimer 1985, 43). Here there is not a restricted but a generalized exchange, involving a substitution and transvaluation of money for death. Like the Nazi slave laborers, there is a temporal delay and reliance on an institutional mediator, life insurance, which is premised on the monetization of loss.[4] This settlement came 85 years after the events, between 1915 and 1922, in which Turks slaughtered up to 1.5 million people. According to New York Life, 8,000 policies, including 3,600 by Armenians, had been sold in Turkey before the outbreak of World War I, when sales were stopped. New York Life settled 300 policies before the massacres and another 1,100 after, leaving 2,200 unresolved. As integral part of the deal, New York Life also agreed to a non-quantifiable form of rectification: to publish the names of the policyholders in major American as well as ethnic newspapers.[5]

On the surface, this case appears to be about money substituting for the memory of loss. A life insurance company agrees to pay monetary compensation for deaths that occurred in a genocide. The company pays designated heirs of the victims, most likely of a third generation removed. Given the rather large amount of money and time required to pursue the claims over 85 years and the rather paltry sum in dispute (approximately $10,000 per person), the pursuit of money or profit cannot be the primary drive behind the desire for rectification. Rather, it appears that the primary reason for the persistence of the memory of death would be the desire for historical recognition, a fuller account and an accounting, of the injury—the massacre, the genocide—by others, any others, Americans, Europeans, or Turks. This was indeed part of the settlement, in the agreement to publish names of the victims in newspapers.

Here, as with Nazi slave labor, money is supplementary, though also necessary to complete the indemnification of the memory of loss. The unwillingness of Turkey and the rest of the international community to recognize Armenian deaths is most probably the primary reason why several generations of survivors have vigorously held onto their memory of loss, or to put it another way, why memory's obligation to the dead, the *Schuld* (debt and guilt), seems to speak without listening.[6] Yet the monetary compensation promised in the life insurance contract also speaks in some way to this memory of loss.

How and from where does money speak to loss? Pierre Nora (1996) comments in his ambitious project on "Realms of Memory" that gold is the memory of money. If that is so, and we have now eliminated the gold standard, then what is money the memory of? We do attribute to money many social meanings—calling it old money, new money, allowance, wage, salary, and dole, for example—all suggesting the social origin of the initial transaction that created value, which creates a possible memory stored in specific "special monies" (cf. Zelizer 1989). But there is a way in which money can become cleansed of memory of its origin over time, which is expressed in the distinction "old money" and "new money." Old money is what the Fords and Rockefellers and Mellons give to us in grants; we no longer inquire into its origin. New money is what media moguls like Sylvio Berlusconi or junk bond kings like Michael Milken or computer innovators like Bill Gates accumulate. Old money is more proper and acceptable than new money largely because we have "forgotten" its origin.

In the case of money as remedy for the memory of loss, I want to turn to the utilitarian argument of Marx and Simmel and suggest that *money cannot transvalue memory, but it can transvalue loss.* That is because money is the memory of nothing; it is an empty signifier free to be filled however one pleases. It is the means for a generalized exchange par excellence. No women for women, or land for land. Anything can substitute for money. Even a "savings account," made by accumulating some "special monies" secured through a specific sort of past labor or inheritance, is freed over time from its past and becomes open to any imagined future. As can be seen from the way in which fortunes are legitimated over time, the longer one has a savings account, the more divorced it becomes from any specific memory of accumulation, the more released it is from the actual moment of original deposit and accumulation. Money derives its link to freedom, not as a negation, for with money one can, if one wishes, afford to cultivate or indulge in memory. Rather, by not being tied to the memory of anything, by being the memory of nothing, money can speak a language without specific content or relation to the past, one of virtuality and freedom.

It is well known that money offers the promise of universal exchangeability and translatability. My contribution here aims to explicate the connection of money to memory, specifically to contemporary memory. Not only did we just live through a decade, following the collapse of the Cold War, of a discourse on money and wealth that seemed to dominate if not colonize most other value domains not only in Europe and the United States but worldwide, but also we are living through an explosion of interest in memory: Fredric Jameson (1984, 58, 65, 67) decries the "colonization of the present by the nostalgic mode" leading to a new depthlessness, a "historicism that effaces history"; Pierre Nora (1996) talks of a "crisis of social memory" and the replacement of the memory-nation with *lieux de mémoire*; Ian Hacking (1996, 73) talks of a new "memoro-politics," where "the sciences of memory have become surrogates for the soul" and provide access to our most essential truths.

Why, at this time, this parallel embrace of memory and money? My argument is that memory and money rely upon, but have inverse relations to, the same issue: accountability. Memory of loss is an account obtained through recall of something learned, experienced, or imagined in the past. Money is what *Webster's* defines as an "archaic" form of accounting: "to give or receive a financial account," involving "counting, remuneration, computation." Both speak the language of accounting, but while memory over time seeks accountability, money over time evades accountability. And since money is the memory of nothing, it speaks orthogonally to or *around* memory as does nothing else. Other symbolic means to address loss—rituals of mourning, commemoration, therapy, and legal justice—can, in fact, with proper mediation and under certain circumstances, affect memory by enabling a social displacement of the loss. But they are all themselves caught up within memory, establishing a relationship of accountability to it, trying to access and speak to something that rarely and only under the most unusual circumstances listens. Money, by contrast, does not rely on access to memory in order to relate to loss. It speaks to loss directly. But as to the memory of loss, money always enters into a relationship with this memory as supplementary, perhaps necessary for a full accounting as part of a generalized exchange, but secondary to the mediation of retribution and commemoration as forms of restricted exchange.

Relating the Collective to Money and Memory

In the twentieth century, Germany and Germans have been located within the community of nations on the perpetrator not the victim side of the question of *Schuld*. This guilt has been addressed in modes ranging from the redress obligated by the "war guilt clause" of the Versailles Treaty in 1918, to the trials, reparations, and commemorations following World War II. My interest has been precisely in how this "loss" has become a "memory of loss," a German memory of the issue of reparations. Within two decades of World War II, Germans had largely internalized the narrative of the victors (which also became a global narrative): that Germans collectively were responsible for the harm they had inflicted, which required active redress, and that Germany itself required an external remedy (the presence of Western Allies).

Even after the fault and debt aspects of the *Schuldfrage* of individual Germans were addressed through monetary compensation and the military and criminal courts, the question remains as to what extent Germans were individually responsible for wrongdoing done in the name of the collective that was not or could not be addressed in criminal courts or through reparations. Since the 1960s, this dimension of guilt has been addressed in the civil or cultural domain by public apologies, the setting aside of days of mourning, investigatory commissions, support for historiography, and constructing memorials (*Denkmäler* and *Mahnmale*) and museums—sites of memory intended primarily as provocations to further thought or as admonitions. Most of these cultural responses are what we call "rites of commemoration."

A first postwar generation addressed collective liability through restitution, monetary compensation, and later legal retribution. Or to be more specific, this address was done *for* them, with taxpayer's money, in the name of Germany. The generation presently in positions of power in Germany, a postwar generation called the "68ers" (*Achtundsechziger*), has been the most active in pursuing commemoration, in attempting to redress the memory of a loss inflicted by their parents in the name of Germany as a "restricted guilt" over the Holocaust. Along these lines, the sociologist Bernhard Giesen (1993) has even called the postwar Germans a "Holocaust-nation."

Fault for crimes can be assessed only individually, and monetary debt is calculable; payment releases one from the debt. But guilt, while unstable and taking many forms, speaks a collective or social language of memory of loss.

Individual Experience of Money and Memory

It may be dangerous, but it is also easier to talk about these matters at a collective than at an individual level, easier to generalize about a group when one is not confined to the specificities of individual life histories that resist discipline and reduction to single issues. One might say that this essay thus far has been anthropological but not very ethnographic. Here I will resort to the ethnographic present and provide some of the experiential description that is the necessary referent for collective histories, tracing the relation of money to memory in the lives of two individuals that I know.

During my first full year of fieldwork in 1986–87 in East Berlin, I was paid in two currencies, a monthly stipend in East German "Mark der DDR" and a small sum of U.S. dollars that I could use in the Inter-shops that sold imported Western (mostly West German) goods. The Inter-shops would only accept Western currency, not East German Marks. During my second and third year of fieldwork in 1987–89 in West Berlin, I was paid in West German Marks, which I could also use in the East. After a compulsory exchange of 1:1 for my first DM 25, I could exchange as many D-Mark or dollars as I wanted on the black market for 3 or 4:1. Whatever did not get spent was either thrown away or saved to give to friends as souvenirs of the Communist East. What I want to emphasize is the way East German money, lacking convertibility, was a "special money" (at the time often compared to the play money used in the game

Monopoly). For restricted exchange only, East German money symbolized lack of freedom, and this lack dominated the unification process.

One winter day in 1988 as I was walking with a friend along Friedrichstrasse in the center of East Berlin, I saw a child of about age six discover a one-coin DM on the street. He was filled with pure joy and exuberance, and began to proclaim his finding—"Look mama, look mama!"—in that loud, high-pitched voice of children his age. His embarrassed mother tried, unsuccessfully, to hush him. My friend commented, "If it goes so far, that is the end of us."

We all know what happened next. A year later the Wall came down, and the first thing most East Germans did was to queue in block-long lines to collect their *Begrüssungsgeld* (welcome money) from the West German government. This welcome money was a Cold War propaganda ploy only viable when a few East Germans were able to visit the West, not when the entire population could visit. Three months later, in March 1990, a near majority of citizens voted for a speedy dissolution of the GDR and crowned Helmut Kohl "Chancellor of Unity," justifying this by saying, "Kohl bringt die Kohle" (Kohl brings the bucks)![7]

What followed was the setting up of the *Treuhand,* a formally independent trust with the mandate to "*sanieren*" (manage and restructure) all collective— state- and (SED) Party-owned—property. *Sanieren* soon became "*privatisieren*." Under the operative principle of *Rückgabe vor Entschädigung* (return before compensation) determined by the German Constitutional Court, the Treuhand was to restore property to former owners and to privatize what remained. Its work rekindled memories of the East German state's expropriations and negated two other kinds of memory: the memory of accumulation, and the memory of loss. One might even characterize the Treuhand's work, without exaggeration, as part of a general annihilation of "communist memory": memory of the history of capitalism, of ownership, exploitation, and class relations. In the context of German unification, the restoration of property to its former owners and its distribution to new ones parallels what Marx dubbed the critical moment in capitalism of "primitive accumulation."

One of the major fears that the GDR used in its initial fight for legitimation was that, should East unite with West, West German industrialists would come in and gobble up their land and resources. In my office I have a poster made in 1948, showing the hands of speculators reaching from uncolored territory into the colored land of the GDR, a large red and black hammer posed to crush the attempted land grab. And that is what, from 1990 to 1994, the West Germans and a few other Westerners did, through the Treuhand: they obtained East German property—often without paying anything—simply with the promise that they would invest and modernize and make it profitable.[8]

Profitability was only one, and not all that frequent, effect of privatization. Most privatization resulted in a "second privatization" as West German companies fired workers (calling it "rationalization"), sold off the most profitable parts, and dumped the larger parts that truly needed investment back onto the Treuhand. My West Berlin friend Claudio was hired to do a second privatization of the largest East German energy *Kombinat* (trust). He failed, for reasons that should be studied, but since all of the documents are under *Datenschutz,* the far-reaching law protecting data from public access, I doubt if any researcher will ever get close to them in my lifetime. Indeed, among West Germans there is no official support for, and very little interest in the memory of, either the first or second privatization—or, more accurately, in this late-twentieth-century moment of primitive accumulation. There is, on the other hand, widespread interest in the issues of restitution and compensation, to which I will return later.

My leftist West German friends were highly critical of the East German turn to Kohl in two successive elections to save them from economic plight and lead their integration into the West. They attributed this to GDR naiveté and stupidity, which the East Germans knew and resented, contributing to an alienation of new and old interest groups that should have been working in alliance—East German socialists, leftists, and workers, the small group of environmentalists and dissidents from West German Greens, Social Democrats, and "68ers." Nothing more pointedly symbolizes the one-sidedness of unification than *die Abwicklung,* the "bringing to completion" of East German institutions through "scientific" evaluation, meaning the firing of East Germans and the closing of their institutions, all in the interest of renovation, renewal, modernization. Needless to say, there was no comparable evaluation of West German institutions. Some West Germans undoubtedly benefited from this, especially those in professions with replicas in the East such as banking or academics or administration. But what most West Germans remember is the *Solidaritätsbeitrag,* the (initially) 7.5 percent monthly contribution to solidarity that is automatically deducted from and specially marked at the bottom of each paycheck. Ten years later, they are still paying. So went the first decade of "unification": two historical trajectories, unable to speak to each other, and now two fundamentally different histories of money and memory, of memories of loss and amnesia about accumulation.

I sat with my friend Arnim and watched the results of the first free election of March 1990, which led to the dissolution of the GDR, from the headquarters of the old Communist Party (renamed PDS: Party of Democratic Socialism). Arnim told me he voted for the Social Democrats, but in 1995 he rejoined his old nemesis, the PDS. Feeling he must resist the dominance of the West and defend the interests of the dispossessed, he is now active in PDS public events, including anti-fascist and anti-xenophobic actions.

Arnim is a citizen with a specific history of memory and money, which is then interpellated *im Namen Deutschlands*. Only through the history of this collective *Volk* can we understand Arnim's memory of loss and money in his life. But for his conscious, adult life, Arnim was an East German for 51 years and a German for only the last decade. His own personal history is one of a sequence of dramatic losses, starting from the loss of his uncles in the First and Second World Wars, the loss of his home and flight with his mother and brother from the Soviets and thus his physical displacement, the attempt of his panicked mother to drown him in her fear of advancing Russian soldiers, and, in 1950, the loss of his family's elite clothing manufacturing business. Nonetheless, Arnim had a stellar career in clothing sales because the large *Kombinat* that absorbed his family business retained him and members of his family, even giving them high positions. He joined the SED in 1958, but in 1974 he was kicked out of the Party. Arnim then withdrew from this career and became what in the GDR was called *asozial*. Since rents were low, health care free, and food and entertainment cheap, he could live well as long as he kept his monetary needs to a minimum. In short, Arnim has three competing sites of memories of loss—which we might designate as the Holocaust and World War II, the GDR, and Unified Germany.

Although both states and societies engaged in legal retribution for the Holocaust and World War II during Arnim's childhood and youth, it was only the West German state that engaged in the monetary compensation part of *Wiedergutmachung*. (The GDR did engage in restitution.) Hence, this West German history of addressing memory of loss with money, of German money redressing losses committed *im Namen Deutschlands,* is not one that Arnim experienced but one that he inherited.

Today Arnim speaks, awkwardly, the West German language of *Schuld* and *Wiedergutmachung* that he has recently inherited. Given the total dominance of West German concepts and speech in the unification process, this language is *the* mode of articulation for Germans of his generation without which he would not be heard. Arnim grew up feeling absolved from guilt through the official GDR position of anti-fascism. As a child, he had been part of the "Timur movement," based on a character in the novel *Timur and His Gang* by Soviet author Arkadi Gaidar. Timur stood for the best qualities of a young communist, a cross between a Bolshevik Boy Scout and an ideologically trained Hardy Boy, committed to selflessly serving others in the struggle to emancipate mankind. Unification processes worked relentlessly to smash whatever was left of Arnim's idealism, and the entire edifice of GDR ideology, including its commitment to anti-fascism, was delegitimated and declared a myth. Arnim now assumes he shares with other Germans a *Schuld* for past injuries inflicted and that these require additional redress.

I asked him what precisely this *Schuld* entails and what is its relation to money. Arnim says he is aware, and in fact supportive, of the legal retribution done by a first generation of postwar West Germans and of a second generation's commemorative work—public apologies, days of mourning, critical historiography. At the same time, he is uncertain about whether this redress requires further monetary compensation or the building of the large Holocaust Memorial near the Reichstag and Brandenburg Gate. Instead, he emphasizes the need to show solidarity with other contemporary victims of violence, which may also mean that Germans make a disproportionate monetary contribution to peacekeeping efforts, as they currently do in budget politics of the European Union. This does not mean, he emphasizes, following the dominant argument of his party, the PDS, that Germans should engage in military combat outside the country proper, even if its intent is to stop genocide.

In this way, Arnim works through and against the hegemony of the West German memoro-politics, but his opposition is not total. At a macro-level, he shares with West Germans the fact that the unconditional *defeat* and then the Allied *occupation* of nearly a half-century were enabling losses. These two conditions, defeat and occupation, presented the opportunity for an individual accounting at the level of fault and debt and some consciousness about guilt, the three dimensions of *Schuld*. Ultimately, the defeat enabled Germany to transform its relation both with internal difference and with its neighbors. What he does not share with West Germans is the history of money.

These enabling losses were experienced as gains by another friend, Kolja, who worked with me from the summer of 1989 through 1995 on a project on Jewish repatriation to Germany. Kolja was born in 1954 in Kazakhstan in what his mother, in 1989, before the GDR began dissolving, still called a "work camp" instead of a gulag. At the time, his father was in exile in Siberia, banned to a gulag there in 1937 in a Stalinist purge of German emigrants. Both parents, as Communists and Jews, left Germany for Paris in 1933 and then voluntarily left Paris for the Soviet Union in 1935, where they eventually picked up Soviet citizenship. They didn't return to Germany until 1956, when Khrushchev released the last group of prisoners of war and German detainees. As committed Communists, they of course returned to the East, as his mother explained to me, even though they could have gone to West Germany or to England, where the Kolja's maternal grandparents lived.

German defeat and Soviet occupation were initially emancipatory for Kolja's family because their experience of exile and loss meant that they were relieved of the kind of burden of *Schuld* that other Germans carried. And Kolja's family was subject to both German and Jewish fates. In East Germany, the family was even rewarded in small ways—a better apartment, political agreement with the ideology of the "Worker and Farmer State." His mother worked as translator of Russian and English newspapers for the Politburo. That Kolja's brother escaped to the West a week before the Wall was built and the family did not see him for another 11 years was a real blow, especially to Kolja since he was emotionally closest to his brother. But the family explained it as a burden of the Cold War that many German families experienced and hence not one for which they were personally singled out.

In 1988, after a long period of unemployment, Kolja began working for the Zentrum Judaicum, a document and cultural center for Jewish activities financed by money from the American Ronald Lauder, son and heir to the Estée Lauder cosmetics empire. Lauder was interested in supporting Jewish culture and the memory of Jewish life in East-Central Europe. By 1990, after the opening of the Wall, Kolja was heavily involved in memory work: helping Jews who lived outside Germany, nearly all from the West, reconstruct their histories in and around Berlin. By 1992 he was spending a large part of his time aiding in the research of claims for restitution of Jewish property, the majority of the claims being in the Prenzlauer Berg, the district where Kolja worked and lived. Several times, Kolja took me on walking tours of the old Scheunenviertel near Alexanderplatz, the poor and densely populated Jewish district before the war. Kolja was highly ambivalent about these restitutions.

Morally, of course, it was important to return stolen property. But the legal firms often had to hunt hard to find legal heirs to much of the property, and then some of the distant relatives, once located, were unenthusiastic about the restitution. Kolja found that it was not the loss of property with which the heirs were primarily concerned but the memory of this loss and the events surrounding it. Any attempt to transvalue this memory of loss threatened to "cheapen memory." Very few of the heirs had any memory of the actual property, and those that did had not seen or heard of it for half a century. In the meantime, most of the property had indeed been transformed—with new buildings and new neighborhoods—and most of the claims involved not actual victims but the inheritors of the initial dispossessed. Nearly all cases seemed headed toward a monetary compensation. At bottom, then, was the fact that compensation would end up speaking not to loss but to this memory of loss, as if such memory could be transvalued into money. This was precisely the turning of *Schuld* into *Schulden*, guilt into debt, that the actual injured parties had always wanted to avoid.

Kolja observed that in practice most restitution involved simply paying intermediates—law firms and distant relatives—a fee before taking the property out of the hands of its current renters and users. In the GDR, much of this property had been administered by municipal authorities and used by non-elites. Now it was put back onto the open market at a much higher price than if it had been merely privatized, making it unaffordable to East Germans like Kolja himself to buy, since East Germans had very little individual savings. Restitution meant, in effect, dispossessing current tenants and users and turning this stolen or expropriated property over to West Berlin and West German speculators who then, together with legal firms from the United States, made a profit, some of which went to legal heirs of the injured parties. Not only was this a direct negation of communism, the very antithesis of what Kolja's family over several generations had fought and suffered for, but it was also less about restitution—a form of restricted exchange where the original property is returned to the original owner—than about a form of class redistribution under the guise of restitution. That is, a generalized exchange occurs through a series of substitutions: the original stolen or expropriated property is taken out of circulation or use, turned into monetary value, and then resold in order to compensate legal firms and heirs of victims of the original theft.[9]

During all the time I worked with Kolja, rumors circulated that he was involved with the *Stasi,* the State Security. It was always rumored that many East German Jews were involved with the *Stasi* because, first, many were ideologically committed to the socialist state, and second, they were safe recruits, for who among the non-Jewish Germans would suspect them or could rightly accuse them of complicity? Unification changed all this, since the East and West Berlin Jewish communities had to reunite, and the personal histories of those in the East became public. By 1998 documents turned up proving Kolja had been a *Stasi* employee—part-time, as had most of their employees, but this made no difference. He was fired from his job, and perhaps partly because of this, his non-Jewish wife subsequently left him. In short, Kolja's fate, like Arnim's, is linked to three particular sites of the memory of loss: the Holocaust and World War II, the GDR, and Unified Germany

Unlike Kolja, Arnim seems to have adjusted well to claiming either East German or German identification when it suits either his pocketbook or his memory. Arnim's history is of course not merely of expropriations or losses. This past year he became a beneficiary of the compensation policies of the new Germany. In 1997 Arnim filed a legal claim for restitution of his family business, and he was successful, though not in receiving the original property since that property had been transformed into part of an East German trust and then twice privatized by the Treuhand. He was successful in obtaining compensation: about $10,000, which he hopes to use as a supplement to his small pension and use to take yearly bus trips to Spain. "You wouldn't believe the beauty," he explained, "of the morning sun as I wake up on the bus and we descend from the French mountains into Spain!"

What is clear is that Arnim understands this payment as compensation, not for the memory of loss, but directly for the loss itself. His parents might have had that memory, and this settlement may have been unacceptable to them. But the debt owed to Arnim by the GDR, or the Federal Republic acting in its name, is not about property loss but about an experience of confinement and lack of mobility, and money could transvalue this loss and repay this debt with freedom. Indeed, that is what this money offers Arnim, a transvaluation: not only freedom to indulge in memory, but more importantly, freedom from memory. By being the memory of nothing, money can speak a language without specific content or relation to the past.

As to the memory of loss of World War II and the Holocaust, both Arnim and Kolja are interpellated by the German *Schuldfrage*, though they are historically situated on the opposing victim/perpetrator sides of this question. But since memory of loss cannot be addressed directly, the whole issue of monetary compensation is about something else, certainly about loss, but not about its memory.

3 Public Apologies, Dignity, and Performative Redress

Apologies and Democratic Agency

For approximately a decade, from the end of the Cold War and fall of the Berlin Wall in 1989 to the beginning of the War on Terror in 2002, representatives of states increasingly succumbed to pressure to issue public apologies for wrongs committed in the past. The trend attests to the growing power of victim groups, evinces a novel willingness of states or state representatives to admit wrong, and reveals an emergent global public that was eager to hear such admissions. A wide range of countries issued apologies, such as France for World War II collaboration with the Germans in the persecution of Jews, South Africa for a century of apartheid crimes against blacks, and the United States for a history of slavery and for the persecution of native Indians. Not only did citizens (or ex-citizens, or descendants of citizens) demand and receive apologies from their own states, but states issued apologies to each other, such as Japan to Korea, Israel to the Palestinian Authority and vice-versa, England to Northern Ireland, and Syria to the United States.

This wave of apologies is an integral part of the widespread democratization processes that accompanied the end of the Cold War. Democratic states require the reiteration of principles of accountability to establish themselves as moral authorities that can claim to represent entire communities, as shown in *Settling Accounts: Violence, Justice, and Accountability in Postsocialist Europe* (Borneman 1997). These principles are at the core of the concept of rule of law, and they are enacted in periodic political purification. Political purification entails governments' assuming responsibility for societal criminality rather than displacing it to peripheral actors. In other words, democratic governments that do not periodically cleanse themselves of their own criminal behaviors will tend to displace criminality to non-central groups (e.g., immigrants in France, poor blacks in the U.S., asylum seekers and foreigners in Germany, or ethno-religious minorities in Yugoslavia, Rwanda, and India). Displacement to substitute victims may stabilize countries domestically, but it also perpetuates local injustices because the ruling elites accomplish such displacement by using the judicial system as a political instrument (Borneman 2002b).

Punishing wrongdoers through legal trials is necessary to establish public trust in the rule of law, but it is also insufficient. States must also restore the moral integrity and repair the damaged self-worth of the wronged person. Apologies, whether from a state to a people or from a public commission in the name of a state to an individual, do such work; in the process, they provide a specific means to establish democratic political agency.

Apologies are a form of performative redress that link the fate of the wrongdoer and the victim in a public event, which seeks to defeat the wrongdoer's claim to mastery over the victim. To punish wrongdoers in this way—by linking them to their actual victims—does not compromise their status as persons; in other words, it does not constitute an act of reciprocal revenge. Rather, such public events that acknowledge the wrong confirm the victim and wrongdoer "as equal by virtue of their humanity" (Hampton 1992, 1686–87). They affirm that both victim and wrongdoer are equal, in the sense that both are intersubjective political agents exercising free will, the minimal condition of humanity in democratic states.

The end of the Cold War and its bipolar division of the world eliminated both an easily identifiable external enemy and certain pressures for internal unity. Consequently, demands that were formerly submerged under the pressure for unity faced new possibilities, resulting in stronger victim groups and increasing the articulation of injustices. Local citizen appeals for state apologies, or appeals of states to each other, were a product of this opening, part of a global call for accountability in states that had been undemocratic or where democratization had been frozen. That said, neither the organization of victim groups on a world stage nor pressure for democratization as a form of state legitimation is new to the post–Cold War order. My purpose in what follows, therefore, is not to map out this contemporary period but simply to explicate two cases of apologies that exemplify the accountability work they do in the performative redress of an injury.

Example 1. A state apologizes to other people

On December 7, 1970, West German Chancellor Willy Brandt visited Warsaw as part of his policy of *Ostpolitik* that sought to normalize relations with the USSR and other Eastern bloc countries. During his visit, he spontaneously fell to his knees at the commemoration to the Jewish victims of the Warsaw ghetto. In his diary, Brandt explains what has become known as his *Kniefall:* "An unusual burden accompanied me on my way to Warsaw. Nowhere else had a people suffered as in Poland. The machine-like annihilation of Polish Jewry represented a heightening of bloodthirstiness that no one had held possible. On my way to Warsaw [I carried with me] the memory of the fight to the death of the Warsaw ghetto, which I had followed from my Stockholm exile." Brandt remarks that he "had planned nothing" specific before the visit but felt he "had to do something to express the particularity of the commemoration at the ghetto monument. On the abyss of German history and carrying the burden of the millions who were murdered, I did what people do when words fail them." [*Abgrund der deutschen Geschichte und unter der Last der Millionen Ermordeten tat ich, was Menschen tun, wenn die Sprache versagt.*] Then he quotes a reporter, describing him at the scene, "Then he, who need not have, fell to his knees, for those who do not fall to their knees, but who need to—because they dared not or could not or could not dare." [*Dann kniet er, der das nicht nötig hat, fuer alle, die es nötig haben, aber nicht knien—weil sie es nicht wagen oder nicht können oder nicht wagen können.*] (Brandt 1994, 214, my translations).

Back home in Bonn, some critics attacked Brandt's *Kniefall*, claiming it was exaggerated; others criticized him more generally for failing to secure any rights of repatriation or compensation for Germans who had been driven from their Polish homes at the end of World War II. Furthermore, Brandt's personal history provoked questions about his patriotism, especially in his relations with foreign states. In his teens, Brandt had been an active Social Democrat and therefore made the Nazi blacklist, forcing him to flee Germany when the Nazis seized power in 1933. He sought exile in Norway, had his German citizenship revoked, and became a Norwegian citizen. In 1936 he returned to Germany under a false identity to work in the illegal underground, and in 1937 he went to Catalonia to fight in the Spanish Civil War. When the Germans invaded Norway in 1940, he moved to Sweden, where he spent the last five years of the war. In 1947 he returned to Berlin as a Norwegian press attaché. In 1949 he reacquired his German citizenship and subsequently entered German politics (see Prittie 1974). To some Germans, Brandt's apologetic gesture on behalf of the Germans recalled his wartime resistance, and it suggested disloyalty to the German cause.

The vast majority of people did not, however, criticize Brandt. The immediate Polish reaction was surprise and silence. During the remainder of his visit, no one in Poland mentioned that Brandt had fallen to his knees. Brandt also visited the Tomb of the Unknown Soldier on this trip, but there he laid a wreath without kneeling. Within days, the Polish press praised him and welcomed Brandt's sincerity, a sign of improvement in Polish-German relations. The majority of Germans, especially younger Germans who had not experienced the war, were startled and moved at this act of expiation, because it acknowledged German culpability for both Polish and Jewish suffering. In 1971 Brandt was awarded the Nobel Peace Prize for his efforts in pursuing friendship and peace with the Eastern bloc during the Cold War.

Example 2. A Vindication Commission apologizes to single individuals

Vindication is an act that repairs the damaged self-worth of victims. It is normally a minor concern of justice systems but became critical in Eastern and Central Europe after the regime changes of 1989, when large numbers of people came forward to identify themselves as victims of socialist political regimes and to demand official redress. In East Germany, people claimed to have suffered from numerous state-sponsored activities: the scandalous imprisonment of Social Democrats and Communists in Nazi concentration camps, Stalinist show trials, government kidnappings, removal and forced adoption of children, imprisonment for attempting to flee the republic, extortion in return for freedom to emigrate, and many other acts, such as blacklisting and discrimination in employment.

From November 1989 through March 1990, the East German Roundtable discussed possible remedies for victims of three regimes: Nazi rule from 1933–45, Soviet rule from 1944–89, and the German Democratic Republic (GDR) from 1949–89. On September 6, 1990, the freely elected GDR parliament passed a vindication law dealing with rectification for non-property-related harms. In the preamble to this law, the parliament defended the idea of rehabilitation and justice for the victims as more than a goodwill measure; it was also necessary to establish the legitimacy of the reformed democratic state.

Article 17 of the Unity Treaty, which was passed by the parliaments of both the West German and the interim East German governments, called on the future united German parliament to write a new rehabilitation law that would regulate these claims. But the dissolution of the GDR was followed by a paper war in the federal and provincial ministries, and passage was delayed for more than two years. In this period workers throughout Eastern and Central Europe created Commissions of Vindication) in many different places of employment that operated without legal sanction. In Germany they were called *Rehabilitierungskommissionen,* ostensibly to refer both to the process of restoration, of return to good standing after redress, and to vindication of the victim. Approximately midway through the work of these commissions, in 1992, the united German parliament established an *Enquete-Kommission* (Public Investigative Commission) to inquire into "the repressions of the Soviet Occupation Zone/GDR." It concluded its investigation and issued a final report in 1994 (Bundestag 1994a, 1994b). After some politicians and members of the commission themselves criticized the report for dealing only with the negative aspects of GDR history, parliament established another investigatory commission in 1995.

Between 1990 and 1993, I worked with one of the Vindication Commissions, that for East German Radio and Television. Its head, Herr Grollmitz, criticized the *Enquete-Kommission* for being more interested in "historical abstractions of what went on and in the historical evaluation of this period . . . than in the fate of individual histories." The *Enquete-Kommission* and the general public, complained Grollmitz, showed "only limited interest" in the Vindication Commission's goal of "reestablishing the honor and standing of former radio and television workers."

Although the united German government never directly conferred authority on the Vindication Commissions, it did eventually address their concerns in two laws. On October 29, 1992, legislators passed the "First Law for Settling SED-Illegality." On June 23, 1994, they passed a "Second Law for Settling SED-Illegality." Article 1 of the First Law clarified the scope of the law to be "rehabilitation and restitution of victims of illegal measures of criminal prosecution in the [GDR]." (see Schröder 1993, 350). The First Law established a list of GDR laws that should be considered illegal and identified the victims to be vindicated "insofar as the laws are irreconcilable with the essential principles of a free legal order." It codified the grounds for vindication and calculated financial restitution for categories of victims. The Second Law broadened the categories of victims and increased the amounts of restitution for some groups.

The Vindication Commission for Radio and Television took the form of an open yet limited inquiry, deliberating the nature of the wrong, the plausibility and veracity of the claim, and the possibility of procuring remedies. They primarily considered injuries suffered either directly at the hands of fellow workers or from the political instrumentalization of the workplace bureaucracy. Petitioners rarely made claims directly in the domain of corrective justice; the new German legal system had addressed many material harms immediately by returning property, restoring positions, or granting restitution. Instead, most claims concerned moral injuries: actions that were harmful but not in a readily quantifiable way.

If the Vindication Commission was able to verify a petitioner's claimed injury, it issued a letter of apology. The Vindication Commission for Radio and Television repeatedly used such letters to "reaffirm the political and moral integrity" of the victim. The letters expressed "regret for the repressions and discriminations," for "the destruction of meaningful career development," and for "the severe psychological stress." They offered sympathy for the suffering caused and "condemned the arbitrary measures employed" to isolate and persecute critical voices. The Commission then made the apologies public so that either the findings could be challenged or the larger community could acknowledge the Commission's vindication. Grollmitz asked newspapers and other forms of media to publish lists of people vindicated, which they occasionally did. The Commission could not materially compensate victims, nor did it have the power to go to court on behalf of petitioners, but it did actively engage other institutions in finding material remedies for harm suffered.

If the Commission verified a petitioner's claims, it would offer an official apology on behalf of the company. If a particular individual were responsible for the violation, the Commission would ask for a personal apology. Most of those responsible for violations had already left the company through voluntary retirement, however, so such apologies were rare. The Commission also frequently proposed that the state adjust the petitioner's pension as a form of economic compensation for particular losses.

The Case of Frau Winkler

Berlin's Vindication Commission for Radio and Television verified claims of injury for 75 (out of 100) petitioners; Frau Winkler was one of them. She argued that in the 1960s, while pregnant with her second child, she had been fired from her secretarial job for making political statements critical of the Party and denied unemployment and welfare entitlements. Thereafter, although she had been trained in radio and television production, she could not find meaningful employment corresponding to her level of skill. She believed the *Stasi* (State Security) had informally blacklisted her. For years she had suffered from under-employment and feelings of inadequacy, but she could attribute this only to her own worthlessness. Only with the disintegration of the state and the opening provided by this Commission did she consider the possibility of understanding why she had been singled out for discriminatory treatment. Frau Winkler then sought remedy for "defamation because of a critical position."

After Frau Winkler's second appearance at the Commission, I asked if she would be willing to discuss her case privately. She agreed and invited me to her home, along with Michael Weck, a German political scientist and my co-partner on parts of this research. At her home, I asked Frau Winkler when her problems began. She then related an event, a meeting in her boss's office, attended by the SED Party representative to the company. "*Ich habe gestrippt,*" she said. "*Gestrippt?*" I asked, thinking I had misheard her. Yes, indeed, she confirmed. Her boss, together with the Party representative, had called her into the meeting, where it seemed like she was being framed for making offhand comments critical of the Party. Feeling she would be unable to defend herself, she decided to take them by surprise, and strip.

Frau Winkler interpreted this meeting in her boss's office as confirmation that she had already been placed on a blacklist. If I understand her correctly, her striptease was an act of defiance against a group norm, an attempt to demonstrate *erotic worth* while she was denied *socialist self-worth*. It showed the men who were intent on taking away her dignity—for employment, the ability to work, was surely the measure of worth of the socialist person—that she had another source of worth (her body) and it was inaccessible to them.

Her bosses were, of course, caught off guard (as was I), and they never mentioned the incident again. Soon thereafter she was dismissed from her job, without proper notification. Even though she was a single mother with a second child on the way, and notwithstanding the GDR's pro-natal policy, her appeals for justice were denied. For the next thirty years, she felt socially isolated and frustrated in her career advancement in television and radio.

The Commission did not hear the story of the striptease, but only the details of Frau Winkler's employment history, and they could not verify those exact details. She was not named on any particular blacklist, her employers had not gone out of their way to criticize her in evaluations, and there were no records to verify that she had actually made any politically critical statements. Nonetheless, the Commission determined that her dismissal and punishment corresponded to a general pattern typical of the *Stasi* in the 1960s and 1970s. The *Stasi* seemed to blacklist people who voiced political opinions without taking actual formal legal action against them and without systematically documenting the measures taken. Such people subsequently suffered downward mobility in their careers. The Commission also determined that East German Radio and Television had indeed fired her and denied her benefits while she was pregnant, and this was crucial, because the act was in violation of East German law at the time. That she was later rehired at a lower level served to confirm the punitive nature of the action.

The Commission issued an official apology to Frau Winkler, and it wrote a letter to the West German social security commission documenting her injury and requesting an adjustment in her pension. Frau Winkler's pension was indeed adjusted to correct for the years of discrimination. The state contributed to affirming principles of dignity and accountability when it responded to the Commission's work, and hence it established t its own legitimacy as an impartial moral agent (cf. Rautenberg 1994).

Dignity and Democracy

Performative redress takes on special importance in the context of postwar German law. Article 1 of the West German Basic Law of 1949, which became pan-

German law after unification in October 1990, posits a fundamental, inviolable human dignity as the basis of human rights and many basic property rights. Given the industrial organization of Nazi mass murder, postwar German authorities found it imperative to assert each person's essential and irreducible humanity, a personhood independent of one's social history, legal status, or membership in a community (cf. Schachter 1983, 248–54). The use of the word *dignity* echoes the Kantian categorical imperative that people ought to be treated as "ends in themselves" and never simply as means to an end. The law defines dignity as a pre-political substance, something belonging to human nature as such that cannot be taken away. Formulated as a notion of personhood that applies to all potential subjects in a democratic state, the word *dignity* extends to all humans the high value inherent in the Latin term *dignitas,* which describes persons of high rank or honor alone (cf. Egonsson 1998).

The National Socialist system of valuation had made personhood contingent on membership in the *Volk* community. By erecting the nation as single referent, the Nazi system had reduced large groups of persons—Jews, gypsies, homosexuals—to a purely biological, animal existence. As postwar German authorities struggled to divest the society of Nazi values, they had to supersede the Kantian notion of dignity as an essentially pre-political substance. German authorities began to say that individuals who had suffered or resisted Nazi authority exhibited dignity. Thus, human dignity evolved beyond the realm of the pre-political and became something produced in political action, a substance that could be politically damaged and politically restored. Such values are fundamental to democracies but antithetical to totalitarian regimes, because they originate in the exercise of free will. Tzvetan Todorov (1996, 61) has elaborated on this contemporary understanding of dignity, arguing that people can assert dignity only in a public act; it "must give rise to an act that is visible to others (even if they are not actually there to see it)." Additionally, dignity cannot be gained from group identification, but is always a quality of individuals. In this sense, one of the most common assertions of dignity is an act of refusal to obey a command; the individuals thus assert their self-worth against a community norm.

Needless to say, after a regime change, the very same community whose norms are violated finds itself in the position of conferring dignity upon a person for resisting those norms. This apparent paradox points to a fundamental characteristic of dignity that differentiates democratic states from other states: dignity is both an inherent quality of the person and a quality gained through political action. The democratic subject is by nature both an inviolable, irreplaceable, objectively valuable human (pre-politically), and a political agent empowered within a particular community. If, in democratic states, individuals are granted certain protections and rights merely because they have this fundamental human quality called dignity, they are also capable of affirming, losing, or gaining dignity though the retroactive recognition of behaviors that violate community norms. By contrast, in a totalitarian state, dignity as political agency would ennoble only individuals who act in accord with the state's communal norms.

Especially during periods of regime change, democratizing states require retroactive recognition of dignity in order to reaffirm the importance of community norms, thereby enabling the state to rectify wrongs and reaffirm the possibility for justice. Moreover, a public agent must confer this recognition on individuals whose self-worth has been damaged because of community negligence or malevolence. In bestowing dignity, the community acknowledges that moral norms also apply to the group, and so it must lower itself in order for the victim to regain the self-worth that the community had denied. Such was the task of Brandt in Warsaw and of the Vindication Commissions in states of the former Soviet bloc.

The lack of severity of Frau Winkler's victimization—job discrimination compared to kidnapping, imprisonment, or murder, for example—may in some estimates discredit her demand for justice. But agents of the state had indeed tried to damage her dignity. She, in the face of this assault, asserted her eroticism as a form of self-expression that they could not deny. On the one hand, the East German state treated dignity as political agency to be granted or taken away, while on the other, she invoked it as something pre-political and inviolable. The post-1990 democratizing state, in turn, affirmed both definitions of dignity, with one major difference—dignity was not something it could take away from her, a democratic subject, but only something it might try, retroactively and surely inadequately, to restore. It could confirm her value only as someone who showed courage in exercising free will in resisting the norms of the group.

The Social Significance of Apologies

An apology, writes Nicholas Tavuchis, is a "secular rite of expiation . . . [that] works its magic by a kind of speech that cannot be contained or understood merely in terms of expediency or the desire to achieve reconciliation" (1991, 13). It functions as a performance, in which the intention of the speaker, the content of the message, and the effect on the listener equally contribute to the success of the apology. An apology cannot, then, be understood metaphorically as a "social text," as Paul Ricoeur (1981) proposed, understanding human action generally. A social text, Ricoeur maintained, can convey a message independent of the speaker's intent. A successful apology, by contrast, requires authenticity in the intent of the wrongdoer. That the intent must be clear to the listener (in this case, the wronged person) is also essential.

Nor can an apology function as a "remedial interchange" or as "impression management," as Erving Goffman (1971, 113–14) argued. "Remedial interchange" renders an offense "acceptable" merely through the form of the speech-act, without attention to the way in which the content is understood by the offended party. An apology that merely seeks to remedy a situation or to manage a situation strategically would not be accepted as authentic, since it totally circumvents redressing the dignity of the victim. Authenticity is situated in the performative act itself and in its acknowledgement of the impossibility of material remedy alone. Apologies are, in fact, "predicated upon the impossibility of restitution," writes Tavuchis (1991, 24). That is, material compensation and corrective justice themselves are always suspect, and victims often do refuse monetary awards for restitution; money can never compensate fully for loss and damaged dignity. An apology, by contrast, represents a purely symbolic exchange whereby the wrongdoer voluntarily lowers his own status as a person.

The need for performative redress does not, however, obviate or lessen the need for material restitution (see Borneman 2002a). Acts of material restitution to the Jews, the major victims of the Holocaust, preceded Willy Brandt's apology at the Warsaw ghetto. The Federal Republic of Germany had already given billions of deutsche marks in the name of the German people to the state of Israel, which acted in the name of the Jewish people. The Germans also paid restitution to many private individuals whose private property the Nazis had expropriated. More was necessary, however, to return the German nation to the human community of nations, even in the eyes of many Germans. Correcting a harm is not the same as righting a wrong. For several decades after World War II, national and international trials helped establish Nazi crimes as the ultimate symbol of evil. But trials did not clarify the level of responsibility of other Germans. Expressions of regret by Germans individually tended to sound hollow, for the regret of an individual German could not absolve the German people of crimes committed in the name of the collective. And who had the authority to apologize on behalf of the Germans to the human community for "crimes against humanity"? For some 25 years, no gesture seemed adequate to this task.

Brandt's apology was successful only because it was a symbolic act intended to right a wrong. He fell to his knees before the Polish people, in front of a monument to Poland's shattered Jewish community. The spontaneity of his gesture reinforced the authenticity of his expression of sorrow, as did his own lack of culpability in Nazi crimes. He apologized as the highest representative of the German people in the name of the German people. The Polish people accepted the sincerity of his act, and the apology inaugurated a new phase in the relations between Germany and both the Poles and the Jews it had persecuted. That the Poles were both victims of Nazi policies and at times collaborators intending to exterminate European Jewry complicates their victim status but not the authenticity of the apology.

Apologies, unlike testimonials or confessions of guilt, are not techniques for eliciting truth. Brandt's apology was neither a confession (he had worked in the resistance), nor did it testify to any new truth, as in a trial. His expression of remorse was purely symbolic. The German unconditional surrender of 1945 had served as a confession, and the numerous trials and historical accounts had documented the Nazi crimes. But redressing the wrongs required invoking the German people, who, as a symbolic entity, had come to signify the source of ultimate evil. It took the supreme representative of these people, and one who himself was untainted by these crimes, to apologize for them.

Only such a symbolic purification ritual could transform the German people from a criminal nation to a rehabilitated member of the international community. Purification required, first, a form of self-punishment: an obligation to relive the sorrowful events. Second, it required an act of reconciliation with the victims, in this case the Poles (including Polish Jews). Thus, an apology, while reciprocal, is also asymmetrical: while there is an exchange, ultimate responsibly always lies with one side. Paradoxically, through the act of reaffirming the value of the other, the wrongdoer (the German people) reestablishes its own value. Brandt's apology was effective only on the basis of an admission of the German people's categorical unworthiness—expressed by a collapse to his knees and speechlessness—before their victims, Poles and Polish Jews.

But how exactly does the German people reassert their national identity after admitting national culpability? The national symbolism of the apology depends not on its illocutionary meaning but on its perlocutionary effects. Today Brandt's act of remorse has been memorialized as a constitutive act of the German people in the post-unification German Historical Museum in Berlin. This museum serves to reinterpret the history of the German nation in the context of European political and social movements. Alongside recordings of other famous events in twentieth-century German history, including the building and the opening of the Berlin Wall, a looped video recording of Brandt's *Kniefall* plays continuously. The museum displays it amidst other objects of everyday life of central emotional importance to Germans like automobiles: the Nazi-era Volkswagen, the West German BMW, and the East German Trabant. More than half of the 22 written testimonials in a book published about Brandt following his death mention his Warsaw apology

(Engholm 1992). Many German secondary schools teach about the apology as an integral event of self-definition. It is a common topic on television talk shows, especially among members of the first postwar generation, who identify the apology as one of the first times they were either proud of a German statesman or proud to be German.

The use of the apology to define and establish one's relation to the referent nation presents a profoundly new type of constitutive act. By invoking a state apology as a form of self-identification, the Germans acknowledged the role of the Other in shaping their own nationhood. Brandt was paying tribute to the damage done to the Other as a condition of the German people's own future constitution. In this respect, the apology is an act of care that reverses roles of perpetrator and victim (cf. Borneman 2001). It vindicates the victim and rehabilitates the wrongdoer.

By apologizing and admitting categorical unworthiness, Brandt constituted the German people not as presence but as lack thereof, as a void in need of the recognition of the Other. The nation's incompleteness and emptiness is a necessary condition, as Claude Lefort (1986) has argued, in democratic states. By contrast, leaders in totalitarian regimes or in states whose democratization has frozen portray the nation in their own image and then fill in this referential space with their own visions and power. Instead of asserting that the German nation could determine its own identity, Brandt acknowledged the essential role of the Other, Jew and Pole, in redefining German identity.

The apologies of the people's Vindication Commissions to individuals worked in a comparable manner to Brandt's state-led act of contrition. Those who had suffered East German state-sponsored injustice came before the Commissions seeking the performative power of the apology to purify them, vindicate them, and enable them to resume life with a restored sense of value. The Commissions took upon themselves the work of lowering the nation's status to restore the unjustly damaged self-worth of the victims.

An apology alone, however, cannot complete the work of redress. Other actions must support it, such as punishing perpetrators through legal action, contesting accepted truth in public community forums, conducting critical historiography and museum education, constructing monuments to mourn victims, as well as providing material compensation (cf. Maier 1991; Offe 1992; Schaefgen 1994; Senatsverwaltung 1996; Weber and Piazolo 1995; ZERV 1993, 1994, 1996). Most of the individuals who came before the Vindication Commissions did desire material help, in the form of increased pensions or access to meaningful employment, and in some cases the law did eventually provide for corrective justice. Yet the Commissions' work was primarily symbolic and came in the form of apologies. This symbolism is a major factor in explaining the peaceful nature of regime transformation in East Germany, despite its creation of new forms of injustice through privatization and redistribution of property. The tranquility of the German transition stands in sharp contrast to that of other newly democratizing states of the former Eastern bloc. The former Yugoslavia is an extreme example of the alternative to performative redress: retributive violence that precludes taking the rectification of moral injuries to others seriously.

4 Reconciliation after Ethnic Cleansing: Listening, Retribution, Affiliation

Reconcile: to render no longer opposed. What conditions might make possible reconciliation after violent conflict? This essay addresses reconciliation in the aftermath of the ethnic cleansings and ethnicizations of the twentieth century. It neither elaborates a specific case nor makes detailed historical-cultural comparisons. Its potential contribution is theoretical and temporal: identifying contemporary psychosocial logics and processes integral to reconciliation after violent conflicts. In particular, it focuses on the role of the "third party" and argues for cultivating "practices of listening" after a violent conflict. The arguments presented can apply to reconciliation after conflicts other than those specifically referred to, but I restrict myself largely to a temporal diagnostic of the extreme case of what is today called ethnic cleansing: the attempt, through measures ranging from forced relocation to extermination, to eliminate from a social body, in whole or in part, a group based on identification as ethnic.[1]

I define *reconciliation* not in terms of permanent peace or harmony but as a project of *departure from violence.* To reconcile is an intersubjective process, an agreement to settle accounts that involves at least two subjects who are related in time. They are related in a temporal sense, not in that they necessarily have a shared past or even think of themselves as sharing a concrete future. Consensus about visions of the past or future—in modern parlance, a collective memory—may make reconciliation easier, but it is not necessary. The expectation of social consensus often presupposes what Laura Nader (1990) has dubbed "harmony ideology," and it may in fact awaken counterproductive drives to recover a lost whole or to produce a community without discord. Rather, to reconcile, different subjects must agree only "to render no longer opposed," which means sharing a present, a present that is nonrepetitive (Moore 1987). To agree to a present that does not repeat requires creating both a "sense of ending"—a radical break or rupture from existing relations—and a "sense of beginning"—a departure into new relations of affinity marked not by cyclical violence but by trust and care.

Traumatic Loss after Ethnic Cleansing

After ethnic cleansing, victims, and to some extent perpetrators, are engaged in a struggle whose stakes are much higher than mere survival. Hostilities and violence may continue in some form, but physical survival is a solvable problem. It is, on the other hand, one that resolves very little. At a deeper, existential level, survivors suffer from despair, an agony or melancholy of inconsolable and inarticulable grief. Despair, following Kierkegaard, does not result from an inability to live, but from "the disconsolateness of not being able to die. . . . What keeps the gnawing pain alive and keeps life in the pain . . . is the reason why he despairs . . . because he cannot consume himself, cannot get rid of himself, cannot become nothing" (1974, 342). Because most survivors cannot die, they are continually confronted with the psychic, social, and political tasks of dealing with the ever-present loss of those who did die. They must, in some way, attempt to recuperate or redeem this loss.

Yet the profound loss suffered in an ethnic cleansing—the unbearable loss of loved ones as well as the damage inflicted on one's own standards of self, irrespective of whether one is perpetrator or victim—is never fully recoupable. Some sense of the loss continually reappears, and because of this continuous and uncontrollable reappearance, survivors remain, necessarily, in a state resembling melancholy, unable to detach themselves from the love object or (as Freud would have it) prone to repetition compulsions.

The possibility of nonrepetition, then, rests on the recuperation of losses that are impossible to recuperate, the reconciliation with an end to which there is no end. This paradox is the key to reconciliation after ethnic cleansing. Two common attempts to recuperate loss are physical reproduction and revenge.

Recuperation of Loss through Physical Reproduction

Following an ethnic cleansing, in the face of a loss that cannot be articulated and that is unrecoupable, perhaps the most common attempt at recuperation is compulsive physical reproduction by victims. One might think that physical reproduction following ethnic cleansing is a positive transformation of a loss into a life-affirming event. But I think this interpretation is dangerous: first, because it does not take seriously the fundamentally paradoxical logic of such projects of recuperation; and second, because it does not acknowledge the likely dramatic consequences of trying to recuperate loss through physical reproduction.

Recuperation is impossible because of the nature of traumatic loss, which is experienced as a temporally delayed and repeated suffering of events that can be experienced and grasped only retrospectively (Caruth 1996). Loss that becomes traumatic is characterized by not having been experienced at the time of the occurrence. During an ethnic cleansing, some central aspect of the loss remains unregistered and escapes recognition at the actual time of happening; language and the ordering mechanisms of the symbolic order fail to register what is often called "the unspeakable." In other words, the event is only experienced later, if at all, as it returns to the victim unbidden, frequently as a horrifying silence that cannot be spoken—hence, our difficulty in detecting, understanding, or treating such an experience. Trauma resists any solution.

The suffering of traumatic loss cannot be stopped or overcome by presenting the possibility of return to a prior state of innocence or fullness. A recovery that might be a reconciliation, a departure from violence, is possible only, as Serge Leclaire (1998, 3) writes, if the loss is "relentlessly mourned and mourned." To assume a definitive end to this mourning is to place oneself in a limbo, "in the milky light of a shadowless, hopeless waiting." Indeed, an end to the despair is afforded only by the deliverance of death—that is to say, suicide. The victimized are thus challenged to begin anew without a material end; they are challenged to create an end and a departure that paradoxically also acknowledges its fictional character, a beginning that does not deny the loss.

Impatient with relentless mourning, to deliver themselves from this waiting, many survivors have babies. The arrival of the child changes the nature of the waiting, but it does not end the despair. Though it cannot recuperate a loss that is unrecoupable, it changes the waiting by presenting a potential fullness to fill the absence. Immediate physical reproduction after ethnic cleansing is the substitution of a child for the loss of a loved one, a living substitute for the dead. The child might well be the product of an act of love, and is likely thought of as a new beginning. But it carries with it the despair, the inability to die, that motivates much of the survivor's grief. Immediate reproduction perpetuates this despair by passing it on to the child, who then grows up bearing the parental expectations, their unfulfilled wishes and hopes, of recovering the loss suffered in the initial ethnic cleansing. The child is brought up in the light of these expectations. This wonderful child, the child of hope and despair, is asked to deliver the parents from their waiting. But deliver them where? Herein lurks a likely repetition of the violence, a strong motive for revenge, for the child to begin a new cycle of what Maurice Bloch (1992) calls "rebounding violence."

While rebounding violence may be potentially present in every time and people, its motives are always specific and historical. Today, reproduction after ethnic cleansing is situated within the global movement of ethnicization. An increase in ethnicization, a recovery, reinvention, or intensification of ethnic belonging, is observable in places across five continents, especially in states that legitimate themselves through ruling majorities. It is also a salient tendency among people who have been the victims of ethnic cleansing, especially among those who remain at the site of the violence or who are displaced but wait to return, those who are asked to reconstitute the social in living space marked by the memory of violence. In the last several decades, ethnicization has often accompanied separatist or secessionist demands. Some of the most prominent targeting of violence (and counterviolence) has followed rumblings of autonomy among Tamils in Sri Lanka, Kurds in Turkey and Iraq, Palestinians in Israel, various ethnic groups (Croats, Bosniaks, Macedonians, and Albanians) in Yugoslavia, Timorese in Indonesia, and Chechens in Russia. Milica Bookman (1997) has analyzed the use of procreation, largely by victimized groups, to obtain political dominance in these circumstances as a "demographic struggle for power."

Certainly, not all survivors of persecutions or attempted cleansings subscribe or submit to this strategy: reproductive motives vary within any group, and individuals who live in more permanent diasporas and who do not dream of a physical return act within a different political milieu with respect to sites of memories and structures of opportunity. There one can observe a plurality of strategies to recuperate losses, some of which entail neither procreation nor ethnicization.[2]

By contrast, this most recent wave in ethnic identification is usually furthered through procreative strategies. It is often talked about as a kind of "fundamentalization," wherein the group turns in on itself, engaging in a further purification of its principles, a nostalgia for autochthony, an obsession with origins and roots, and a clear demarcation of itself from other groups. Such a turn inward, or inner purification, not only appears to complete, in a putatively voluntaristic spirit, the ethnic cleansing initially perpetrated on the group, but it also institutionalizes a further "cleansing" of the group by enforcing endogamy on its members (Borneman 1998b). No marriage with ethnic Others. Studies conducted among post-Holocaust Jewish communities tend to confirm this hypothesis about the relation of violent cleansing to coerced endogamy.[3] Ethnographic studies over time are necessary to test the hypothesis in other places and to follow changing generational dynamics within different opportunity structures and in different places. But my impression is that it holds for most of the ethnic cleansings and violent expulsions of the last several decades—in Guatemala, Sri Lanka, East Timor, Bosnia, Rwanda, Kosovo, and Chechnya, to name some examples.[4]

If compulsive reproduction follows ethnic cleansing, it is directly related to, if not caused by, this ethnicization at the social and political levels. However understandable at a personal level, immediate reproduction after ethnic cleansing permits the fiction of a recuperation of loss through substitution of the living child for the dead. New group leaders who understand their purpose to be the reconstitution of the social, or *ethnie*, frequently instrumentalize this fiction in order to create and mobilize followers. Insofar as their authority is tied to an ethnicization of the group, political leaders encourage the illusion of recuperation of personal loss through substitution of the living child for the dead loved ones.

In today's world, the legitimacy of rule in most states—their recognition by other states and by their own residents—is based on the support of a numerical majority that can claim to represent the social. Such ruling majorities are never easily configured around a single ethnic affinity. After an ethnic cleansing, however, a multiethnic majority is yet more difficult to produce, since it usually requires reconciliation between the victimized group and the victimizer. Hence, a popular contemporary strategy to reconstitute the *ethnie* is to narrow its scope, to politicize and actualize it through a politics of long-term endogamous reproduction. So-called mixed marriages are the antithesis of this politics of exclusion. Endogamous pronatalism, then, substitutes a demographic strategy of a future numerical majority for a strategy based on other, more inclusive principles of present-day affiliation. In this way, the sociopolitical logic of ethnicization feeds off the attempt to recuperate an individual loss through physical reproduction.

In short, ethnicization is a politics of repetition. It is more likely to lead to a perpetuation of, rather than a departure from, violence. If the preconditions for reconciliation are a desire for nonrepetition and an appreciation of the intersubjectivity of the present, then reconciliation is improbable if not impossible without rethinking reproduction, without a new and more inclusive—that is, exogamous—politics of the domestic group.

Attempts to recuperate individual losses—other than procreation and ethnicization of the group—are worth exploring. Under what condition do women and men actually refuse ethnic reproduction after such violence? What forms of social inclusion and participation might lead women, specifically, to reject their own instrumentalization for the purposes of a politics of repetition of violence? Certainly, factors such as access to education, active inclusion in political life (the democratization of decision making), and expanded economic opportunities will substantively change the nature of a subject's relation to the social, making it less necessary to submit to compulsory reproduction as a means of recuperating losses.

Studies are needed that focus on those individuals (and their strategies) who successfully resist the pressures of ethnicization, compulsive reproduction, and rebounding violence. My own research, conducted with Jeffrey Peck, on German Jews who returned from exile after the Holocaust to East and West Germany, suggests that such individuals do exist and that their strategies vary with the degree and kind of social exclusion/inclusion. Many of those who returned did in fact immediately procreate; but significantly, most engaged in exogamy, and most resisted the pressures of immediate ethnicization. And nearly all of their children continued this trend, not finding it necessary to live out the wish of recuperation of parental loss (Borneman 1996; Borneman and Peck 1995). Above all, they resisted the understandable motivation of revenge and the group dynamic of rebounding violence.

Physical reproduction of the *ethnie,* then, is not a universal but rather a specific mode of recovery from ethnic cleansing. It tends to create a sense of continuity instead of a radical break or rupture from existing relations. Moreover, it relegates women to the presumably apolitical role of mothers of the future (cf. Enloe 1993). The sense of beginning that might be associated with the birth of a child is an illusion in this case, since the baby represents the wish to return to a prior state of wholeness and innocence. Especially today, given the political uses of pronatalism to support ethnic majoritarian projects, leaders tend to emplot new children within a narrative of recovery and recuperation. Because such endogamous physical reproduction denies the intersubjectivity of the present, it deflects from the work needed to reconcile social groups and actually increases the likelihood of a repetition of violence.

Possible alternatives to ethnicization would subscribe to more inclusive forms of affiliation and accord more generally with principles that articulate *care*— reciprocal but nonegalitarian practices that affirm intersubjectivity (Borneman 2001; Tronto 1993). Care might even take the form of an expedient politics of sterility, focusing radically on the present, in recognition of the immediacy of the need for reconciliation. In the aftermath of an ethnic cleansing, reconciliation calls for nothing less than an ethics of *caring for the enemy.*[5]

Recuperation of Loss through Revenge

Much like physical reproduction, revenge is an attempt to do the impossible: to recuperate a loss through the righting of a wrong—a wrong that, in truth, cannot be corrected. Revenge is a reciprocal exchange, a form of turn taking in which individuals or groups engage in reciprocal violence. But it is an exchange that is the opposite of caring. After violent conflict, revenge takes many forms, from reciprocating one's own suffering by expelling the expeller to creating myths about the eternal evil of the ethnic Other. Often motivated by personal frustration with continued injustice, individuals act to solve their own problems where jural authorities, or the state, will not or cannot act. In the anthropological literature, the principle of revenge is frequently equated with forms of justice administered by the state, but revenge distinguishes itself from legal redress in two crucial respects.

First, revenge is the arbitrary, narcissistic exercise of violence in which there is no accountability except to oneself (as part of a narrowly circumscribed group) and to a personal memory of the dead. Traditional "blood feuds" may be more orderly and less arbitrary than revenge as pursued by individuals in that a sub-stitute victim is chosen methodically, but they nonetheless reject any interven-tion by a third party to end the violence. In the attempt to "annul the crime," another crime is committed against another innocent subject. Second, revenge enacts a repetition by degrading the value of the wrongdoer (or the group of wrongdoers) in the same way that the original violence denied the value of the victim (or group of victims). The only difference from the "initial" violence is that those victimized have been, or hope to be, perpetrators at some point in the cycle. Revenge reenacts violence and therefore increases the likelihood of further rebounding violence.

That the state frequently fails in its pursuit of justice admittedly exacerbates revenge motives, as does the fact that many states themselves actually initiate much of the violence that then rebounds against them in the form of "terror." But a personal act of revenge, however organized and regulated by group norms, simply perpetuates rebounding violence. Ultimately, the arbitrariness of rule by "men of honor" insures a politics of repetition. The alternative to revenge after ethnic cleansing is, as I will make clear below, a legal reckoning with the violence, an invocation of the principles of the rule of law to settle accounts. Legal judgment fosters a sense of ending, which in turn facilitates the rebuild-ing of networks of trust and principles of accountability. That these networks of trust—specifically, trust in local judiciaries, police, or any third party to the conflict—often do not yet exist is, admittedly, a major challenge for any effort at reconciliation.

Here I would like to address two separate but complementary legal processes as alternatives to revenge, as modes of possible departure from violence, elements in a politics of nonrepetition. The first is witnessing; the second is the legal redress of violence, or what might be called *retributive justice*.

Witnessing, Truth-Telling, Trust

Witnessing is a kind of cultivated listening and is especially important in initiat-ing the healing of the wounds left by a violent process such as ethnic cleansing.[6] It involves the listening and speaking of at least two parties, and its intended end is *truth-telling*. It is primarily associated with speaking, with giving voice to individuals who have been silenced, but here I want instead to concentrate on witnessing as an act of listening, on the relation of speaking to the listener, a third party, after a violent conflict. A first step is to bring into discourse the silenced voices of victims. Experiences of harm and suffering, of being victimized by violence against oneself and one's group, are articulated and heard publicly. Such articulation has an immediate social effect in that it often contributes to the attribution of causality, ultimately leading to the possibility of symbolically righting the wrong, including making legal claims on perpetrators and holding them accountable for their wrongdoing. Courts, however, are only one forum in which witnessing can have an impact; others include familial discussions, neighborhood meetings, public hearings, and ritual events. Such forums should not be seen in competition with each other but as alternative sites for truth-telling.

The social practice of witnessing and its intended end, truth-telling, differ significantly from the social practice of confessing and its intended end, forgiveness. For one thing, the testimony of a witness tends to focus initially on the fate of the victim as a documentation of personal experience and affirmation of respect; confessing focuses primarily on the perpetrator. For another, witnessing is usually voluntary; confessions are frequently coerced. And thirdly, the primary effect of truth-telling would be to remedy a relationship, to effect a change in a social situation, whereas the primary effect of forgiveness is to induce a psychological state within an individual independently of whether the harm or relationship has been redressed socially or legally.[7] Without redress, forgiveness may therefore actually be harmful—conducive to a repression, or forgetting, of the initial conditions that lead to the harm. Such forgetting increases the likelihood of unconscious repetition. Witnessing, then, is victim oriented, noncoercive, and intended to redress a social situation through truth-telling.

Most recently, in Latin America and South Africa, the act of witnessing in controversial truth commissions has contributed to reconstructing a public sphere where truth—the truth of concrete lived experience—is itself given a value.[8] What do I mean by the "truth of experience," and how does one assign a value to it? To be sure, experiential accounts of overwhelming and traumatic events are in themselves incommensurable, and their veracity is often questionable. But the effects of truth-telling are far from the same for each account, and those effects—the perlocutionary force of speech—can be evaluated.

When is truth-telling trivial, and when does it make a critical difference? For a truth of experience to make a difference, to have a measurable effect, it must contradict or risk something—a risk, in the first instance, for the person speaking, but also for the listener, who might feel compelled to act differently based on the effects of what is said. A truth of this kind cannot merely confirm a general dogma but must also refer to a specific instance, signifying one outcome among a set of alternatives. In the aftermath of violent events, such truths have the effect of creating openings and points of departure. It is in this sense that Hans-Georg Gadamer, in his magisterial *Truth and Method* (1975), construes new experience as possible "only through negative instances. . . . Every experience worthy of the name runs counter to our expectation. [A true experience] involves an orientation toward new experience. That is why a person who is called 'experienced' has become such not only through experiences, but is also open to new experiences. The perfection of his experience, the perfect form of what we call 'experienced,' does not consist in the fact that someone already knows everything and knows better than anyone else. Rather, the experienced person proves to be, on the contrary, someone who is radically undogmatic; who, because of the many experiences he has had and the knowledge he has drawn from them, is particularly well equipped to have new experiences and to learn from them" (319). Truth-telling makes a difference, then, when the disclosed experience elicits an orientation to new experience.

The value put on speaking the truth also has a significant impact on establishing *networks of trust*. These networks include not only neighbors' relations with one another but also citizens' relations with the state and, in particular, with the courts and the justice system. By networks of trust I do not mean a reinvention of the civil society that Alexis de Tocqueville found in 1830s America, as recently proposed by Robert Putnam (1995) and Francis Fukuyama (1995), with reinvigorated family values and local bowling clubs. Putnam, in particular, casts civil society in the image of a historical past—pre-electronic, pre-mass communication, pre-suburb, pre-megalopolis—anchored in the institution of a strong nuclear family. In his own celebration of family values, Fukuyama presents Chinese Confucianism as a model for a certain scale of trust and economic organization. Familial-based trust, however, seems everywhere to reinforce forms of clientelism that—as is observable in postwar Italy, Belgium, and Germany, for example—easily turn into the social ill we call corruption. Clientelism shares with endogamy a similar function: to circumscribe the group and ensure the exclusion of outsiders. An alternative politics, in an age of intensified interaction between local and global differences and of dispersed families of different form, requires reimagining solidarity and sociality, not in terms of integration and consensus in a civil society, but in terms of difference in a dissensual community (Osiel 1995).

Solidarity in a dissensual community cannot be created through the invocation of "familiarity," a "shared past," or a "shared culture." Instead of proposing the People as One, solidarity must begin with acknowledgment of the heterogeneity of life projects, open toward cultural differences and new experiences of sociality (Kymlicka 1995; Lefort 1986). Here it is important to underscore the relation of witnessing and truth-telling to the creation of networks of trust. We might begin by looking to the Czech dissident, later president, Václav Havel, who explored "living in truth" as a central theme in his plays and essays, although he did not make its connection to trust explicit. Writing as a dissident about life under the repressive state-socialist regime (what he called a "post-totalitarian system"), Havel developed this concept in his 1978 essay "The Power of the

Powerless." The time in question was one of social stagnation, when the brutality of the post-1968 Czech state had given way to a cynical compact with its subjects: activity in "civil society" was permitted, but only to the extent that it did not present any possibility for the development of social networks of trust outside of those organized or co-opted by the state itself. Explicit oppression was replaced with a form of internalized violence aimed at the integrity of the individual's relation to the social, at sowing suspicion through lies and rumors between neighbors and friends.

Against this violence and distrust, Havel proposed "[l]iving within the truth [which] covers a vast territory . . . full of modest expressions of human volition, the vast majority of which will remain anonymous and whose political impact will probably never be felt or described any more concretely than simply as a part of a social climate or mood" (1986, 84–85). His plea at the time was not for more social clubs but for a more personal accounting and taking responsibility for everyday relations, a turning away from "abstract political visions of the future toward concrete human beings and ways of defending them" (93).

Rebuilding the integrity of the social—or, in the terms of this essay, an enduring reconciliation—must start with a social climate that encourages individual departures from violence. Such a climate is made possible through a continuous practice of truth-telling about the everyday, through witnessing and a double rebuilding on the basis of trust: between neighbors, and between citizens and the state. Those who listen to this truth-telling, who thus constitute the community within which truth-effects ripple, are rarely ever merely local actors. In most places today, relations with neighbors are no longer primarily face-to-face, and no group has the luxury of constructing its world independently of other groups. Relations between citizen and state may no longer prioritize issues of defense and internal security, which in any case are increasingly difficult for states to provide without the aid of suprastate organizations.

Trust, in other words, must be reestablished under new conditions of the production of truth, conditions that embed the individual, the ethnic group, and the truth-effects in larger and more global concentric circles—networks—of others. Caring for the enemy, then, becomes an essential aspect of any ongoing reconciliation. This said, an elaboration of the conditions necessary for the establishment of trust must reckon with the forms of affiliation that are specific to a given place. The institutional forms in which any society incorporates networks of trust—friendship, kinship, residence in neighborhoods, membership in parties, clubs, or social movements—will inevitably vary. What is certain is that no attempt at reconciliation through stretching the horizons of forms of local affiliation will succeed if the diverse and locally contingent character of such forms is not taken into account.

Listening, Witnessing, Accountability

What is the relation of witnessing as an activity to principles of accountability? Witnessing fundamentally involves speaking and giving voice, but it must be preceded and followed by listening. To listen is a motivated practice that differs from hearing in that it always involves listening *for*. Following an ethnic cleansing, this mandates listening for truth. In German, this difference between hearing and listening is clearly drawn in the distinction between *hören* and *zuhören*, the prefix *zu* indicating to, at, in, on, by—to come closer to the hearing, and to hear for something. To listen for everything is to hear a cacophony of sounds; what is called noise. But to listen for truth entails a complex interpretative and evaluative process that goes beyond documenting experience per se.

Listening is a practice, an art, similar to that of reading or speaking. It is not passive but interactive, involving soliciting, questioning, and weighing competing accounts, as well as hearing. Listening can be learned and cultivated, and some individuals are far better at it than others. I am suggesting here that we rethink the very practice of listening—both what should be listened for, and who might be the best practitioners of listening after violent events. Potential listeners include not only members of truth commissions, friends, neighbors, anthropologists, and historians but also professional observers, such as the Organization for Cooperation and Security in Europe (OCSE), UN "monitors," and individuals who work for Human Rights Watch and Amnesty International.[9] Professional "observers," in particular, might redefine themselves as "listeners" and actively cultivate the art of listening for the truth. Such listening does not mimetically reproduce the speech of suffering but listens specifically for potential departures from violence. What does this entail?

The significance of listening is not directly linked to its timing, although such timing itself has significant effects on the production of true accounts. Listening for the truth in conflictual situations would occur ideally at the moments when violence is initiated, but that is usually impossible. It is in the interest of perpetrators of harm to delay the timing of listening, with the result that third parties are limited to documenting the violence's escalation or are confined to retrieving the fallible work of memory. Hence, the simple presence of professional listeners at a moment of escalating conflict may actually make potential perpetrators of harm pause before committing acts of violence.[10]

Likewise, the question of when this listening is turned into voicing, or witnessing, is a matter of the political control of timing. Political in character, too, is the question of the forums—familial, neighborhood, television, courtroom—in which the voicing, and the allocation of accountability, takes place. The timing of voicing truth claims based on listening requires sensitivity to the specific character of place and context, to the politics of the present. In other words, the effect of truth-telling on establishing wrongdoing, socially and legally, is highly context dependent. But the nature of listening is not. Hence, the telling of some truths has no effect until years after the actual experiences are listened to and documented. This delay in fact heightens the significance of professional listening during the unfolding of an event. A delayed impact was demonstrated, for example, in the prosecution of many Nazi war criminals, such as Adolf Eichmann, in which wrongdoing was assessed and allocated in Jerusalem more than a decade after the crimes had occurred in Germany.

Today, those who record the perpetration of atrocities must often reckon with such a delay and perhaps with an extraterritorial judicial process as well. Such is the case with Yale University's Cambodia Project of simply listening to witnesses and gathering evidence of Pol Pot's crimes without any immediate hope of a reckoning; with the attempt in Britain to prosecute Chile's General Augusto Pinochet for murders more than two decades after they were committed; with the attempt in Senegal to prosecute Chad's Hissène Habré for political killings, torture, and disappearances a decade after his murderous rule; or with the UN tribunal prosecution of accused Bosnian war criminals who remain at the top of the local hierarchy.

My focus on listening here is not meant to discount the importance of voice, which has received much recent attention in the human and social sciences. Voicing projects, however, tend to emphasize the authority of the location of the speaker and to be concerned with the constructedness and autonomy of discourse—as over and against the truth-value of the message and its relation to listeners. Such empathic recovery and voicing on the part of oppressed minorities, motivated by their claims of injustice, often even contributes to ethnicization. And it fails to direct us to the ineffectiveness of speaking if no one listens, and to the question of how and on what basis one should act upon listening, should it occur.

A serious limitation of many of the truth commissions of the 1990s is that they explicitly delinked telling the truth from any retribution. Separating the search for truth from the administration of justice was pointedly the policy of South Africa's Commission for Truth and Reconciliation, which has quickly become the model for independent investigatory commissions.[11] Benefits accrued from the harm inflicted on others—especially through privileged access to land ownership and education—were never taken away from most perpetrators. Instead, the vast majority of victims were left without material redress and most often admonished simply to forgive rather than seek justice. In many cases, the voicing of suffering served to reenact trauma without directing any attention to the punishment of the institutional agents of the violence. That said, even if perpetrators had been made to listen, a temporal delay in legal retribution was to have been expected—and is to be expected in the future. The frequent necessity of negotiating with perpetrators during periods of regime transition requires compromises in the pursuit of justice in the short run. My point, however, is that listening, witnessing, and retribution cannot be delinked in a project of reconciliation over time; they are conceptually part of the same complex.

To contribute to reconciliation, this complex requires public forums—including newsprint, radio, and television—where participants in widely dispersed communities feel compelled to listen, to weigh, and to judge competing accounts. Ultimately, such forums will lead to an open acknowledgment of dissensus, of the ambivalences and complicities inherent in the exercise of power. They may even lead to public conflict and to aggression directed toward those who have truths to tell. But because this acknowledgment affirms the power of truth-telling in creating a public sphere, it is in the interest of democratic publics. Hence, it will likely lessen the cynicism that usually accompanies revelations about the workings of power generally, and it introduces the possibility of transparency and accountability in social relations, thereby preparing for the building of trust. In short, third-party listening, as a necessary precondition to giving voice, creates the possibility for departure, for a sense of ending, rupture, and break with the past.

A sense of ending is made possible only by breaking hegemonic silences concerning the nature of loss and its attempted recuperation in relation to the sources of violence and its modes of reproduction. The cultivation of listening as a concrete social practice contributes to making a public sphere that is vigilant, critical, and engaged. While educated and critical elites are important for this public sphere, they are insufficient without diverse popular participation. Many of the nascent public spheres in Latin America, Europe, and much of Asia, for example, are initially peopled by marginal actors—women or minority groups— whose interests are diverse and dissentious, and hence not easily appropriated and instrumentalized for the purposes of ethnicization.

The success of interventions by international nongovernment organizations in support of "civil society projects" may in fact depend largely on their ability to listen to these marginal or dissenting voices. It is frequently the case that pressures for unity after a violent conflict silence voices of difference, displacing violence formerly directed at an external enemy to marginalized groups within a society or even to women and children within one's own domestic group. Listening to marginal actors is important because they often have the greatest interest in departing from patterns of rebounding violence. With the most to gain and the least to lose, marginal actors are also willing to take the greatest risks. Their voices deserve our attention, then, not because of the extremity of their suffering or the location from which they speak, but because of the risk they embody in speaking the truth. Listening for the truth in the aftermath of violence, while crucial for long-term reconciliation, only actually becomes truth, as Michel Foucault (1980) would argue, when plugged into practices and systems of power. Listening must therefore be complemented by a process of legal and institutional accountability, to which I now turn.

Legal Retribution

Unlike witnessing, which rests on truth-telling and listening for the truth, a legal accounting in the domain of retributive justice is concerned with symbolically affirming the distinction between right and wrong (Hampton 1992). Retribution does this by means both of punishment—taking away the advantage accrued from wrongdoing—and of vindication—affirming the value of the victim. As mentioned above, the truth must first be told in practices of listening and witnessing in the public sphere before courts can consider competing accounts. Hence, legal retribution is always in some sense delayed. Moreover, courts are only formally independent of the other branches of government, which makes it difficult for them to participate in truth-telling when it may implicate members of the executive or legislative branches. And making judicial appointments and setting the budgets, as well as determining types of criminality, are very much political decisions that rest with executive and legislative actors. Furthermore, if courts convict, they need the cooperation of the other branches of government to enforce their rulings and carry out their sentences.

This embeddedness within political processes contributes to pragmatic delays in the legal reckoning with injustices, delays in legal investigation and prosecution that result in trials decades after the actual occurrence of harm and wrongdoing. But if reconciliation is never merely an individual act but always a social one, then an eventual settling of accounts involves the punishment of evil and the rewarding of good by a higher authority, with judgment rendered through regularized procedures by a recognized court of law. Such a process is integral to making possible a departure from violence after ethnic cleansing. Departures, then, are not a matter of finding the proper balance between remembering and forgetting, but of reconciling the self and the group with the permanence of loss. This memory can best be reconciled when courts reaffirm, with the authority of the state behind them, the fiction of "an end."

In *Settling Accounts: Violence, Justice, and Accountability in Postsocialist Europe* (1997), I argued that legal accountability is not just desirable but also necessary, although only in democracies. Unlike other political forms, democracies require a form of strict accountability. The stability of a democratic regime is dependent on a formally autonomous legal system that can invoke principles of accountability and apply them to members of the executive and parliamentary branches of government. Such legal accounting is never capable of redressing all of the wrongs perpetrated—it cannot recuperate the losses suffered in an ethnic cleansing. But its significance derives not from the efficiency and comprehensiveness of its prosecutions but from the political efficacy of prosecuting select, symbolically significant cases—what might be called a *ritual purification of the center*—and thus creating a sense of ending to the set of injustices. A ritual efficacy is thus the measure of the success of nonarbitrary institutions of law that are positioned above individual men and women and are independent of particular social groups. Such legal institutions, if they make good-faith efforts at justice, nurture networks of trust among disparate individuals and between citizens and the state. This trust, in turn, relieves victims, or victimized groups, of the need to take justice into their own hands—that is, it takes away one of the prime motives for personal or collective revenge.[12]

A further step in this direction was made in 1998, when 120 nations agreed to set up a permanent International Criminal Tribunal in The Hague. Formally independent international tribunals are presently at work establishing accountability for ethnic cleansings in the Balkans and the attempted genocide in Rwanda. In 1999, an alternative UN joint war crimes tribunal was proposed for Cambodia, in which Cambodian and foreign judges would try former political and military leaders of the Khmer Rouge in a single trial. That these tribunals lack their own effective enforcement powers, and are dependent on national judiciaries and armies for exacting compliance with international judgments, presents a formidable obstacle that may eventually doom their efforts. Also an obstacle is the fact that such supranational courts are not democratically constituted and therefore make no pretense of representing majorities. Without the support of democratically elected majorities, courts risk a legitimation crisis. This is especially so when they base their judgments on "human rights" in the defense of injured minorities or on appeals to the cosmopolitan ideas of intellectual elites. Unlike civil rights, human rights have no democratically organized or territorial constituency. To the extent that national legal authorities reconstruct their own domestic legitimacy by appealing to an ideology of universal human rights, as against particular legislated or constitutionally anchored national civil rights, the two levels of legal authority work not in opposition but in tandem. However, at the moment, this is not what is happening in most nondemocratic states. The worst perpetrators of abuses and the most powerful states, of course, will be the most sensitive to the issue of legal sovereignty and will insist on the discreteness and indivisibility of their sovereignty.

Obstacles to enforcement are present for all judicial systems; however, they are simply more formidable for those in their formative stages and for those lacking the naturalized sovereignty claims of state-run legal systems. The legitimacy of the decision of a court, national or international, may ultimately be based not on the claim that it represents the will of the majority but on the claim that it is "right" or represents the "truth" as determined through impartial and fair procedures. But truth or rightness is also always perspectival, and the acceptance of legal findings as "right" is contingent on many factors.

The legitimation crisis surrounding human rights norms will involve a lengthy struggle, one unlikely to be resolved in the near future. But this was also the case historically in establishing the legitimacy of decisions made by national legal courts, including those within Europe. That struggle has never really ended, because any court is always confronted with demands to respond to three legitimacy claims simultaneously: the particular testimony of harm and the need for redress, majority public opinion, and the demand to represent an abstract "right" or "truth." In each and every context, the timing of the prosecution of cases is a strategic decision that is legitimated over time as "ordinary" people are asked to abide by legal judgments. While popular acceptance of legal judgments by international courts—or by local court judgments that appeal to international standards—may be desired, a degree of popular acquiescence may be the only effect immediately obtainable. Acquiescence, after all, also contributes to legal legitimacy.

The time lag in the popular reception of legal judgments will undoubtedly affect their efficacy, but not in ways that can be clearly foreseen. Legal efficacy is a processual feat, never achieved at the time of judgment or sentencing. The crucial factor at present is that international tribunals, like national courts, make good-faith efforts, through the time-tested procedures of the rule of law, to listen for the truth, witnessing and documenting the harms perpetrated and procuring remedies for them. Passing and enforcing judgments is crucial, but it is only the last step in a settling of accounts that itself will remain open to memory work over time. Retributive justice merely creates a sense of ending by stopping the cycle of rebounding violence, thereby inaugurating the possibility of mourning the losses and articulating alternative beginnings.

Reconciliation and Peacekeeping

In sum, I have argued that reconciliation is an agreement among antagonistic subjects to depart from violence in a shared present. This present requires both domestic and governmental initiatives to restructure principles of affiliation. Our ability to imagine departures from violence is hampered by inadequate understanding of the relation between alternative responses to personal loss and the possibilities of justice. The first term in the relation, responses to personal loss, alerts us to the importance of principles of care, networks of trust, and an inclusive political vision that can suggest alternatives to the politics of endogamous physical reproduction and the potential effects of its instantiation as ethnicization. The second, the possibilities of justice, alerts us to an alternative to revenge and rebounding violence: a system of national and extranational legal accountability, embodied in the principle of the rule of law.

Imagining departures from violence has not been a major project among anthropologists or other social scientists. But if we are to contribute to reconciliation in the many communities in which we work, then such imaginings are an essential part of our work. They are perhaps the major contribution we might make to what are called international peacekeeping efforts. Since the latter part of the twentieth century, regional, national, international, and transnational actors and organizations have increasingly been challenged by the escalation of violence and the proliferation of ethnic cleansing. In each situation, formally external or third parties, such as the United Nations, are being asked to respond. Among the militaries of many industrialized nations—the United States, Canada, Australia, and Europe, in particular—peace efforts increasingly supplement, and often replace, coercive military operations. Or at least that is their explicit intent. "Peacekeeping efforts" are formal attempts within a particular locality to end "hostilities" and bring about a "reconciliation," a nonrepetition of events, after a period of intense violence—in the most extreme scenario, after an attempted genocide. In this essay, I have tried to address such efforts and obstacles to them in a new way.

Unfortunately, even if we grant good intentions, we know that most peacekeeping efforts fail or are failing. This essay suggests that the failure must initially be addressed by something as modest as cultivating the art of listening. Listening is part of the professional ethos, if not always of the practices, of anthropology. This resource, when further professionalized, might be taught and shared with peacekeepers. It is a fact that peacekeepers are rarely asked, as anthropologists are, to understand the local in its own terms and to reflect self-critically on the process of arriving at that understanding. They frequently see the "native's point of view"—an expression coined by Bronislaw Malinowski, the *Urvater* of fieldwork-based anthropology—as culturally fixed, intransigent, and as more an obstacle than a cultural difference and aid to peacekeeping. But taking the native's point of view as the starting point of a relationship is indispensable, even more so now that we realize that the native has many and conflicting points of view.

How then, indeed, "to render no longer opposed"? Any new solidarity, to the extent that it is possible after violent conflict, would be based, not on common culture, but on acknowledging the nature of differences in their layered registers of local and global articulation. This acknowledgment is possible only when different forums for truth-telling exist. Like anthropologists, peacekeepers are professional third parties who could be trained to listen, specifically for departures from violence. When stationed at the site of violence, both anthropologists and peacekeepers could serve as crucial witnesses. Because witnessing is oriented not toward any coercive harmony but toward perspectival truth-telling, it presents the most propitious opening to communication within and across social groups. It is through the creation of an open dissensus that individuals will be enabled to seek new forms of affiliation and to demand a public transparency that invokes principles of accountability.

Like anthropologists, peacekeepers themselves enter strange settings not as neutral observers but as additional signifiers of difference within dissensual communities. Regardless of how we perceive ourselves, we are always subject to projections on the part of the local imaginary. Once peacekeepers enter as bodies with money, tools, guns, and access to other worlds, they become constitutive of the shaping of local cultural processes.[13] If they cannot help but play an active role, they can try to direct the local articulation of difference into a particular form: one oriented toward witnessing, listening for the truth of experience, enacting more inclusive principles of affiliation, and encouraging personal and legal accountability through governmental reform.

On the surface, this particular vision may seem Janus-faced, for it assumes both *Realpolitik*—the omnipresence of interests and power—and *utopia*—the possibility of a departure from violence. That, indeed, is the condition of any analysis of reconciliation that does not evade the fundamental paradox of the task: to facilitate an ongoing recuperation of a loss that is not recoupable. I have tried to bring a certain understanding of contemporary anthropology to bear on the problem of ethnic cleansing and peacekeeping. This anthropology insists on the primacy and professionalization of the activity of listening. It calls for knowledge that is intersubjective, fundamentally reflexive and relational, and that requires an often uncomfortable encounter with alterity. It challenges us to intervene simultaneously on the side of accountability, trust, and care for the Other, including the enemy.

5 The State of War Crimes following the Israeli-Hezbollah War

This essay examines the state of "war crimes" today by thinking through why the prosecution of war crimes has been frustrated in the 2006 Israeli-Hezbollah War in Lebanon. It focuses on legal issues regarding the conduct of war (*jus in bello*), and critically analyzes how the threat of prosecution due to the use of excessive violence might affect the different tactical and strategic "self-interests" of the belligerents. Finally, it makes an argument in favor of when principles of proportionality may trump principles of equity, and assesses the political efficacy of prosecutions in this case. This war brings to light several paradoxes in the field of international justice generally, or international humanitarian law more specifically, and suggests a certain contemporary impasse in the prosecution of war crimes.

The war lasted for 34 days, from July 12 to August 14 in the summer of 2006, and pitted Hezbollah (Party of God) paramilitary forces against the state of Israel. In Lebanon it was dubbed the "July War"; in Israel, the "Second Lebanon War." But since this war was not primarily either about a period of time or about Lebanon, I prefer to call it, after its major belligerents, the Israeli-Hezbollah War.[1] Claiming to be responding to a July 12 raid by Hezbollah forces into Israel, in which they abducted two Israeli soldiers and killed three others, and to a failed rescue mission in which five more soldiers were killed, Israel launched massive airstrikes and artillery fire on the Lebanese civilian infrastructure, an air and naval blockade, and a ground invasion of southern Lebanon.[2] During the conflict, 159 Israelis were killed, most of whom were soldiers. However, about 41 civilians were also hit by some 4000 Katyusha rockets and mortars indiscriminately fired by Hezbollah forces from Lebanon into northern Israel. Another 997 were injured (seventy-five "seriously" and 115 "moderately"), and approximately 300,000 Israeli civilians were displaced.

On the other side, 1,191 Lebanese were killed, nearly all civilians. One third of those killed were children under twelve, including about 43 Lebanese soldiers and police, 74 Hezbollah and 17 Amal combatants. Further, some 4,490 Lebanese were wounded, and approximately 900,000 were displaced. Israeli attacks obliterated several villages and sections of Beirut and Tyre, set some forests in the north afire, caused an estimated $280 million in agricultural damage, and in targeting power stations and oil refineries, unleashed an oil slick in the eastern Mediterranean whose environmental damage is estimated to be $64 million. Moreover, a July 25 airstrike on a UN peacekeeping post in Khiyam left four United Nations Interim Force in Lebanon [UNIFIL] observers dead.[3]

Perhaps the most controversial of these attacks was the artillery units' use of white phosphorous shells (which cause painful and often lethal burns), and the air force's dropping, indiscriminately in civilian areas, of at least 1,800 cluster bombs containing 1.2 million cluster bomblets around the south of Lebanon. Neither weapon is banned by international law, but 90 percent of the bomblets were scattered north of the Litani River in the final 72 hours of the assault in rich agricultural land outside the "Katyusha" range for targets within Israel.[4] At the time of the UN-brokered ceasefire that ended the armed conflict, more than 100,000 of these unexploded bomblets were causing, and will continue to cause, accidental deaths into the indefinite future.

The facts of this international armed conflict are well documented, and on the surface they constitute convincing evidence of several kinds of violations of the rules of war. Indeed, a three-member commission of the United Nations Human Rights Council [UNHCR], sent to Lebanon to probe charges of "systematic targeting and killing" of Lebanese civilians by Israel, concluded in a November 21, 2006 report that Israel was guilty of "excessive, indiscriminate and disproportionate use of force against Lebanese civilians and civilian objects" in the war. At the same time, the commission found evidence of Hezbollah's "using UNIFIL and Observer Group Lebanon posts as deliberate shields for the firing of their rockets."[5]

International machinery in the form of the International Criminal Court [ICC] was established in The Hague in 2002 as a treaty-based "court of last resort" to prosecute such violations (after July 2002) in cases where national judicial systems are incapable or unwilling to do so. However, it appears at present highly unlikely that there will be a prosecution for the violations of either side.[6] This is not simply because Israel, and its major supporter, the United States, have refused to participate in the ICC or recognize its jurisdiction, or that Lebanon also has not acceded to the *Rome Statute* of the ICC, or that Hezbollah and its allies would resist any prosecution of its own actions, perhaps directly targeting witnesses and judicial officials. Many Lebanese and Israelis have dual citizenship, that is, citizenship in a signatory nation, which means that members of the Hezbollah forces or the Israeli military, members of so-called "objector nations," could still be prosecuted or appear as plaintiffs before the ICC. In addition, there could be a prosecution on behalf of the UN peacekeepers "apparently deliberately target[ed]" in Khiyam.[7] The reasons for the lack of prosecution of war crimes must, therefore, lie elsewhere.[8]

Conduct in a War and Commencing a War

Rules to limit the type and extent of violence permissible in war are the oldest of judiciable wrongs in the international sphere, though their evolution has not been continuous.[9] The statute that established the ICC makes war crimes part of a trilogy of human rights violations.[10] It contains three articles: Article 6 regulating genocide, Article 7 regulating crimes against humanity, and Article 8 regulating war crimes. Article 8 is by far the lengthiest and most detailed of these. All three offences have been conceptualized as involving excessive violence, primarily of state militaries or groups modeled after them (e.g., irregulars, guerrillas, militias), and because of their exceptionally heinous nature, they have no statute of limitations.

War crimes are not only the oldest of international offences, but they also distinguish themselves from the others in that all groups, at least during any period of intense armed conflict, have a peculiarly strong self-interest in upholding the rules against them. Unlike the regulation of crimes against humanity and genocide, rules of war intend to limit the cruelty and destructiveness (egregious violence) that the enemy can legitimately inflict. Rules of war are about protecting oneself from the aggression of the other and not the other from one's own aggression. A secondary aspect of self-interest rests in the assumption that if the violence in armed conflict is limited in type and extent, then such conflicts will not expand, and reconciliation between the belligerents after the war is more likely. These self-interest motives should, theoretically, give war crimes a particular advantage over the other two types of human rights violations and lead to an international consensus on their regulation, but that is clearly not the case; their nature and the conditions under which such violence is actionable, in the legal sense, remain as essentially contested as ever.

For several reasons, my focus will be on legal issues regarding the conduct of war (*jus in bello*) and not on the legality of initiating war (*jus ad bellum*), although the laws of war cover both categories of offence. The Nuremberg precedent, strictly speaking, like the *Kellogg-Briand Pact* of 1928 before it, reinforced a belief that was not so foregrounded in the declarations of The Hague Conferences of 1899 and 1907 or the Geneva Conventions of 1929 and 1949: that one could hinder a conflict by identifying and prosecuting the party who commences a war. According to this belief, the supreme international crime is that of commencing a war of aggression, also sometimes called "crimes against peace," because it is the crime from which all war crimes follow; and, equally important, it was assumed that the threat of prosecution for commencing a war would prevent future wars.

First, the evidence from the last century overwhelmingly disproves these assumptions. All war crimes do not follow from the commencement of a war (for example, it is possible to commit a war crime through strategic assaults, such as the massacre of 9/11, without actually commencing a war or even intending to do so). And if, following the Nuremberg precedent, the threat of prosecution for such action had deterred future wars, then we would not have witnessed the sheer number and brutality of armed conflicts, and of recurrent wars, in the Cold War and post–Cold War periods. Especially since Nuremberg and the Geneva Protocols, examples of states, both weak and small, and of non-state groups initiating war are simply too numerous to support the hypothesis that the threat of prosecution has acted as a deterrent. To be sure, I am still of the opinion that we should support international efforts to prevent the planning, preparing, or initiating of wars of aggression. But there is little reason to expect the threat of legal prosecution for commencing a war to be a deterrent to armed conflict generally. This deterrent must come from a source, if not outside, then at least one not primarily dependent on law. The establishment of the ICC and its unique ability to threaten an international prosecution is unlikely to change this logic.

Second, except perhaps in new wars with little history of conflict among the belligerents, it is nearly impossible to establish fairly that one side alone is primarily responsible for commencing a war. In the case at hand, Israel and Hezbollah both claim, plausibly enough, that the other initiated the war; and both can indeed legitimate their claims if one grants their respective periodizations of when the conflict began. Pointing to the immediate abduction of soldiers, Israel has a very good prima facie case that Hezbollah's actions forced it into an equally aggressive response. Alternately, however, Hezbollah's Secretary-General Sheikh Hassan Nasrallah claims that the abductions were a response to four prior Israeli actions: occupation of the Shebaa Farms, violations of Lebanese sovereignty, holding of prisoners, and attacks on Lebanese civilians.[11] These claims may be, and usually are, dismissed as specious, but not because they are factually incorrect. Rather, they are disputed as to their significance in a chain of events over time. As with most long-running conflicts, the date of and responsibility for the origin of excessive aggression is subject to an infinite regress. In any conflict that endures, there is usually a point in time, and usually fairly early during the hostilities, when the victim also becomes an aggressor. For this reason, as in all long-running conflicts, it is not possible to arrive at a fair or just conclusion about who is solely or primarily responsible for commencing the war of 2006. Each claim regarding "commencement of armed conflict" is correct from its own perspective about the temporal sequence of events.

Third, assessing one party as solely responsible for commencing a war is often used as justification by the (then recognized) victim group for not conforming to the rules about how to conduct war fairly. In this way, the question of the origin of the war serves to deflect one's focus from a question that can be subject to realistic assessment and legal regulation: not how to stop aggression but how to deter excessive violence. How, after an ongoing conflict becomes defined as a "war," might the threat of prosecution for war crimes subject the belligerents to legally binding rules specifically limiting the type and amount of permissible violence?

War Crimes in the Israeli-Hezbollah War

What are the alleged war crimes? The UN Commission of Inquiry report concludes that the conflict was an "international armed conflict" (fulfilling the first condition of Article 8 of the statute that established the ICC), and that the "basic corpus of international humanitarian law" and "international human rights law" are applicable, specifically to Israel, Lebanon, and Hezbollah.[12] As required by its mandate, this UN Commission largely restricts itself to the damage Israel inflicted in this war. Nonetheless, it also finds evidence of Hezbollah violations. For neither side does it specify which war crimes specifically may apply.[13] My purpose here is not to construct a case against either Israel or Hezbollah, but merely to establish that there is abundant evidence, outlined above in the first section of this article, as well as in the necessary statutes, to make a war crime prosecution of both sides possible. To present some initial order, we can identify under Article 8 of the ICC statute minimally three war crimes that might apply to both Israel and Hezbollah, two that might apply primarily to Hezbollah, and six that might apply primarily to Israel.[14]

Of those crimes that apply to both:

Article 8 (2) (a) (iv): War crime of destruction and appropriation of property. Article 8 (2) (b) (i): War crime of attacking civilians. Article 8 (2) (b) (v) War crime of attacking undefended places.

Of those that apply primarily to Hezbollah:

Article 8 (2) (a) (viii) War crime of taking hostages: "The perpetrator intended to compel a State, an international organization, a natural or legal person or a group of persons to act or refrain from acting as an explicit or implicit condition for the safety or the release of such person or persons." Article 8 (2) (b) (xxiii) War crime of using protected persons as shields: "The perpetrator moved or otherwise took advantage of the location of one or more civilians or other persons protected under the international law of armed conflict."

Of those that apply primarily to Israel:

Article 8 (2) (a) (iii) War crime of willfully causing great suffering. Article 8 (2) (e) (iii) War crime of attacking personnel or objects involved in a humanitarian assistance or peacekeeping mission. Article 8 (2) (b) (iv): War crime of excessive incidental death, injury, or damage: "The attack was such that it would cause incidental death or injury to civilians or damage to civilian objects or widespread, long-term and severe damage to the natural environment and that such death, injury or damage would be of such an extent as to be clearly excessive in relation to the concrete and direct overall military advantage anticipated." Article 8 (2) (b) (ix) War crime of attacking protected objects. Article 8 (2) (b) (xi) War crime of treacherously killing or wounding: "The perpetrator invited the confidence or belief of one or more persons that they were entitled to, or were obliged to accord, protection under rules of international law applicable in armed conflict." Article 8 (2) (b) (xix) War crime of employing prohibited bullets.

Relating Tactical and Strategic Self-interest to the Prosecution of War Crimes

We return, then, to our central paradox: At the very moment when the international machinery for trying war crimes has been set up—above all, the ICC—and when the means of documenting and publicizing such crimes have expanded and become widely accessible globally, it is nearly impossible to prosecute major geopolitical perpetrators on the world stage. It is, at the same time, proving entirely possible to prosecute perpetrators from geopolitically marginal conflicts such as Yugoslavia, Rwanda, the Democratic Republic of Congo, Uganda, Liberia, and Sudan. But prosecutions are stymied of the active belligerents within the geopolitical center, a broadly defined Middle East—that is, the United States in Afghanistan and Iraq, Russia in Chechnya, and Israel and Hamas in the occupied Palestinian territories, or Israel and Hezbollah in Lebanon.

The obvious structural reason for this paradox is one of self-interest, and it has limited analytic utility: those in positions of power tend to escape justice, irrespective of the category of crime allegedly committed or the jural system in which they operate. The powerful states control, if not the rules, certainly the conditions of their enforcement, and they have sufficient incentives to offer, or punitive possibilities to exact, compliance or silence from their allies, and to enable them to escape accountability for international crimes. According to this logic (which the current administrations in the U.S., Russia, and China all embrace), a self-interest motive is compelling because, first, one might be powerful enough to go it alone; second, the international machinery can and might be used unfairly against superpowers; and third, one might need the flexibility to violate international norms in order to gain an advantage over enemies perceived to be more ruthless (and criminal) than oneself.

While the merits of unrestricted national sovereignty and self-realization in obtaining immediate tactical advantages in war are debatable, this go-it-alone logic is seriously flawed strategically over the long term because it ignores how self-interest is always defined in an intersubjective process over time. Since long-term balances in types of power are unpredictable and subject to reversals, it might be wise to support institutional stability at the international level in order to minimize the effects of contingent, unplanned events. Yet the term "self-interest" in the conduct of war tends to be employed only in a tactical sense—with the assumption of autonomous actors in a short time frame, in part because strategic interests appear, by comparison, speculative. Who can predict the long-term consequences of victory or defeat in a war? Both Hezbollah's provocation and Israel's response were predicated on assumptions of tactical advantage with no serious regard for long-term relations between neighbors. Since the possibilities for self-delusion are infinite, delusions about self-determination often assert themselves over reality checks, especially when recognition of reality requires the integration of imagined long-term relations with others into one's own immediate self-interest.

Rationalized Indulgence in the Conduct of War

This confusion about self-interest leads to a related paradox: that the apparent moral progress, historically in the definition and acceptance of the legal category "war crimes" since the Nuremberg trials after World War II, is not in any way matched by a lessening of the brutality of means, the cruelty and destructiveness of action, in war. This framing may appear to be a mere repeat of the "Dialectic of the Enlightenment" argument of the Frankfurt School,[15] but let us ask more methodically what this dialectic might mean if indeed it is integral also to the historical logic of war crimes.[16]

The evidence seems to suggest that there is an inverse relationship between violence and legal progress in specifying war crimes, in that moral advances in the consciousness of regulation of violence foster perverse effects, like the devious employment of cruelty and the simultaneous self-deceptive repression and rhetorical rationalization of wishes to debase the other through excessive injury. These cruel wishes are, then, notwithstanding rational agreement on moral regulation, acted out when conditions permit. Contemporary examples of this kind of indulgence in war are legion. For example, what do we make of the increasingly brutal behavior of the militaries of the two Cold War superpowers and their non-state opponents: the U.S.'s indefinite detainment and torture of suspects in the War on Terror, its use of waterboarding and sexual humiliation in Abu Ghraib in Iraq, as well as Iraqi insurgent beheadings of Western mercenaries and bodily mutilation of civilians; the brutality of Russian bombing, killing, torture, and abductions in Chechnya, as well as the barbarity of the Chechen resistance in the Moscow theatre hostage crisis and the Beslan school siege. In both of these cases, rationalized cruelty parallels moral progress in defining the limits of the use of violence in the conduct of war.

What about Israel and Hezbollah? The UN Commission of Inquiry report of late November 2006 accuses Israel of lack of respect for the "cardinal principles of armed conflict: . . . distinction, proportion, precaution," and of "collective punishment of Lebanese civilians" for Hezbollah attacks. It specifically takes Israel to task for the damage to "civilian infrastructure," arguing "that damage inflicted on some infrastructure was done for the sake of destruction"; and for the use of cluster munitions, which, while not illegal per se, amount to "a de facto scattering of anti-personnel mines across wide tracts of Lebanese land . . . to act as a major impediment to the return of IDPs [internally displaced persons] and refugees, as well as threatening the lives and livelihoods of those who have chosen to return."[17] As well, the explicit goal stated by the Israeli Defense Force of the "removal" of Hezbollah, or of "Hezbollah strongholds," presupposes the possibility of separating Hezbollah forces from the civilian population, whereas the so-called "strongholds" were in fact civilian spaces. For example, the Beiruti residential suburb of al-Dahiya was a dense residential space with both Hezbollah Party organizations and markets, apartment buildings, mosques, and the like.[18]

Israel's response to the charge of indiscriminate and disproportionate use of force has been equivocal. On the one hand, it quickly fired one general, set up an internal State Commission of Inquiry to assess its own behavior, and prepared a legal staff to advise and defend the individuals who were responsible for the attacks in Lebanon. On the other hand, Israel's rhetorical defense has been to insist on total innocence, that because Hezbollah deliberately operated within civilian areas, its own attacks against Hezbollah targets in populated areas were of "military necessity" and therefore not a violation of international law.

Additional support for this defense, documenting Hezbollah's tactics, especially those of hiding among civilians, came in early December 2006, in the form of a 300-page report with videos, authored by Reuven Erlich, a retired lieutenant colonel who now heads the Intelligence and Terrorism Information Center, which has close ties with the Israel Defense Forces [IDF] and maintains an office at the Defense Ministry. Erlich specifically asserted that his report "could offer a response to allegations of human rights organizations on why the Israel Defense Forces operated in civilian areas."[19] Hezbollah's counterargument, in the words of Nasrallah, is that because "Zionists behave like there are no rules and no red lines . . . it is our right to behave in the same way." Both sides offer in effect the same weak argument: that they are justified in engaging in war crimes because the other side is engaging in them too, and not to engage in these crimes would be to grant the other side a tactical advantage in war. Much as an automobile driver cannot legally exceed the speed limit because the cars in front of him do, the fact that Israel or Hezbollah disobey the law does not waive the other's obligation to obey.[20]

Equity versus Proportionality

If both sides are correct in their accusations of war crimes (and the available evidence supports the claims of both belligerents), then the principle of equity requires that both sides be prosecuted for their conduct in this war. Although the current geopolitical configuration makes any prosecution unlikely, in an ideal world of justice, the principle of equity in prosecution is a precondition for justice. But given that we must act and decide under non-ideal circumstances, the question that follows is: Does this impasse with regard to equity of prosecution (that both parties deserve punishment) always trump the principle of proportionality (that the violence deployed was excessive and disproportionate to the threat)?

To talk of the principle of proportionality requires, in this case, a comparison of excessive brutalities and relative threats. This is an unpleasant task, but it would be irresponsible, even cowardly, to merely conclude that this conflict was one of equally wrong belligerents engaged in equally excessive violence in response to an unchanging and equal threat; in which case, to be fair either both or neither should be prosecuted.[21] A closer look at the argument of proportionality in light of strategic self-interest might recast the equity argument in more relative terms.

Given the asymmetrical nature of the power between Israel and Hezbollah— a powerful militarized state versus a small militarized social movement—might not the strategic self-interest motives of the more powerful party to uphold international norms for moral conduct and refrain from war crimes be stronger? If Israel, as the militarily stronger party, upholds the rules of war, is it more likely that Hezbollah will also have an interest in doing so? Yes. This follows because not only is Israel capable of inflicting more damage on Hezbollah than Hezbollah on Israel, but also the international community can in reality put much more pressure on Hezbollah to refrain from aggression (e.g., withdrawal of funds or weapons) than it can on Israel (which has its own economy and weapons production system, much less to speak of its nuclear threat). Hezbollah is often seen as a mere puppet of Iran and/or Syria (without which it would presumably collapse), while Israel rarely defers to the authority of its major benefactor, the United States. In short, Hezbollah compliance with the rules of conduct in war is in the interests of Israel, and such compliance might follow merely from Hezbollah's weakness vis-à-vis Israel.

The argument about restraint does not work in both directions, however. Hezbollah restraint alone will not increase the likelihood that Israel restrains from excessive violence. Ultimately, Israel counts on its military superiority, and it enjoys relative impunity from punishment for its behavior in wars with its Arab (or Persian) neighbors. Nor is Israel likely to reward Hezbollah in some way for upholding the international norms that limit the violence it can inflict on Israel. Hezbollah, for its part, only came into existence in 1982 as a militia precisely to inflict violence on Israel in south Lebanon during what Israel dubbed the "First Lebanon War." It was a response to an Israeli invasion (the intent of which was to eliminate attacks on Israel by Palestinian refugees who had been displaced from Israel), and over time thought of itself as taking the place in the south of the Lebanese state, which could not pose a threat sufficient to force Israel to end the occupation. In 2000, Israel suddenly withdrew, and today Hezbollah, of course, takes primary credit for this end. My point is that Israel existed without an enemy on its northern border for more than twenty years (Israelis, in this period, used to even vacation in Lebanon), and Israel would seem to have a compelling self-interest in eliminating the conditions that gave rise to and sustain Hezbollah.[22]

In point of fact, the behavior in this last war contradicts this logic of asymmetrical restraint: Israel behaved as if its self-interest is neither to calculate the proportionality of the threat, nor to refrain from excessive violence, nor to address the conditions that sustain Hezbollah forces. By contrast, Hezbollah, perhaps fearing complete destruction, neither used its longest range missiles nor became more aggressive as the war continued. Perhaps this was because Hezbollah merely lacked the means to do the same thing as Israel. Certainly, both sides stated openly their wish to inflict maximum pain on the other.

Yet the behavior of Israel is distinctive in that it suggests a fully conscious, unambiguous flaunting of the rules of conduct in war. Israel directly bombed not only infrastructure that could be used by Hezbollah but also ambulances, medical facilities, Red Cross vehicles and relief personnel, fleeing groups of refugees, refugee centers, cultural and archaeological sites, churches, and mosques. It bombed not only Hezbollah targets but also engaged in 30 direct attacks on UN peacekeepers, UNIFIL, and Observer Group Lebanon positions. The IDF mass abducted people with the last name of "Nasrallah" and even re-bombed the city of Qana, a site where the IDF had massacred refugees in a UN center during the First Lebanese War. And then there was the order to "flood," as one Israeli soldier reported, the south with cluster bombs after plans for the ceasefire had already been finalized and preparations for withdrawal were well underway.[23]

The pattern of brutality here is not uncommon in war: as a conflict endures and the enemy does not go away, the violence of the warriors and the rhetoric of their leaders become more extreme. Frustrated by its inability to destroy Hezbollah's military capabilities, which, because they were camouflaged underground, could not be seen from the air, Israel was forced into comprehensive use of ground troops in search-and-destroy missions. At the same time, it continued the useless and indiscriminate air assault, expanding the types of targets and weapons deployed. In this mess, on the verge of retreat or even defeat that they could not admit to themselves, the Israelis exacted a final price and did it quickly; in the last seventy-two hours, before withdrawing its troops and returning to civilization, which is certainly where they eventually want to be— to rules of restraint, and to the laws regulating aggression in war. This resort to excessive and disproportionate violence before the end was, in fact, rational and consistent with one major goal of Israeli policies since 1982: to make south Lebanon uninhabitable for now in order to create a larger buffer zone on Israel's northern border.[24]

According to this logic, Israeli use of excessive violence did in fact have a strategic, long-term interest: controlling and structuring the future of Lebanon so as to maximize its own security. And it resorted to this violence only after being frustrated in its immediate goal of retrieving its abducted soldiers without giving up any prisoners itself, which was soon supplemented by the rationale of turning Lebanon's population against Hezbollah so that other Lebanese would eliminate that part of themselves that the Israelis identify as an adversary. But the violence unleashed in pursuit of this interest had the perverse effect, from the Israeli perspective, of uniting large segments of Lebanese society with the fate of Hezbollah (and silencing others). The Interim Report of the Winograd Commission, while avoiding any talk of excessive violence or military conduct, said as much, focusing directly on the policy failure to make immediate goals serve long-term interests through a military campaign. The report leaves unquestioned, however, the kind of future imagined by Israel's warriors and the public who supported them—Israel as an autochthonous island surrounded by adversaries.

The buffer zone argument proves crucial to the imagination of the future, but it is of limited explanatory power to explain conduct that includes the commission of war crimes. Each year brings improvements in weapon technologies, so that while Hezbollah missiles of today may not reach Tel Aviv and Jerusalem, few doubt that these limitations will hold in a few years. And didn't this massive destruction of things that are Lebanese both elevate the status of Hezbollah among the Lebanese specifically, and among Arabs and Muslims generally, guaranteeing the production of a future generation of anti-Israeli fighters? This future was, of course, not only about the buffer zone, Hezbollah, and the Lebanese, but also about the Israelis themselves, about preserving an image of themselves as invulnerable and therefore to secure some kind of "victory" at all costs before leaving.

By comparison, Hezbollah's terror of Israel, specifically the hiding of its forces in civilian areas, the cross-border abduction of soldiers, and the indetermination of its targets—where will its rockets and mortars land?—also constitutes war crimes. But the issue of the proportionality of violence to the threat is relevant here, and it relativizes the issue of equity of prosecution. The responses of the two belligerents were not at all proportionate to each other's aggression, and as the conflict progressed, the Israeli response became excessively violent and increasingly disproportionate to the relative threat.

To be sure, Hezbollah's abduction of Israeli soldiers was a grave miscalculation. Nasrallah himself admitted that he did not anticipate the way Israel would respond. In the past both sides had periodically engaged in abductions, eventually resulting in prisoner exchanges. But in this case the abduction became the trigger for war, with Israeli leaders assuming that Hezbollah could not survive its superior assault weapons. Hezbollah did survive, however, and in the public opinion of the Arab world, if not of Europe and America, it won this round of conflict, this war. It did not "win" because it inflicted more damage on Israel and forced it to retreat, however. Hezbollah won because of how it survived as the weaker party in its conduct of the war: by holding back some of its arsenal. It did not use the longer-range missiles it supposedly possessed. It did not target Tel Aviv, Israeli refugees, Red Cross officials, or sacred sites. Nor did it use poisons or cluster bombs or the like against Israeli troops. In other words, Hezbollah's response, its lobbing of mostly cheap Soviet- and Iranian-made rockets onto the Israeli civilian population, while certainly criminal, was proportionate to the threat, and proportionately a lesser crime.

Despite its official rhetoric insisting on the elimination of the state of Israel, Hezbollah was reckoning with the continued existence of its neighbor, and it kept open the possibility for peaceful coexistence. That is, Hezbollah's violence in this war was in the spirit of a sacrifice that risked the immolation of all of Lebanon and all Lebanese in order to inflict damage on Israel, but it did not aim to annihilate Israel. Israel's violence, by contrast, had no element of self-sacrifice; it was directed initially against all "Hezbollah strongholds"—meaning most of the Shi'a population of the south—but it soon extended to all Lebanese in the assumption that the annihilation of Hezbollah and destruction of Lebanese infrastructure would save Israeli lives in the future. So at this point the conclusion to be drawn about the prosecution of war crimes is that the insistence on equity (to be fair, one must prosecute all guilty parties) should not always trump the argument of proportionality (the violence inflicted must not be excessive but relative to the threat). That is, justice demands in principle that Israel be prosecuted regardless of the status of a potential prosecution of Hezbollah.[25]

The Political Efficacy of Prosecution for War Crimes

This leads us to a final paradox arising from this war, about the political efficacy of prosecution for war crimes in creating justice. Why engage in the contentious prosecution of the conduct of war if such action is likely to be ineffectual? Such prosecution would be efficacious if it led, minimally, to any one of three conditions: to better regulation of the justifications for and conduct of war; to more measured use of force in war; or to improved conditions for peace after the conflict has ended.[26] A legal prosecution, then, is a relative goal to achieve an end, not an end in itself. And since few wars today are merely for and about a narrow set of belligerents, efficacy of prosecution for conduct is contingent on many actors within a regional political dynamic.

What would a prosecution of Israel and/or Hezbollah for war crimes do? Trials cannot, after all, bring back lives or undo destruction. But they can, perhaps, contribute to trust in a legal system and bring about some version of justice. Long-term peace, according to the logic of the post-Westphalian state system, is contingent on trust in the rule of law—that is, in deferral of conflict resolution to the official instruments of justice, considered superior due to, for example, the predictability of law's application, the nonarbitrary interpretation of legal statutes, and the regularized and impartial enforcement of law. Equity is a key element in building trust. But trust is difficult to create without equity.

And it is precisely the lack of equity in prosecuting all those presumed guilty that often, at least in the short term, produces perverse effects. Prosecutions considered one-sided foster cynicism; they result in groups turning inward (including increased public support for whichever strong man or woman is in power); they can even destabilize political systems, which increases the likelihood of uncontrolled violence.

Justice systems within the larger Middle East are not particularly trusted; they are known neither for their impartiality nor for their ability to retain much independence from the executive branches of government. Political systems in the Middle East generally maintain stability more by sheer force than the threat of law. For both belligerents, Israel and Hezbollah, the issues of jurisdictional level and trust in a legal verdict are central. A prosecution of Israelis for war crimes without a concurrent prosecution of Hezbollah may serve as an issue to unite the Israelis further against the entire system of international justice, especially when Israelis are engaging in an internal debate, albeit largely restricted to political organs, about their conduct in the war. Since the ICC is charged with prosecution only in those cases where national judicial systems refuse or are unable to act, it may be best at present to merely support the internal forces for justice in Israeli society and refrain from any attempt to threaten Israelis with external punishment. On the other hand, the threat of prosecution alone may facilitate a process of internal judicial investigation into war crimes, if not prosecution for them. A judicial intervention can cut either way.[27]

A prosecution of Hezbollah for war crimes now, even with a concurrent prosecution of Israel, would also be unlikely to produce trust among its followers in the international legal system or make conditions for peace more propitious. The Israeli assault, by strengthening Hezbollah's position and claim to leadership within internal Lebanese politics, has in fact tremendously destabilized Lebanon's already fragile political system.[28] It has created awareness and sympathy for the demands of Hezbollah's followers for more political inclusion within Lebanon, and it has increased the status and solidarity of Shi'a followers of Islam vis-à-vis their generally more conservative Sunni counterparts throughout the Arab world. Any prosecution of Hezbollah would likely exacerbate and harden the Lebanese sectarian fault lines, already frayed by the attempt, internationally organized, to prosecute those suspected of assassinating the former prime minister, Rafiq Hariri, a Sunni Arab, in 2005. In response to a prosecution for war crimes, Hezbollah forces may target witnesses and prosecutors for assassination, much as it appears Syria has assassinated Lebanese public figures who dare to voice criticism of its role in Lebanon (including its alleged role in the murder of Hariri).[29] Should there be a prosecution, Lebanon's democratic reform movement from the "Cedar Revolution" of 2005 would likely further splinter, leading to a strengthening of Syria's control over Lebanon's diverse domestic constituencies—the inverse of the intent of the reform movement, and, in this case, of Israel. Without political stability, the stability of judicial organs is precarious, and without cooperation between the two—the executive must enforce judicial decisions—there can be no trust or, one might say, satisfaction, in what prosecutions can or do achieve.[30] The state of war crimes, in this case, is at an impasse.

6 Terror, Compassion, and the Limits of Identification: Counter-Transference and Rites of Commemoration in Lebanon

Dream Work: Counter-Transference in Late Summer 2002

We often imagine countries and cities as mythical dreamscapes—cornucopias of prosperity and abundant pleasures. For much of the twentieth century, Lebanon and Beirut evoked such a dreamscape: a glorious past of cosmopolitan Phoenician traders transformed into modern French-Arabic fusion; cool mountain homes overlooking the warm Mediterranean sea; and a capital city, Beirut, that showcased intellectual, cultural, and economic surprises. But a more recent memory, of the violent civil war that raged on and off for seventeen years between 1975 and 1992, has filled the cup of plenty with sorrows. My own dreams, as well as those of my Lebanese friends, about and in Beirut tend to situate these recent memories in these dreamscapes.

I had such a disturbing dream on a summer night in late August 2001 as I was preparing to leave Beirut to do fieldwork in south Lebanon. Shortly before my first visit to Lebanon, the south had been liberated from an Israeli occupation that began in 1985 and ended, abruptly, with a complete withdrawal, on May 24, 2000. Hezbollah (Party of God), the victorious organizers of the resistance, called the withdrawal "emancipation." It was unexpected and stunned everyone, including the Lebanese to the north, who were suddenly charged with integrating and administering a territory and a people poorer, less educated, less skilled, less developed than themselves—in short, backward—for which, in the past, they had often shirked responsibility and, under Israeli control, had assumed only a representational or ideological alliance. I was trying to understand Lebanese notions of punishment, how, specifically, "collaboration with the enemy"—meaning, with Israel—was understood and dealt with, and how this relates to the post–civil war integration of "Lebanese society," whatever that might mean.

Before this trip to the south, I dreamt that I had been accused of improprieties—the word in the dream was "harassment"—while teaching at Cornell University, though I am now and was in the dream also a professor at Princeton. I expected these improprieties to be sexual in nature, and once in the dream I placed myself at the American Anthropology Meetings, where I met up with some of my male students, with whom I am perhaps more demonstrably physical in my affection than are most professors. But at the time I was unable to recollect an actual offense, and this inability to specify the wrong jarred me out of my sleep, sweaty even though the sweltering heat and humidity of the Beirut summer had already passed into a deep warmth softened by the occasional ocean breeze. I woke up because in my dream I did not know, I was unable to specify or act upon, what or to whom exactly I had done wrong, and this disturbing sense of having committed an offense of which I was unaware kept me awake for some time.

The next day I related the dream to a friend I will call "H.," a Shi'a who grew up in the south, who had agreed to accompany me on this trip. He first told me of his vivid and strange dream of the previous night in which he woke up dead. Then, as we drove in search of his grandfather's former villa in the mountains of the south, he offered an explication of my dream: There was a connection between my former career with horses and the word *harassment*, which is related to the French word *haras*, meaning a stud farm, a place for the reproduction of horses.

Then H. moved to the difference between the French words *manège* and *ménage*, which parallels a discrepancy between my former and present life. In the former, I was working with horses (in a riding school, a *manège*) and leading a life of "floundering and lust," as in a *ménage à trois;* presently, I work in the academy and lead a more restricted "life of couples." There are French expressions for this difference, "*J'ai fait mon ménage*," versus "*Je suis en ménage.*" I was bringing my domestic life from the time I worked with horses, prior to reentering academics, into a dream of the present. My past impropriety, or "harassment," is haunting me today.

H. also thought my not knowing of this "harassment" was related to the English double "no/know": both to my inability to "know" the wrong (which awakened me in the dream) and to an inability to say, or to accept, "no" from others (which constitutes the legal impropriety of harassment). I delighted in these clever observations, plausible in the Lebanese context, where conversations among those in the educated middle class constantly switch registers from English to French to Arabic, sometimes within the same sentence, though most often speakers digress into the language with which they are most comfortable or which they were using at the time of an experience, usually French or Arabic. This situational linguistic competence is also part of a larger economy: mostly French for intellectual or philosophical topics, mostly Arabic for intimacies. English tends to be an adult language, for academic or commercial use, a language for communicating with outsiders (such as myself), while Arabic and French are learned with the affection and discipline of childhood.

H., who was working on a master's degree in philosophy, had been the evening news anchor for the French television station in Lebanon. With the rationalization of its workforce, he received a settlement and was most recently writing the jingles for some ad companies. His control of all three languages is so playful and exceptional that it puts my own linguistic skills to shame. Hence my own explanation of the dream was more prosaic, or "flat-footed," as I said to H. On the one hand, it was about my identification with Lebanese collaborators during the Israeli occupation, who also insisted that they were doing nothing wrong—just feeding their families, finding unskilled work as maids or day laborers in San Diego-style Israeli homes and in the irrigated green fields on the terraced hills on the other side of the frontier; or, in select cases, cooperating in administration of the occupation in the arrest and detention and interrogation, including torture, of Lebanese resisters—Israel called them "terrorists"—to the Israeli occupation. But also, H. and I had several days before discussed J. M. Coetzee's *Disgrace,* a novel that greatly impressed me because Coetzee uses allegory without abstraction and without displacing the scene of South Africa outside its own temporal and physical space.[1] South Africa is a crime scene, for sure, but Coetzee resists resolving the great anxieties of rape and placelessness among the whites, or of the desire to be merciful to animals by euthanizing them, into any emotional gain for the reader. He tells a great mythical story that nonetheless speaks directly to a specific time and place.

In *Disgrace,* Coetzee tracks the fate of a middle-aged professor, a man of the mind, who has an affair with an unenthusiastic but passive and seemingly willing young coed. She sinks into a kind of moroseness, perhaps because of this liaison. At least that is what her parents think, that the professor is the cause of their daughter's malaise, and they insist that the university fire him. Ultimately, it is the professor's own diffidence, however, that leads to his firing, whereupon he visits his daughter, a lesbian who has moved to the country to build a farm. During the visit, he begins working at an animal shelter, his only compensation being the mercy he gives. His daughter is raped by black thugs, organized by her own head servant, to whom she agrees to sign over rights to the land, hoping this will enable her anticipated baby, whose father is black, to remain and inherit in the new South Africa. In the end, the white professor stands fully disgraced: unable to teach, a failed father lacking authority of any sort, without place or location from which to speak in the new South Africa—except, perhaps, as one who cares for abandoned animals nearing death.

My dream positions me, like the figure in Coetze's novel, speechless and in need of punishment. My dream of punishment anticipates, I suspect, failed expectations in my fieldwork in Lebanon, a conflict between my superego (about what I should do) and my ego (about what I am able to do).

Collaboration and Punishment in South Lebanon

South Lebanon, at the time of my visit, had two large memorials to the Israeli occupation, one an emptied detention/interrogation center in Khiam, the other a memorial to a massacre in a former UN shelter in Qana. We intend to visit both.

The detention center in Khiam is now a museum. It sits at the top of a hill overlooking the valleys below and, indeed, much of the south. Like most of the former Israeli outposts in the south, it was once a fortress, dating back to one of the Crusades, then used by the French before the Israelis expanded and partly modernized it. Friendly, bearded, soft-speaking Hezbollah men greet H. and I and tell us to park our car near a rusting military water tank left behind by the occupiers. The first object we pass, on our right, is a set of small, lacquered, hand-held missiles used in the resistance, so glossy that they look like the candied marzipan for which Lebanon and Syria are renowned, though unusually large, as if stricken by elephantiasis. On our left a man is selling a children's book, *Sharon al-Shareer* (Sharon the Evil One), camouflaged in a cover marked simply "May 25" (the date of emancipation). The cover depicts a dream montage that includes a photo of Sayed Hassan Nasrallah, the Hezbollah leader, a woman's eyes, a resister setting fire to a flag, and the golden dome of a mosque. The book tells the story of children with stones defeating the evil Sharon and driving him from their land. I buy one.

Then we go through the actual rooms and barracks. Yellow metal plates attached to the walls state in Arabic and poorly translated English the function of the spaces: "A Typical Individual Room Before Red Cross Entry," "A Collective Room After the Entrance of the Red Cross in 1995," "A Room for Investigation with the Help of the Traitors," "The Hall of Torturing: Burying-Kicking-Beating-Applying Electricity-Pouring Hot Water-Placing a Dog Beside," "An Open Space for Sun: Ten Minutes Every Ten Days For Females." The plates intend to singularize the administrative cruelty of Israeli detention methods, to draw attention to the rationalization of all tasks and functions: this room for torture in interrogation, that for cooking, another for washing, for sleeping, for the jailers or the detained, for women or men, a space for solitary confinement, for visits with non-prisoners. My first thought, though, is that one could probably find this evil in every continent, perhaps even in a museum of a detention center. On one wall, over an Israeli flag, the graffiti reads: "Who are the causes for War?" On another wall: "All Jews Must Die."

The room for women's access to the sun is slightly larger than but otherwise similar to the others: a cement slab floor of about two square yards. H. dubs it a "sun deck." I laugh. But shortly after, H. feels queasy and has to leave. I walk on. The yellow plates emphasize an important distinction between rooms constructed before and after the Red Cross was granted access to the prisoners. After the Red Cross filed a report, most detainee rooms were enlarged, and beds replaced cement floors for sleeping. Most rooms have no windows, and most are just large enough for a prisoner of moderate size to lie prone on the floor or to turn around in while standing up. Two special rooms are equipped for electric torture, the metal conductor grids still hanging from the ceiling, the actual machines and devices, a guide tells me, taken back to Israel. I am surprised the Israelis did not destroy more of the evidence before they left, but I am told they left in a hurry. The prime minister at the time, Ehud Barak, simply pulled out the troops one night, an evacuation that the Israeli public seemed to expect but that left Lebanese scrambling for positions. Hezbollah, with a large on-the-ground resistance during the occupation, was the best-organized force to step into this vacuum. They kept their weapons, despite UN resolutions to the effect that they should disarm, and more or less took over policing the south.

The outer courtyard maintains the recently abandoned look, except for four paintings, unmistakably Hezbollah art: computer-generated, glitzy painted images of doves flying above fists grasping AK-47 assault rifles and smashing through walls, of crescents, stars of David, and wrecked tanks—symbols of muscular victory and cruelty, Islam and peace. Against a wall leans a large portrait of Nasrallah, Hezbollah's leader, and mimeographed photos of slain fighters are posted on the wall near the entrance. It strikes me as odd that the museum gives the names of some specific Lebanese victims, claimed as "martyrs" to the cause, but does not name any Lebanese collaborators. Only Israelis are singled out for culpability. Later, a friend who had visited within weeks of the withdrawal, in the summer of 2000, told me he remembered having seen a list of all suspected collaborators—but, then again, now he is unsure what he actually saw. Within the first several years of the Israeli withdrawal there was, except for a few isolated examples, a notable lack of local recrimination—let's call it revenge—against people who helped to inform or administer the Israeli occupation. In the late summer and fall of 2002, however, I began to hear a few rumors of local extortion practiced by Hezbollah against Christian groups.

How the south was "administered" during and immediately after the occupation is a question of perspective, and there are many. The more I ask about local details, the more fragmented the picture. During the occupation, the south remained formally a part of the state of Lebanon; its residents retained their Lebanese citizenship and were more or less free to move back and forth between northern and southern Lebanon. Some, in a labor capacity, commuted to Israel. Although UN "observers" and "peacekeepers" were stationed on the border between Lebanon and Israel and had a minimal presence in some of the villages, they seemed to have little effect on how either the Lebanese or the Israelis conducted their affairs. Israel still bombed and surveilled and made their presence known at will; the Lebanese reacted and adjusted. Except for Hezbollah, and to a lesser extent Amal, the groups that organized not only the resistance but also assumed the basic functions of the state during the occupation; they provided minimal social and public assistance, primarily health care and infusions of outside capital that kept local economies from collapsing. Israel was concerned solely with its own security and military goals: to deploy the entire south as a "buffer" or "security zone" devoid of people. Hence, they sought to keep the area backward educationally, culturally, and economically.

As for Israeli torture of civilians, I had already met a victim, in 1999, on my first visit to Beirut. A taxi driver, upon hearing that I am American, revealed that he is Palestinian and said, "America is good, a friend." He then stretched his gnarled hand across the seat and showed me a scar on his wrist and a stub of a fingernail that, he said, had been yanked out during one of his ten years in Israeli prisons. He then pulled his T-shirt over his right shoulder, and with each gesture his eyes flashed more angrily, to show me a gaping hole he also got in prison in Khiam—and he wanted me to touch it, which I did. He still has the key to his family house in Haifa, and he gestured to show me what the key looks like. His grandfather had taken it with him when he was evicted. "America is good," he repeated, "a friend." Clinton didn't like Netanyahu, he said in response to a question, and Barak represents some hope. "But there is no place for Jews in Palestine," he said. "They should leave." To where? I ask. "Wherever," he replied. "To Africa." This was my first exposure to a claim of Israeli torture, my first confrontation with bodily evidence, and I realized how inextricably this present episode of Lebanese-Israeli history is wound up with the Jewish-driven expulsions of Palestinians in 1948.

Largely because of this Israeli policy within what is now Israel and in the south of Lebanon, between 1978 and the time of the Israeli withdrawal from Lebanon, the population in the south declined from 600,000 to an estimated

65,000, with most of the refugees settling in the southern suburbs of Beirut. The long-term impact of making the south secure for Israel was to make it unsafe for local residents, its demands for collaboration poisoning relations between members of the various sects. Long-term insecurity was also ensured through the Israeli policy of planting approximately 70,000 land mines all over the south, which UN personnel (UNIFIL, to be precise), mostly Africans experienced in mine removal on their own terrain, are presently trying to find and remove.

At the end of May 2002, within a week of the "liberation," 6,000 south Lebanese, mostly members of Israel's former proxy militia, the Southern Lebanese Army (SLA), and their families, left Lebanon—mostly to Europe via Israel, with at least half reportedly sent to Germany. Within six months of the liberation, military tribunals began to hold marathon sessions up to three times a week, charging 2,200 Lebanese—including some of those who had already left the country—with collaboration and handing down 800 verdicts, frequently reached after two or three minutes of deliberation. Of those who had left, 202 returned within six months; others have been trickling back since.

Defense lawyers worked out a plea bargain deal with prosecutors to divide collaborators—those in "contact with the enemy"—into four categories.[2] The first was for those who had worked in Israel, the second for those who had worked in civil administration, the third for soldiers of the SLA, and the fourth for those who had worked in intelligence/security. Conviction for the first two categories resulted in a fine of approximately $200 and a period of detention, which in most cases had already been served between the time of the initial arrest and release. SLA soldiers got six to eighteen months prison; intelligence/security employees, six to fifteen years. Only one officer of the SLA surrendered; most were sentenced in absentia. By October 2001, 54 high-level collaborators had been sentenced to death, all in absentia, meaning that they would be granted a retrial if and when apprehended. Although death by hanging is legal, its execution had been suspended after Lebanese President Emile Lahoud took office in November 1998.[3] Many sentences were immediately appealed, first to a supreme military tribunal, then to a civilian court of cassation, and both the tribunal and court reversed some verdicts or lessened sentences.

Israeli occupation policy had allowed one Lebanese per family to work in Israel, provided that each family also offered one man to work for the SLA to protect the "security zone." Most of those who did not agree with this policy either vacated their land and residence and became displaced "internal refugees" in the rest of Lebanon or worked covertly with the primarily Shiite Hezbollah resistance movement. Hezbollah supported its associates, in turn, with currency from abroad, most of which likely came from Syria or Iran, or from diaspora

Lebanese in Australia, Europe, or the United States. Israel enforced its employment policy across sectarian lines, so that 50 to 80 percent of the SLA members were Shiites, depending on their proportion in the local population. Consequently, some 2,000 Shiites surrendered immediately after the Israeli evacuation, knowing they had no place to flee. Muslim lawyers, under pressure not to defend the accused, were often themselves then accused of collaboration, though none, to my knowledge, were punished.

Hezbollah objected to any suggestion of a general amnesty, as had been granted following the civil war in 1991, insisting that individuals had to engage in "repentance" (*tawbah*) as the means for political purification before that could be considered. The term *tawbah* is taken from a Shiite religious interpretation of the "door of repentance" (*bab el-tawbah*), through which one must pass in order to leave the cycle of earth and enter a new cycle of time. By insisting on the applicability of this condition (purification through the door of repentance) in the military-political-jural domain, Hezbollah ended up accommodating its religious doctrine to, instead of trying to replace, the secular legal institutions of the Napoleonic tradition. Lebanon retains a legal structure similar to the one the French had imposed. One official explained to me that although Hezbollah's public stance on collaborators was radical, in practice they were pragmatic and political, often arguing leniency for some families, exile for others who might vote against them. In other words, for Hezbollah, a territorial displacement (exile) could substitute for a process of purification leading to a temporal metamorphosis (emancipation into a new order). Some people with whom I spoke concluded that swift legal action by the Lebanese state effectively took the place of what would most likely have been popular violence against collaborators. Since most southern Lebanese who strongly wanted to condemn collaborators also shared in the difficulties of survival during the occupation, a great measure of ambivalence marked popular attitudes.

In the reckoning with Israeli occupation, equally if not more significant than legal punishment are rites of commemoration: the symbolic retribution in cultural work, such as turning sites of Israeli torture and murder into museums, which are to be visited ritually with no foreseeable end.

The Qana museum is the twisted wreckage of a massacre in museum form. As such, it is older, better financed, and more elaborate than the memorial of Khiam. A small Shiite village, Qana was the site of a 1986 Israeli massacre of 106 Lebanese civilians (with another 120 wounded), at a shelter within a UN peacekeeping base by several direct hits from Israeli missiles (800 people were in the shelter). Some UN soldiers in nearby buildings were also killed, and they are allotted a separate and large memorial on the same site, which lists their names and country of origin (most were from Fiji). At the time, Israel, caught in a war of attrition, its occupation stalled and ineffective at preventing cross-border attacks, launched "Operation Grapes of Wrath," a 16-day artillery and naval assault, ostensibly to wipe out Hezbollah bases. The Israeli government claimed that it was unaware of civilian presence at the UN base in Qana, but a UN investigation later suggested that, since there were several direct hits on the base, it had likely been deliberately attacked.[4] The day of the massacre, April 18th, is now an official day of mourning throughout Lebanon.

H. and I are the only guests when we arrive at the Qana museum, and H. parks his car directly across from the site, which is on the main street of the village. A young man, dark-haired, with large, alert eyes and a full mouth, immediately comes over to accompany us through the exhibit. H. says that his witnessing to visitors like me is considered a form of religious service. The first room contains a photo documentary of the massacre. He had memorized a lengthy story for each picture, and he seems to dwell on the most gruesome photographs of the dead, with their bloody body parts strewn around the site. I tell him, "I know this story already." "But I want to tell it to you," he replies matter-of-factly.

I am too disturbed by the graphic images to remain polite, so after a few minutes I simply abandon him while he talks, and I walk into the next room, a large space with an exhibit of the artwork of college students inspired to paint the event, what the exhibit calls a "Holocaust." But the guide follows me, and I become increasingly irritated as he continues to narrate the story of the massacre, in an assured, measured, monotone voice.

To overcome this irritation, I try to eroticize him, in particular his mouth, which appears to me sensuous but also crooked, as if some injury or birth defect was preventing the full range of movement of his lips. I think, perhaps I am projecting crookedness onto his mouth in order to distance myself from his voice-over. The pictures with small texts beneath are themselves sufficient, in my mind, to portray the enormity of the Israeli crime. I find the comparison with the Holocaust overwrought, an attempt to bestow significance on a massacre by elevating it to the crime of genocide. Nonetheless, the museum guide's demands on me follow a very correct and rigorous logic, which begins with the presupposition that the Holocaust is the sine qua non of modern terror and suffering. It follows that all subsequent experiences of this kind will be measured by the standard of the Jewish Holocaust.

However, I want to resist what I take to be the political instrumentalization of my empathy, an attempt to turn compassion into anti-Jewish sentiment. The Jewish Holocaust was a German event, the Qana massacre of Lebanese Shiites an Israeli event. Separate, singular states, societies, historical eras, genealogies, sequences of events—and crimes. This young man appears to want of me not only empathy for his losses but also a revision of my understanding of the Jewish Shoa. I leave a donation and convince H. to exit the city without first having a coffee, as is our custom.

An Arab Dream

During this trip to Lebanon I also visited Aleppo, Syria, accompanied by two Beiruti friends, H., who also accompanied me to southern Lebanon, and a friend I will call Ahmed. Because nothing of political significance in Lebanon could take place without at least tacit approval of the Syrians, I thought it important to include Syria as much as possible in any research on Lebanon. After our first night, Ahmed wakes up sweating, even though the air conditioner has overly cooled our room, and he relates the following dream:

"I came to your place, not your home in Princeton, but a very big villa, like a suburban house, with marble floors, perhaps like our hotel, a remodeled fifteenth-century villa. You are sitting on a couch, and you are the host. You are showing a film made by Derrida."

I am puzzled: Does Derrida make films?

"There are many other guests, children and families, and people of all ages, women and men. The film is extremely violent, a kind of collective violence, a massacre—people are cutting each other up. I wonder why you are showing this film to these people. It seems inappropriate. Yet I am not disturbed, for I've seen this film before. The film begins near the end, and only then proceeds to the beginning. Nothing really happens with the spectators, who just sit quietly and watch. I myself was never afraid. No one acts out; in fact, there is no shock effect. But I ask, again, why are you showing this film? Although I had seen it before, actually you and I are the intended audience; the others are an unintended audience, only spectators.

"There is another scene, also in the dream, something about cruising, but the guy I am interested in goes out with you somewhere instead. He likes you."

The three of us discuss this dream. It is the memory of a traumatic event, and it brings this memory into the present. It is an encounter with this memory that invites Ahmed to make sense of his own trauma—the Lebanese civil war that accompanied his childhood and youth. Syria prompts memory of the war because he spent many happy summers with the family of his nanny in Syria. And perhaps Syria, being a majority Sunnite country, had seemed a respite for Ahmed, who was raised in a Sunni family but in a country where over the course of the war Sunnis were increasingly marginalized and threatened by sectarian divisions. Unlike H., whose entire childhood was spent in Lebanon during the war, Ahmed spent one year away, in Africa with a brother. But that escape from the war was also separation from his parents. Thus, it is perhaps propitious and more "safe" for Ahmed to dream of the Lebanese trauma in Syria, a place he associates with childhood innocence.

The sequence of the film screening, from end back to beginning, replicates the latency inherent in trauma—that the original scene is unrecoverable, and recognition is possible only in reverse, after the fact. Ahmed says the images in the film were painting-like, but still very violent. He remembers someone in the dream wearing red, but in the Derrida film you could not see the actual victims. He situates me as the intellectual guide inviting others to react by screening the film. I am actively intervening, as I do in fieldwork, showing the victim's story from within the trauma, while Ahmed is placed in the screening, having to watch others watch the slaughter, which is subjecting him to a kind of sadistic moment. But, then, I am not the author of the film. I am merely screening a film produced by someone else, by the philosopher "Derrida." Moreover, Ahmed is not frightened by it, since he's seen it before and he is, like Derrida, adept at reading.[5] The audience, being like a family, with mothers and kids, also seems familiar with the film's story and experiences no shock in viewing. The audience is, in fact, truly spectral because they have no apparent relation to Ahmed and are not themselves placed in the trauma. They just watch, which is perhaps the key to their culpability, the culpability of the protective Lebanese family that could merely watch and not intervene in the war.

Ahmed's dream was partly provoked by an encounter we had had the previous night with two Syrian-Armenians, a dentist who resides in Aleppo and an interior designer who moved with his family two years ago to Paris but visits every summer. We are sitting, at around midnight, in a café in a series of many Aleppian cafes, all of them full, across from the huge twelfth-century citadel built to defend Aleppo against the Crusaders. Men are engaged in lively conversation as well as in chess and card games and backgammon, and there is much smoking of the nargileh. Everyone is pleasant and relaxed; I detect none of the tension that I associate with the dictatorships with which I am familiar from fieldwork in the Communist regimes of East-Central Europe before 1990.

Conversation with the designer switches between Armenian, French, and Arabic, while the dentist speaks perfect English, as do my Lebanese friends. The dentist states that he enjoys discussing politics. I ask him why Aleppo appears to me to be such a free place, when they are living under a dictatorship in what is supposed to be a condition of unfreedom. He says that the ubiquitous pictures of Assad are a joke to the Syrian people. I should not take them seriously as indicators of any behavior. People put them up and ignore them. The government has no fear of public places, he says, it is only large gatherings in private that they fear. "Are there any social movements or public demonstrations here?" I ask. "The only demonstrations here are pro," he remarks and smiles.

I ask about Hama, the place where, in 1982, the brother of Hafez el-Assad, Syria's political father, massacred some 30,000 to 40,000 members of the Muslim Brotherhood, who at the time were intent on toppling Assad's secular regime. (On our way to Aleppo, my friends and I had stopped in Hama, a bustling old city that Assad had spatially reorganized, bulldozing the center, in an attempt to efface any traces of this event, and moving it to another space a kilometer away.) Because our friend's responses were open and articulate, I risk asking him the delicate question of his reaction to this violence. I struggle to phrase a question, not wanting to use the word *trauma,* and there is no Arabic equivalent. But as he hears me say the word, he uses it himself in turn, making my struggle look silly. "Is Hama a trauma in Syria?" I ask. "No," he says, "the event does not at the moment exist."

He suddenly switches registers, becoming personal and emotional. As a child of five, he remembers, he heard stories of the massacre that occurred at the time, but nothing like that could be discussed, he says, and it will not be for a very long time. Along the way, he introduces the phrase, "the Syrian trauma." I sense some guilt in this admission, a guilt concerning his silence after the fact of mass murder. Then he tells us a story of how, as a young adult, he gave directions to two German tourists. The police quickly picked him up and took him in for questioning. As he tells the story, it takes on a live allegorical quality as the fact of intimidation becomes palpable. We notice a man at another table, who at first did not seem to understand English, listening intently to us.

The conversation then turns to lighter affairs—the effect of redirection by my Lebanese friends. It is likely that for our Armenian acquaintances another violent event lurks behind the Syrian trauma of Hama, the not-so-distant and still widely ignored Armenian genocide in Turkey. I dare not ask about this event unless they themselves introduce it, which they do not. Aleppo was the first stop on the exodus of those who escaped the Turkish slaughter. From Aleppo, survivors went on to Lebanon, Iraq, the West. These two families stayed.

Later I ask my Beiruti friends if they were bothered by my intervention, during which they remained unusually silent. They both admit discomfort, which leads to a discussion of how I conduct fieldwork, of my provocative questions, and of their role as mediators, friends, and informants. On this particular evening, they had agreed between themselves without telling me to let me ask people more intrusive questions, since I had not yet talked to anyone in any depth. Some of our Syrian acquaintances seemed to want to counter a common Lebanese conceit: that Syrians are less educated or sophisticated than the Lebanese, that they are not informed, not intellectual, and perhaps because of political restrictions incapable of understanding what is going on around them.

My friends return to Ahmed's dream. Ahmed is taking over my desire, they say, as in the cruising scene, but he ends up deserting me, or being left out, without understanding on what basis. Although I occupy the place of the phallus, it is unclear whether Ahmed desires me or merely my roles. In the dream, Ahmed is unaccustomedly passive. I place him in the film screening without forcing him to do anything. I set the grounds for engagement, for questions, for viewing, which in some ways parallels a deconstructive reading, hence the invocation of Derrida. In the cruising scene, Ahmed is in a position where he wants to, and in fact should, take over the role of initiating interaction. But he is reticent, reluctant to provoke or risk improprieties, afraid of the potential consequences and responsibilities that may result. His consciousness of propriety trumps his curiosity.

In our actual conversation with the two Armenians at the café, Ahmed stopped himself, as in the dream, from engaging ethnographically before he even began, because he thinks it inappropriate to ask. After our initial conversations with the two Armenians, he tells me, his initial desire was to know more about their relation to Aleppo, to language, to their minority status in Syria. A wide-ranging discussion ensued, into the wee hours of the morning, after I had already retired to the hotel, but it stayed away from what might be politically inappropriate. Yet the Armenians we met and observed in Aleppo, including a group of young girls in their twenties, appeared far more confident and self-assured—of themselves as a distinct group, of their minority status—than Armenians appear in Lebanon.

My own presence as ethnographer reframes our encounter with the two Armenian men, however; it redefines them as collaborators (not to speak of the applicability of the naïve, older ethnographic term "informant") in a way they are not when merely talking to Lebanese. My presence undoubtedly invokes the specter of police interrogation. I am, when in the Middle East, always a suspicious person; my generation, my nationality, my profession, my unmarried status—and above all my questions—create the profile of a probable spy. Those who speak with me are, in most cases, flaunting the rules of political censorship and thereby putting themselves under suspicion of betrayal. In fieldwork, it is marginal men, sexually, socially, politically, who mediate "culture" for me, who provide initial contacts and initial explanations. And I have seen these same men mediate for many other foreigners, irrespective of gender or sexual interest. With me they are collaborating in the dual registers of the sexual and the political, and because these registers are so fundamental to social order, they are betraying the secrets of social organization. My Lebanese friends stress to me that I cannot choose in which register to operate. Neither I nor they can separate, for instance, my intellectual from my purely personal interests, and this creates on the one hand excitement and intimacy, but on the other discomfort, because it leads them to suspect my motives for knowing about either register. It demands of them either conscious collaboration or distance.

While in Aleppo, we go to one of the oldest hammams, where I meet a Palestinian man in his early 20s, there with his father, a refugee from Israeli expulsions in 1947. The young man had arrived in Aleppo two weeks earlier, he said, freshly deported from Texas, with only a year left to complete his studies in business management. I do not know whether there was justifiable reason for his deportation, but at the very least he deserved a hearing and an explanation, which he did not get. My intuition, drawn largely from his demeanor, the way he tells me his story without self-pity, tells me that he is a false suspect in the new War on Terror, a scapegoat in the aggressive attempt to find a source external to America for its insecurities and to then deport it. I apologize to him, first for myself, then for my country, though I am not in a position to make amends, and I express my wish that he eventually return to the United States. I know, as I utter this wish, how silly and ineffectual it must sound to a young man who, in reaction to the 9/11 massacre in New York, is deported for belonging to the categories Palestinian and Arab.

Departure

On the morning of September 5, I wake regularly every hour, anticipating my departure. At 7, I arise and give Mohammed a wakeup call on his cell phone, as he had requested. He shows up a half-hour later to drive me to the airport. Mohammed drives a "service," the Beirut taxi that charges a standard 1000 lira ($.75) and takes you to the general area in which you are going, picking up other passengers along the way. Inevitably, there is conversation with the others in the cab and much exchange of local gossip. When I jumped into Mohammed's service several weeks before, he ignored the other passenger and chatted with me about his daughter's local chess successes and about my research. I took down his number and employed him several times to drive me longer distances. Whereas most drivers try to charge me more than the standard fare, on my first ride with Mohammed, he refused to take a tip. On the way to the airport, a mere fifteen-minute drive from where I was staying, he surprised me by telling me that he liked me. No Beiruti had done that before, at least not so directly. "I like you too," I replied. He explained that I reminded him of a British man he had met, back in the early '80s, who had taught him English. I was just like him, he said.

On the ride to the airport, he tells me about what happened to the British man in 1986, an event that I subsequently verify. The United States had bombed Tripoli, the Libyan capital, looking for Gaddafi but instead killing mostly women and children, including Gaddafi's 16-year-old daughter. Shortly thereafter, "Arab revolutionary gunmen," as they were called in the press, abducted this man in retaliation for British cooperation in the bombing of Tripoli. At the time, Mohammed's friend was preparing for a trip to London to visit his mother. He was held for one day, then executed.

"That's very tragic," I mumble, unable to come up with a more adequate condolence. Mohammed does not remain silent, however. He quietly talks about other murders in the more recent past, one a Muslim man who killed several Christian co-workers, motivated, Mohammed thought, by sectarian hatred.[6] On a trip the previous day, he had pointed out to me a spot on the road where the only son of a wealthy acquaintance had been killed in a traffic accident. And on one of my other trips with Mohammed, he had told me of the murder of his 16-year-old nephew, another only son, in Detroit.

This accumulating confidence and intimacy begins to overwhelm me, and Mohammed slows the car to a crawl to have enough time to complete the story of his British friend's murder. "There was a lot of violence back then," I say. "The security is much better today," he reassures me. I am still puzzled as to why Mohammed chose this moment, the morning of my departure, to implicate me in his loss.

Mohammed parks the car and, always gently smiling, demonstrates the hospitality for which Arabs are famous: he carries my bags to the passport control, then waits for me as guards check my identity, then waits for me as my luggage passes through the infrared sensors, then waits for me as I recede into the distance and pass through a door that blocks further vision. He worries, and he cares. *Le souci des autres.*

Accountability

We get caught up in other people's dreams and nightmares, and they in ours. We are implicated in other people's massacres, and they in ours. Ethnographic fieldwork, as I am depicting it, is the search for ethical modes of engagement with these implications. In the process of mutual exposure and discovery, of unexpected transferential and counter-transferential projections, we hope to sharpen our descriptions and analytical perspectives without sacrificing nuance.[7] If knowledge results from these interactions, it will not be disinterested but will be reflexively generated, the outcome of both conscious and unconscious collaboration, repressions, displacements, surprises, disappointments, cares, and discomforting worries. Unlike other modes of knowledge production, engaged fieldwork does not allow for bracketing these conditions of interaction in order to get to the facts or to represent them, for these conditions are, in fact, the key to understanding what the facts mean.

Rites of commemoration, in the context of the museums at Khiam and Qana, make a demand on us, the viewers, for recognition. They are similar to events staged for performative redress, such as truth commissions and apologies, except that they do not intend a break with the past but rather a memorialization that links the present to the past in an ongoing repetition of visits. In such memorial sites, we might expect that victims of terror make demands that we automatically empathize with their losses, demands to which we are obligated to respond. But identification with their suffering should not be automatic. A fuller understanding of events and therefore a deeper recognition of their meaning awaits the process of making conscious to ourselves what happens in our encounters with the facts and our emotional reactions to them. For anthropologists, such encounters reveal the possibilities of collaboration and critical understanding as well as the limits of knowing, saying, and identification—in order to objectify and make sense in writing of the terror on display.

Several tensions in this process are especially salient in ethnographic work on violence and terror and in work, such as medical anthropology, where suffering is central. There is the tension between identification with the suffering of all victims, who themselves compete for the compassion of outsiders, and imputing agency for suffering to particular individuals, groups, or states. Identification with all suffering alleviates anthropologists of the need to be reflexive and critical. Imputing agency might result in demands for accountability and punishment, including our own. It might, for example, demand taking some sort of responsibility for a "foreign policy" with which most anthropologists would voice disagreement but that is nonetheless executed in our name, with our often-silent complicity. That American foreign policy, in my case, included support for the Israeli occupation of southern Lebanon, the period in which torture and massacre occurred.

These tensions have paralyzing and dulling effects on anthropological accounts: insistence on compassion for all; pre-editing accounts of certain ambiguities in interactions, above all of our own vulnerabilities; refusal to take sides in the interests of balance, neutrality, or objectivity; or refusal to entertain the possibility of punishment. There is, among many anthropologists, also recourse to a popular and secure formula: "society against the state," which expresses itself in the tension between sanitizing our accounts of victim groups and giving them voice, while self-righteously criticizing all forms of state violence, even though state violence—the force of law—is often one of the necessary means to secure protection against further terror.

A simple transferential relation to the other, a desire to either neutrally voice the other's suffering or to presume to act on it with methodological prescriptions in hand, is a *hysterical identification*—made possible by effacing one's own participation in the recovery and further life of the other's experience. The conditions of interaction are suppressed so as to maintain an innocent identification with the suffering other. Fieldworker anxieties about exposure and duplicity then make us complicitous in the modes of deception of those we study. Identities are secured, communicative possibilities are foreclosed, and a deeper understanding of the implications of intersubjective knowledge is not reached.

Even as we continue to document the trajectories of violence and victimization, we should resist the seduction of a facile identification with victims of terror and the imaginary satisfactions obtained therefrom. This identification survives by pretending to be something else, something like the voice of unmediated or unadulterated suffering. In an effort to foreclose the possibility of questioning both the pretense to suffer and the recognition of its instrumentalization, as well as degrees of responsibility and one's own personal investments and failures to adequately address this suffering, the pretenses and investments shift over time as what they mask is symptomatically revealed. Instead, we might make conscious distinctions between suffering and the pretense to suffer, between our investments and our findings, and we might risk assigning agency to the harms perpetrated by those who use their own suffering as justification for the injuries they inflict on others.

Postscript, August 23, 2006

As I make final changes in this manuscript, Israeli warplanes have systematically destroyed the infrastructure of Lebanon in a month of daily bombings, and the vast majority of the murdered are civilians who were fleeing the attacks. Approximately one-fourth of all Lebanese, including 500,000 internal refugees, ran from this willful and inexcusable assault. Estimates of destroyed Lebanese infrastructure (road, bridges, buildings) total over $3.6 billion. Much of this infrastructure had been rebuilt in the very period—four years—that has elapsed since I first delivered this essay as a talk. Israel has claimed that it is only trying to provide security to its citizens by destroying the Hezbollah militia and securing the release of two captured soldiers. European governments have criticized Israel and evacuated their citizens; the U.S. government has officially approved of Israel's efforts, even expediting the shipment of sophisticated arms to Israel; the rest of the world has watched.

PART 2 Regime Change, Occupation, Democratization

Part Two focuses on the meaning of "regime change" and the American occupation of Iraq. Chapter 7, written initially in the fall of 2002, shortly before the occupation, is both a temporal diagnostic and an exercise in anticipatory reflection. It asks what regime change might look like should the United States invade Iraq; and, by means of a comparison with the Israeli occupation of South Lebanon and the American occupations of Germany and Japan, it asks what responsibility the United States assumes if indeed it occupies Iraq, and what the possible or desirable sorts of regime changes might be. That occupation and regime change has indeed come to pass, of course. Chapter 8, written two years into the occupation, is a sequel and follows events through to 2006. It assesses the occupation in terms of the announced goal of a "global democratic revolution" and interprets it as a form of coercive gift exchange and an attempt to export political form. Since this intervention escalated the levels of violent conflict, leading to further war and ongoing occupations, it asks specifically how to understand the United States' motive of democratization and speculates as to the likely longer-term consequences of the occupation. I am retaining the openness of the inquiry in the spirit of anticipatory reflection in which these essays were written, and in chapter 8 I have added more factual information without changing the substance of the argument. Chapter 9 suggests how German acceptance of defeat might inform the Israeli-Palestinian conflict. It asks about the conditions whereby the external ascription of defeat and collective punishment might result in an internalization of this ascription and an acknowledgment of defeat.

7 Responsibility after Military Intervention: What Is Regime Change? What Is Occupation?

Responsibility after Military Intervention

The George W. Bush administration argues that two responsibilities warrant a military intervention in Iraq: "elimination of weapons of mass destruction" and "regime change."[1] We do not know what this intervention looks like, whether it will be another in a sequence of disastrous encounters with Iraq, or whether it will inaugurate a new relationship with the United States and a new system of rule in Iraq specifically, or the Middle East generally. The administration, for its part, acknowledges reluctantly, if at all, the shortcomings of the last intervention, that of Bush Sr. in the Gulf War, as well as the chilling results of other interventions in Iraq during the Cold War. However, it summarily dismisses this history as irrelevant, for this is a new type of "global war on terrorism" where history is no compass for the future. We have entered a new era, we are told: America is more powerful than any hegemon has ever been in world history; the executive of this hegemon can now determine its own limits on power and its exercise.

As outlined in the official White House document "National Security Strategy of the United States," released on September 17, 2002, and available on the Internet, wars such as the one planned against Iraq are integral to this new era, both to promote "freedom, democracy, and free enterprise" and to maintain permanent U.S. military superiority over all other earthly powers, both friendly and adversarial. Such muscular rhetoric could mean either that the United States is recklessly and compulsively pursuing war again, in an effort to mask its first failure and to divert the public from ongoing failures in domestic policy and in the declared war on terror. Or, conversely, it could mean that the United States is now rectifying a failure or fulfilling a responsibility that, in the first instance, in the Gulf War, it had evaded. I find very little evidence for the second interpretation. But since the decision to wage a preventive war against Iraq appears to have already been made, it is more useful to inquire what it might mean to fulfill a responsibility following military intervention.

Permit me, however, a brief digression to explain why I think this war, or insistent preparation for war, is not about responsibility to an Other but a mask and diversion. I am not alone among American intellectuals in thinking that something is disturbingly wrong, even dangerously mad, in the scope of thought of the current American administration. There is a Nietzschean *Wille zur Macht* at work that is strangely at odds with the vision most Americans think the United States promotes; public opinion within the United States thinks of itself as a democratic system of governance under the rule of law. The Bush administration's notion of responsibility appears limited solely to those individuals who brought it to power or who might sustain its rule. Domestically, its policy is driven by relentless class warfare—permanent tax breaks for the rich, freedom for corporate entrepreneurs, appointment of judges who oppose any notion of a governmental obligation to the less well off or poor. It does not hold itself responsible to its own citizens, not to mention any obligation to "foreigners," and it operates with a total disregard for legal conventions, domestic or international. That was clear already in its no-holds-barred behavior to manipulate the Florida vote and the entire legal system so as to produce a win in the 2000 presidential election. Internationally, this disregard is apparent in its withdrawal from the Kyoto Treaty on the environment; in its obsessive efforts to destroy the new International Criminal Court; and, in its total disregard for the Geneva Conventions regarding the treatment of prisoners of war, as the United States holds "unlawful combatants" (a category that does not exist in international law) captured in Afghanistan, or handed over by Pakistan, at Guantanamo Bay, Cuba, in "indefinite detention without trial."

Leaders of this administration have no interest in other points of view; they consistently lie and dissimulate when confronted with contradictions, and yet they assume that they are always speaking not only for the entire United States but also for civilization as a whole and indeed the world.[2] "Our challenge," wrote Secretary of Defense Donald Rumsfeld, perhaps the most powerful member of the ruling elite, "is to defend our nation against the unknown, the uncertain, the unseen, and the unexpected" (Rumsfeld 2002, 23). Imagine that—a defense against our phantasms and insecurities! Could this be anything other than an attempt to provide security from the Devil—from the evil that knows no territorial boundaries, takes many forms, and is never fully knowable, certain, seen, or expected? Only God could offer this kind of security—and this is precisely the position of the Bush administration—they see themselves as God-ordained crusaders chasing after the Devil. The rest of us are reduced to the status of believers and followers, whom the administration defends against unbelief. How can one take seriously such megalomaniac design, except that it comes from the world's most powerful designer and therefore must be taken seriously because what they say and do has consequences for us all?

In this spirit of understanding the consequences of military intervention, I will return to the second interpretation and ask what might be the outcome of "regime change" after this war on Iraq if the United States indeed tries to rectify a failure and fulfill a responsibility. The first responsibility, "elimination of weapons of mass destruction," is itself hopelessly utopic and admits a great deal of ambiguity (what counts as weapons of mass destruction?) and hypocrisy, not least because the United States has the world's largest repository and is the major exporter of such weapons and has even, in the 1960s, tested biological weapons on its own soldiers but has no intention of eliminating such weapons from its arsenal.[3] Since no human system of control is foolproof, eliminating weapons of mass destruction and their proliferation would be possible only if the United States submits to elimination of its own weapons. At best, this discussion pertains only to who controls access and use of such weapons, requiring another line of strategic and ethical questioning altogether. I will comment only on the second responsibility, "regime change," which might actually be achievable; and I will do so from my own expertise, which is not in political science or international relations but in social anthropology. That is, I am concerned with aspects of the social, of rebuilding the social body and its culture after violent conflict.

Conceptualizing Regime Change

In terms of ideal types, there are at least three ways of conceptualizing regime change, all of which reference different meanings of the word "regime." The first is the most straightforward, what we used to call *overthrow of the government,* in the pre-Vietnam period of bipartisanship of American foreign policy, when there was little oversight of the CIA. This meant replacing, usually by means of a military coup, men at the top with new men at the top friendlier to our interests. To offer a few of our most successful overthrows: in 1953 of Mohammad Massadeq in Iran (followed by the repressive regimes of the Shah and then the Ayatollah); in 1954 of Jacobo Arbenz in Guatemala (followed by military rule and the murder of more than 100,000 civilians over the next 40 years); in 1963 of Ngo Dinh Diem in South Vietnam (eventually followed by a total collapse of the south and Communist takeover); in 1970 of Salvador Allende in Chile (followed by the Pinochet military dictatorship). In retrospect, the historical record—American success—looks bad. All of these interventions overthrew democratically elected governments and resulted in different forms of tyranny; most of them led to regimes that we also eventually opposed, or that opposed us, which should make us wary of confusing regime change with a mere overthrow of the government.[4]

Nonetheless, this abysmal U.S. record should not lead us to oppose overthrowing all government—Hitler's Germany, Stalin's Russia, Idi Amin's Uganda, the Khmer Rouge's Cambodia, for example, which all were governments of such extreme brutality that one should have actively supported an overthrow, independent of any consideration of what would come after them. What role the military plays in this overthrow is a strategic issue. The problem with overthrow is when responsibility is limited solely to military intervention and the replacement of enemy leaders. The second and third conceptualizations of regime change demand more than change of government.

The second conceptualization is *military occupation and colonization*. It may involve overthrow, but it also demands changes in the formal behavior of the country and its people toward others, meaning primarily toward its former enemies, the occupier's state and people. This usually begins with military intervention or its threat, but it also entails forms of co-optation and collaboration, the use of carrots and sticks in a longer-term occupation. Here, I will use the example of Israel's occupation of south Lebanon from 1985 to 2000. In this second understanding of regime change, some responsibility is in fact assumed after military intervention, but it is limited to a self-interested colonization during the period of occupation. There is no enduring commitment to changing the other. Withdrawal of the occupying force is usually prompted by some large-scale failure, and at that point formal colonization ends, as does responsibility to the enemy.

The third conceptualization of regime change involves transforming social organization and culture, what I call *"caring for the enemy"* (Borneman 2001). By care, I am referring to the Heideggerian elaboration of *Sorge,* meaning what one worries about but also what one cares for and cares about. Such a notion of regime change frequently begins with military intervention and a change at the top, but it entails a more thorough change of the forms of authority that generate or support the government or kind of regime one regards as unfriendly. The intent is to change the internal fabric, the culture, and patterns of a society—what political scientists try to operationalize (for other purposes) as a "regime": the values, norms, and rules of governance.

In early October 2002, the Bush administration began floating two historical models for a post-intervention Iraq: the American occupations of Japan and Germany following World War II. These two successful examples from the last century do indeed suggest certain possibilities and limits for regime change in Iraq. Alternately, we cannot draw such lessons from the unfolding dramas following interventions in Bosnia, Kosovo, and East Timor, because those outcomes are still uncertain. The defeats of Hirohito and Hitler were followed by six-and-a-quarter and four years of military rule, respectively, and changes from Imperial and Fascist authority structures to democratic and rational-legal ones, followed by much longer periods of oversight and intervention in civil life. In Japan, the Emperor-God was immediately forced to become human; in Germany, Nazi leaders and their symbology were immediately removed.[5] But the change in leaders was followed by a thorough transformation of institutional forms of political representation, educational systems and their contents, legal structures, and family hierarchies. In other words, changes in government structure were accompanied by changes in what British anthropologists would normally call "social organization" and Americans term "culture." Responsibility after military intervention, in this usage, is to bring about a thicker sense of regime change: transformations in social organization, culture, and patterns of authority, the expectation of an enduring change in that society and in one's relation to it.

All three of these interpretations of regime change—overthrowing the government, colonial military occupation, and caring for the enemy—have been employed at various times by members of the Bush administration when talking about Iraq. Since I am unqualified to speak about the strategic game of deciding which governments to overthrow and when, I will deal only with these last two understandings of regime change and briefly compare the 15 years of Israeli occupation of south Lebanon with the 45 years of Allied (Soviet and U.S./British/French) occupation of Germany.[6]

Colonial Military Occupation: Israel in South Lebanon

I turn to the Israeli military occupation of south Lebanon largely because I know it best. There are other examples that admit of more ambiguity, and hence insight into other sorts of problems, but Lebanon has a dominant and non-unified Muslim majority, like Iraq, and I have been doing ethnographic work there since 1999. This occupation is a clear example of a failed intervention—it did not produce any of the outcomes that the Israelis intended; the situation for all parties concerned got worse instead of better. It did not render the enemy less hostile to Israel. In fact, it facilitated a radicalization of some southern Lebanese, and it created popular support for an enduring, militarized resistance on Israel's northern border.

During the occupation, the south remained formally a part of the state of Lebanon; its residents retained their Lebanese citizenship and were more or less free to move back and forth between northern Lebanon and the south (and some, in a labor capacity, to Israel). Although U.N. "observers" and "peacekeepers" were eventually stationed on the border and had a minimal presence in some of the villages, they seemed to have little effect on either the Lebanese or the Israelis. Hezbollah, and to a lesser extent Amal, the two Lebanese resistance groups created with the aid of other states (primarily Syria and Iran, but also Israel), had not only organized the resistance but also moved into the vacuum of the state and provided minimal social and public assistance, primarily health care, and infusions of outside capital that kept local economies from collapsing. Israel was concerned solely with its own security and military goals: to deploy the entire south as a "buffer" or "security zone" devoid of people. Hence, they sought to keep the area backward educationally, culturally, and economically.

In this aspect of policy, they succeeded. Between 1978 and the Israeli withdrawal, the population in the south declined from roughly 600,000 to an estimated 65,000, with most of the refugees settling in the southern suburbs of Beirut. Also, part of making the south secure for Israel was to make it unsafe for local residents: Israel planted approximately 70,000 thousand land mines all over the south, which UN personnel (UNIFIL, to be precise), mostly Africans experienced in mine removal on their own terrain, are presently trying to find and remove.

In short, Israeli occupation did lead to a regime change, but it was the opposite of what they intended. Israel did rid the south of the PLO, which in 1982, when Israel made its first large-scale military intervention, had set up a kind of de facto government in the south. But not having prepared the people of south Lebanon for anything other than collaboration with Israel's security apparatus against their own state, or menial labor in Israel, or resistance, the Israelis have now turned formerly friendly neighbors into enemies.

Caring for the Enemy: Allied Occupation of Germany

Contrast the Israeli colonial military occupation of south Lebanon with the regime change in Germany following World War II. Is there still any doubt about the outcome? Germany today is one of the world's most prosperous and civil places to live. It has not only made friends of its former enemies, turning relations of enmity into ones of care, but it has also become a country known for strict adherence to principles of *Rechtsstaatlichkeit* (the rule of law), and for the activity of its citizens in promoting the unity of Europe as well as friendship and democracy elsewhere. This all sounds simplistic and cliché-ridden, because one doubts that such radical changes in social organization and culture can be effected in half a century. This doubt about the possibility of such social change—despite, or perhaps precisely because of, the major Cold War social engineering projects creating "Americans" and "Soviets"—surfaces in the widely accepted "joking" about the specter of Nazism in the future of Germans. I do not mean to suspend critique here, but we should take the evidence of transformation in Germany and among Germans seriously: from the model for descent into criminality in the first half of the twentieth century, to a model of reform in the last half of the twentieth century. Postwar Germany is an argument for military intervention, occupation, and regime change—if this model is exportable in any limited way. What were the essential conditions for this transformation?

Following the Nazi defeat and unconditional surrender in 1945, conditions for an occupation and regime change in Germany were certainly more propitious than for Israel in Lebanon or than they are for the United States in Iraq today. The two world wars had wholly delegitimated German government and paternal authority generally; internal divisions were not ethnic or religious but ideological; and large segments of the German population supported the various occupiers with little reservation. Under these conditions, it was relatively easy for the occupiers to transform Germany from an enemy into a friend—in fact, into two ideological friends, one of the Soviets, the other of the Americans. Yet this radical and dramatic postwar transformation was not automatic and cannot be explained away as merely propitious; there were many forms of German resistance, and the country was in absolute chaos at the end of the war.

Following the war, a general "sovereignty crisis" at all levels—transcendent, territorial, political, economic, and domestic—quickly led to a set of hardly imaginable conditions: four occupation armies, each with its own policies, a divided capital, hundreds of thousands of male prisoners of war, a massive market for sex with German women (the export of a symbolically significant number of war brides), and ultimately forty years of political division. Because the Allies differed on how to stabilize, they initially divided the country into two and organized it according to two opposed economic and political principles: capitalism and liberal democracy on one side, and socialism and a one-party state on the other. Whatever differences in strategy, however, they agreed on the necessity of creating a stable legal and political order and in establishing systems of cultural exchange, minimally within their own occupied parts of the divided Germany, in order to train and influence the future generation of German leaders and the direction of German society. These kinds of exchange programs were an essential part of the stabilization of Germany, and through them the different Allied occupiers competed for the loyalties of Germans. For example, between 1945 and 1949, before the founding of the two German states, the Russians, in particular, were known for lifting the curfew in their zone for nightclubs and entertainment, for encouraging musical performances and opening theaters and movie houses. The Allied occupation was successful largely because it was long-term and non-vindictive (which does not mean the absence of punishment); it fostered extensive exchange between former enemies; and it generally supported the imagining and growth of new domestic, political, and transcendent authorities (see Borneman 1992, 2002a).

Most scholars of Germany and Japan are skeptical about whether those occupations could serve as historical precedents for regime change in Iraq. Shortly before the invasion of Iraq, the Pulitzer Prize–winning historian John Dower asked whether the occupation of Japan might serve as a model for Iraq. "The short answer is no," he wrote, concluding that most of the factors that contributed to success in Japan are absent today in Iraq (Dower 2002). These factors include the following: (1) the occupation had moral and legal legitimacy in the eyes of most Japanese as well as the rest of the world; (2) Japan lacked essential internal cleavages; (3) Japanese fanaticism did not survive the war; (4) the occupation was initially administered by a single charismatic authority (General MacArthur); (5) the occupation was not hastily planned but was the result of long interdepartmental deliberation in Washington; (6) the occupation promoted liberal New Deal reforms in Japan (e.g., land reform, organized labor, progressive civil rights, education, and legal reform) that the current U.S. administration generally opposes; (7) postwar Japan being resource poor, no outside economic interests intervened to produce exploitative carpetbaggers; and, (8) structures of the old regime were able to enact reforms because of the existence of strong prewar democratic traditions.

I am generally sympathetic to Dower's skepticism, but I also support the principle of regime change in Iraq. Most of the factors he isolates for Japan also hold for postwar Germany, though I would add (or emphasize) a few others, such as the significance of demilitarization, legal trials, and administrative reforms; a legitimacy deficit because of the international attention given to the Holocaust; and the national structure of East-West division; as well as Allied interventions to accelerate generational differentiation (that is, promote a younger generation) and encourage changes in patriarchal and familial authority. Also, the crisis in German sovereignty in 1945 led to key modifications in mourning practices, particularly in the memorialization of leaders and in the state's role in remembering the dead. The initial taboo on public discussion of Hitler's self-immolation and the sources of his power, the ban on mourning for Hitler or forms of authority associated with the Third Reich, along with Allied disbanding of many traditional fraternities and attempts to prevent the honoring of fallen soldiers and dead leaders, led to new commemorative practices in both East and West Germany.

German bereavement was privatized and denied the public ceremony that usually accompanies departure from the dead. This privatization was due both to the inability of extant German public figures, in particular those tied to political authority and the state, to initiate mourning practices, and to the new international regime of guilt in which Germans were held responsible for the war and the Holocaust. A major effect of this sequence of events is that in German society since 1945 there has been an aversion to death cults, with limited or nonexistent public mourning for national leaders. Such a policy, I think, of forbidding state orchestration of mourning, would be propitious for a regime change in Iraq, irrespective of how Saddam Hussein is eventually replaced (Borneman 2004d).

Despite these major reservations, I think the United States has a responsibility in ending Saddam Hussein's tyrannical rule, above all because it was instrumental in bringing him to power and helping to stabilize his rule. Ending his rule, if facilitated by the United States and a "coalition of the willing," does not, of course, end this coalition's responsibility to the Iraqi people. Thus the German and Japanese success stories are relevant here, but even they have not exhausted the range of transformative possibilities. We must look more closely at the people and country of Iraq in their own terms, in light of Iraq's own social organization and history, as well as examine more closely the reach of U.S. intentions.

Regime Change in Iraq

The aforementioned U.S. National Security Strategy document lists "freedom, democracy, and free enterprise" as the three most significant elements, let me call them "values" or "judgments," that the United States finds itself responsible to pursue in the new world order. The first question is whether the Iraqi people agree to these three judgments, and if so what they think they are agreeing to. All evidence suggests that most Iraqis would support an overthrow of the government to get rid of Saddam Hussein and his tyrannical rule. But for a regime change to be successful—that is, considered legitimate over time—the people must acquiesce to, and ultimately accept, the changes in values and judgments that we promote, or will promote, during an "occupation," which will in turn generate changes in their own forms of culture and social organization. Our responsibility after military intervention, then, in the third conceptualization of "caring for the enemy," can never be just to our own values (except in the purely hypothetical case that they are identical with those of the people who live under and make up the regime we are changing), but to an exchange, a set of interactions, that readjust relationships that might result in dramatic internal changes in values. Given the unavoidable differences between American and Iraqi understanding of values (and such differences exist among Iraqis also), the moral authority that might accrue to the occupiers after a military overthrow will necessarily depend on the moral authority of the processes by which these values and judgments are reached and realized.

The Bush National Security Strategy does not mention these processes, which require a principled understanding of what I will refer to as law or legality, the framework in which values are debated and arbitrated. Freedom and democracy are not absolute values operating independent of context, but they work meaningfully only within a system of fundamental rights that constrain leaders, that constrain parliaments, that constrain majorities.[7] The first goal of an occupation must be to insist on respect for certain limits on rule, including limits on the privileges of the occupiers. Where legality is not the first priority, violence, civil war, and the disintegration of the state tend to follow, the contemporary examples of which are legion.

Introducing democracy without the rule of law is usually disastrous. Simply reflect on the abuses of power of majorities following the death of Tito in Yugoslavia, and the overthrow of Suharto in Indonesia. Introducing free enterprise without the rule of law is also disastrous, especially when the country is rich in resources—consider the plundering of the Russian economy after the collapse of the system of legality of the Soviet Union, or the ongoing state of siege in Columbia. Trials and the punishment of wrongdoers are of course desirable and perhaps ultimately necessary to establish the rule of law, but as I have argued elsewhere, legal trials may be delayed for generations if they pose an immediate risk of radical political destabilization and a security crisis (Borneman 1997, 2004c).

I am referring here to the basic principles of the rule of law, which, when implemented, are the greatest inhibitor of and threat to tyrannical rule. There are roughly seven essential principles: (1) separation of powers within a state, in particular the separation of the executive from the judicial branch; (2) legality, implying that (a) the people's representatives adopt the law, (b) statues find general application, and (c) the legislature itself is bound by the legislation; (3) sovereignty of statute law; (4) the prohibition of excesses of state authority, or a principle of proportionality of crime to punishment; (5) an independent judiciary; (6) a ban on retroactive legislation in order to foster predictability and legal certainty; and (7) trust in the lack of arbitrariness in the law's application. Although these principles provoke resistance everywhere, in no contemporary culture are they totally foreign. If there is a primary responsibility after military intervention, it must be to guarantee negative freedoms, to the enforcement of unpopular limits on rule. This is, indeed, the major conclusion I drew in a 1997 study of accountability in postsocialist Europe (Borneman 1997, 41–42). And it is the major conclusion that Paddy Ashdown, the high representative of the international community for Bosnia and Herzogovia, drew on October 28, 2002, in summarizing lessons from a decade of UN engagement in the Balkans (Ashdown 2002).[8]

The problem is that limits on rule are unpopular, while representative democracy, in contrast to the rule of law, finds much more resonance among more of the world's peoples. "Peoples" naturally prefer to think not in terms of law and limits but in terms of empowerment and self-rule—especially after the death of a leader, at the peak of a revolution, or at the beginning of an "emancipation." This nearly global consensus about the language of participatory democracy is not matched by any cross-cultural agreement, however, on what might constitute an adequate system of "representation," or what power is actually being yielded in a "delegation of authority," much less to speak of the principles of "popular will" or "majority rule." Democratic arrangements will always be historically contingent, varying greatly by region and place, by local cultural forms of power and authority. This variability often makes the democratic form in one place unrecognizable as such in another.

Anthropologists have documented a vast range of understandings of democratic form as it has materialized following decolonization and the collapse of empires. What is increasingly clear is that locating political authority in the category "people"—that is, government of, for, and by the people—centers social organization around a very unstable, abstract, and volatile source. Elections, which are meant to stabilize this source, must at the same time risk a destabilization every two or four or six years as on election day "the people" are ritually dissolved and reconstituted. Elections begin by dividing along the lines of party, tribe, or sect and end with a hypostatized unity, in the process reallocating the power to enforce or change the rules. The people are disaggregated into individuals who vote and then reunited, a process that holds the potential to reallocate the power to change the rules. In transformative moments, elections dramatize the volatility and divisions of the group, becoming violent events that demand sacrifice (Borneman 2002b). We do not know what kind of political form, much less what kind of democracy, might work for the peoples of Iraq.

Unlike Germany and Lebanon, Iraq does not have a history of democratic self-rule. Like Lebanon, it has only a recent history, colonial and post-colonial, as a unity. Like Germany and Lebanon, however, Iraq has a well-educated population, and we should not underestimate people's ability to learn quickly. An oft-repeated joke in the Mideast goes: Egyptians write, Lebanese print, Iraqis read. But there is no compelling logic to believe that what Iraqis read would lead to unity rather than sectarian division.

In Germany the concept of *Volk* does a great deal of work for democracy, fictionally unifying a heterogeneous mix of peoples across region and class. It is a dangerous concept, but one that also made possible an immediate solidarity between East and West following the Cold War division of the country. Not so in Lebanon, where there has traditionally been little loyalty to the Lebanese people as such but much to sectarian, quasi-tribal groupings—Sunni or Shi'a Muslim, Orthodox or Maronite Christian, and Druze, along with many other smaller sects. With the unifying assumption of a *Volk*, democracy in Germany can afford to be individualistic and organized around multiple parties, a one-person-one-vote for shifting party coalitions. But in Lebanon, the 1989 Ta'if accords ending the civil war fixed the sectarian memberships in the constitution, allotting political power not by person (no census has been taken since 1932) but by group alone.[9] People vote less for an individual than for a position, which is competed for within sectarian lines.[10] I suspect that in Iraq democracy will be, for better or worse, organized along sectarian and ethnic-tribal lines, not individualistically, at least not initially.

My reservations should not be seen as an argument against democracy per se. I am merely, in a Tocquevillian spirit, suggesting its limits as a global moral project, the limits of the responsibility to install it. I merely wish to point to some of the many cultural preconditions necessary to make democracy work. If there is a responsibility after military intervention, it is to the establishment of economic and political stability and to certain negative freedoms, not to a project in the self-realization of the people, however much that is seen by the people themselves as a panacea. In any case, nowhere is the consent of the governed, of the "people," the only moral authority behind a judgment. If military intervention does not bring with it sufficient moral authority for a new regime, which is likely to be the case, the occupiers have recourse to alliances with other forms of authority—religious and customary, for example—that are often accorded more respect than plebiscites or elections. In short, I question the assumption of a universal translatability of a "transition to democracy"—a term commonly used in contemporary political theory. It is not only empirically ambiguous, but I also doubt whether this is possible, and I doubt that it is desirable without first constructing the rule of law.

The Bush administration is, however, simply disinterested in legality as an element of regime change. A legal framework for its occupation of Iraq, and for post-occupation, is not a priority design. Even its promulgation of democracy and freedom is more strategic than moral, more tactical than principled. If its current program for readying the United States for a perpetual war on terror is any guide to how it wants to redesign Iraq, then legality is irrelevant, while democratic machinery is essential. Electoral rituals are necessary to legitimate rule, above all when policies are not consciously designed to deliver much else to the majority than the symbolic satisfaction of electoral victories. But also, in the case of the Bush administration, it prefers electoral rituals to legal process—or to put it another way, electoral rituals as the only necessary legal process, since, with money and resources, they can be more easily manipulated. I fear that philosopher Richard Rorty (2002, 14) may not be exaggerating in his recent characterization of the administration's goal: "to bring about the permanent militarization of the state described in Orwell's 1984."

To be fair, however, the Bush administration may be committed pragmatically, if not ideologically, to the third value listed in its National Security statement: free enterprise. What might it mean to introduce free enterprise as an element in Iraqi regime change? First, it is nothing foreign to Iraq. There is already a great deal of free enterprise, as well as entrepreneurship, not least in organizing ways of circumventing the U.S. and British–enforced UN economic boycott. But if the first two years of the Bush administration's economic policies are any indication, what it most wants, I suspect, are unprotected markets—not free enterprise but free trade, where Iraq's natural resources, particularly oil, can be allocated or exchanged with little or no government restriction. If there are lessons here to be drawn from the introduction of this kind of free enterprise in the Soviet Union and Eastern Europe, then in all likelihood the international trade in drugs, weapons, and women will also flourish with the elimination of Iraq's present command economy and its controls on mobility of people and resources. The most likely consequence of insisting on a regime of private property rights like that which exists in the West is an increase in inequality and social conflict both among Iraqis and between us and them.

A final question has to do with duration: How long does responsibility for regime change extend after military intervention? One might overthrow a government within a day, but the neutralization of a regime is never enough to effect regime change. One also needs to change culture and social organization, and such changes rarely occur within a single generation. It takes minimally two generations, 40 to 50 years, for a shift in authority and for time to stabilize the transfer of power to sons and daughters. The longevity and intensity of the American occupation of Germany is exceptional, and unlikely to be repeated in the near future. Americans have a notoriously short attention span in matters of foreign policy. Presidents seem preoccupied with beginnings, not with caring for the enemy and the process of long-term development. The enduring investment in the rebuilding of Germany had a great deal to do with the half-century-long Cold War. Lacking this political context, and lacking all of the old imperial reasons for intervention—"the White Man's Burden," a "civilizing process," or even a mandate to "economic development"—why should a non-instrumental relationship after a change in government endure? The peoples of the West and the United States are by no means motivated by a mission to resist tyranny everywhere, or to advance human rights. Nor is there much of a consensus in any democracy on the nature of obligation outside kin and nation. Yet the success of any military intervention would seem to depend on a more expansive understanding of responsibility along the lines of care and accountability that I have outlined here.

8 Does the United States Want Democratization in Iraq? Anthropological Reflections on the Export of Political Form

While democratic practices may be ancient and found in many parts of the world, democracy as a political form was developed and refined after the eighteenth-century French and American Revolutions. Its most continuously practiced forms are in Europe and North America, and this Euro-American form of democracy has come to think of itself as a kind of political *Urkultur*, the source from which democratic cultural traits are disseminated throughout the world in a process resembling *Kulturkreislehre*.[1] Driven largely by the economic and military power of the West, democracy, along with many other forms of Western culture, ranging from the automobile to consumerism, have found eager audiences in most parts of the world, especially during the period of decolonization following World War II when the democratic form itself was used against the European powers. Whereas the mixed European experience with this diffusion has led to some skepticism among Europeans about the conditions of its export, the American experience, which itself is an early product of decolonization, has instead led to a strengthened resolve in the United States about its importance. Espoused most strongly by Republican Party "neocons" after the attack of 9/11/2001 but also by many political scientists and human rights advocates, the assumption of democracy as a universal good and as a kind of polity that sought peace with its neighbors led to the belief that the democratic form could be a panacea for overcoming problems of political and economic development, especially in the Middle East.[2] Indeed, the desire to democratize Iraq, specifically, may be the most lasting of the many rationales for the March 20, 2003, invasion of Iraq (termed, at the time, "Operation Iraqi Freedom"), and it may have enduring negative historical consequences for the conditions of exchange of democracy in the Middle East and elsewhere.

What does it mean to export a political form, in this case the ideal of democracy? Is this similar to the export of commodities like sugar, after which entire culinary systems have been reordered (Mintz 1986)? Or is there fundamental misrecognition in the specific logics of exchange and registers of authority that accompany the export of this ideal and make its reception radically contingent on local cultural contexts? And what did the George W. Bush administration specifically, and Americans generally, mean when they trumpeted democracy for Iraq?[3]

The Right Embraces Democracy

At least since the French Revolution, the Western Left has occupied the term "democracy"—whether a Rousseauian participatory, John Stuart Mills electoral, or Lockean liberal version—while the Right has occupied the term "rule of law." For both Left and Right, commitments to democracy and the rule of law, respectively, have been decidedly uneven, often more to the ideal of the People or of Order than to the practice of popular sovereignty or to any enforceable principles of accountability. The polarization of Left and Right in the West around this dichotomy continued until the late twentieth century, with the communist commitment to the People and fascist commitment to Order being two master narratives that helped organize the two poles.

American export of the political form of democracy has, to be sure, a longer and more varied history, not tied exclusively to one political ideology. Though generally associated with the Left, democracy has long been part of America's missionary goals, made most explicitly in Woodrow Wilson's espousal of the sovereignty of the people in his Fourteen Points address on January 8, 1918. Subsequently, not only Democrats but also Republicans took up its appeal, in particular Eisenhower in the project of postwar reconstruction of Europe.[4] In this postwar period, however, the United States employed democratic form strategically, supportive only selectively, when electoral results produced pro-American governments (i.e., supportive in Eastern Europe, but opposed in Latin America); whereas its commitment to global economic development and commerce (under the notion of "free markets") was steadfast, generally viewed as part of the national interest within the context of inevitable "modernizing" projects.[5] This changed with the disintegration of Cold War oppositions following the implosion of the Soviet bloc after the fall of the Berlin Wall in 1989. In the subsequent decade, as democratic elections brought about pro-American governments throughout the former Eastern bloc, democracy's ideological charge promised to unite Left and Right in a single chorus of believers. As the end of ideology, a goal without a clear counter-concept, democracy was left with no competitors to challenge evil tyrants abroad.

In short, a new ideological realignment took shape in the United States following the dramatic failures and collapse of the two twentieth-century oppositional master narratives offered by Nazi Germany and the Soviet Union. This new alignment was no longer dependent on a binary logic: now the Right aggressively espoused democracy, internally in refining certain technologies like precision gerrymandering for electoral advantage and popular referendums to bypass the legislative process, and externally in insisting on replacing dictatorial regimes with constitutional democracies that acknowledge the spirit of the values they understood to be American. At the same time, giddy from electoral victories after the Clinton years that enabled it to represent and rule the world's unchallenged imperial power, the Right appeared to abandon its traditional embrace of law, stability, and order. The George W. Bush administration, under the dominance of the neocon wing of the Republican Party, brought this value reversal into focus in its actual policies. In this process of self-redefinition, the Left and the Democratic Party (which under Clinton came to stand for free trade and globalization) no longer served as a traditional foil for the Right, standing for neither more democracy nor more law.

The appeal to democracy after "9/11" is novel in several respects: first, the particular kind of right-wing composition of democracy's leading disciples and avatars—Bush, Pearle, Wolfowitz, Cheney, and Rumsfeld—all former skeptics of the ideal; second, the place to which they wished to export it, to the Middle East, a region of the world with authoritarian governments and minimal democratic traditions, and above all, to Israel's major adversaries (Iraq, Syria, and Iran); and third, the embrace of participatory, electoral democracy in the Middle East (excepting Egypt, Saudi Arabia, and a few other strategically placed U.S.–friendly states) meant a new valorization of change and self-realization over the conservative tradition of limited government and, above all, stability, law, and order.

The invasion and reorganization of Iraq (Afghanistan, by comparison, pales in ideological significance) has become the formal experiment for this revalorization. Explicit statements to this effect are ubiquitous. Bush himself said before Congress on November 6, 2003: "Iraqi democracy will succeed—and that success will send forth the news, from Damascus to Teheran—that freedom can be the future of every nation. [Applause] The establishment of a free Iraq at the heart of the Middle East will be a watershed event in the global democratic revolution."[6]

To be sure, all the talk of liberty, freedom, and democracy—the most recent triumvirate of values—does not mean that the Right has totally vacated appeals to law or authority, for the Department of Justice, later joined by the new Department of Homeland Security, systematically used law and executive authority to curtail civil liberties at home. This is not to speak of the well-documented rights violations in Bagram Air Force base in Afghanistan, in Guantanamo Bay, Abu Ghraib, and hidden detention centers in other countries that epitomize a cavalier attitude, if not total disregard, for the legal rights of non-Americans. But in its espousal of the doctrine of "unitary executive theory," designed to expand the powers of the presidency during an unending war in all fields at all costs, the commitment to law is not merely the adoption of an alternative vision of law but of a specifically authoritarian version. This version of law, which I will explicate below, resembles in many ways fascism's understanding of law in that it tests the conception of law as guaranteeing a balance of power and limiting the exercise of authority. In sum, the Bush administration's attitude toward American law might be called pragmatic and utilitarian, expressed in a relative unconcern with precedent as principles that codify tradition, and in disregarding international law and conventions as means to limit and constrain others (much less itself). My argument will be that this devalorization of conventional law undermines the principles of accountability that make democracy possible, guaranteeing that the enthusiasm for the export of democracy will remain at the level of fantasy.

The Global Democratic Revolution

In speaking of a "global democratic revolution," Bush was appealing to a mono-theistic and specifically Christian teleology of a global mission (though "Damas-cus to Teheran" suggests a regional preoccupation with the Muslim/Middle Eastern world). A global mission requires a universal equivalent, an entity trans-latable across cultural differences. In this case, democracy serves this function of universal equivalent. Much like "development" is the positive ideological form of activity in the economic sphere, "democracy" is the positive form of activ-ity in the political sphere; both provide a theoretically ambitious and relatively open-ended referent for norms, values, and institutions.

For Americans who hear Bush speak of this global revolution, the export of democracy is a collective gift, something precious and universally translatable, which they can share with others as part of their global mission as a People.[7] A gift, in the classical explication of Marcel Mauss (2000), is an obligatory, asymmetric, and reciprocal exchange, a foundational human activity especially important between groups who would otherwise try to eliminate each other. For Mauss, groups engage in coercive exchange—of words, objects, or people—in order to establish peaceful, long-term relations with their neighbors. Obligatory exchanges entail an imagined future, ensuring that concerns for the present and past cannot dominate social activity. The gift of democracy, then, as one of the explicit justifications for the United States' occupation of Iraq, should be understood, above all, as a coercive, asymmetric, and reciprocal exchange between countries, an attempt to ensure future relations having more to do with self-preservation than with benevolence.

The coercive exchange of democracy, the "global democratic revolution," can be understood as an extension of the idea of the export and exchange of women—as signs or counters—in exogamous marital systems. As Levi-Strauss demonstrated about pre-capitalist groups in his magisterial *Elementary Structures of Kinship* (1971), what is of essential value to the reproduction of the kin—women's reproductive powers—is part of a regularized exchange between groups. The exchange of women, words, and goods enlarges sociality and the units of the social, creating inter-sociality, what today operates on the scale of international relations. Such exchange, as Simmel (1990) argued, is at the center of conflict *and* conflict resolution. It is, above all, the answer to war, a way to prevent the Hobbesian state of nature where each group, however small or large, is concerned only with its own welfare and with keeping its valuables for itself.

But what happens when a group refuses to exchange? What happens when it perceives exchange as voluntary and refuses to exchange its valued signs, whether ideas, technologies, resources, reproductive capabilities, or goods? Mauss was equally clear that groups do not exchange everything, but in fact withhold what is most valuable to them. They do this, argues Maurice Godelier (1998) in a re-reading of Mauss, in order to solidify the group, to establish descent, to maintain something distinct about themselves for the group's own internal cohesion and identity. Withheld objects direct the group not to the future but to the past, to the origin, to sacred objects, talismans, originary myths. So we have an aporia: what is withheld is by definition most valuable to the identity of the group as it views its past, but also the very act of withholding increases the value of the object so that it is more coveted by outsiders, and its withholding may result in war in the future. All groups, then, balance withholding something from exchange, which is oriented to the past (and, while strengthening the cohesion of groups, also threatens to isolate them) with obligatory exchange, which is oriented to the future and establishes inter-group relations.

The majority of Americans as a group are settlers or their descendants and do not appear to withhold anything from exchange. (This argument also holds for former slaves and, to a more limited extent, for native Indians.) In fact, Americans are often considered the paradigmatic *modern* nation, in that they formed solely through exchange, above all an exchange of their pasts for an open-ended future. Made up largely of immigrants whose condition of inclusion has been to reject the primacy of group origin, Americans have been encouraged either to think of tradition as voluntary, something to choose, or to reject tradition as a site of anything valuable or sacred.[8]

That Americans stress the forgetting of origin as a precondition for inclusion is revealed most clearly in the status of the so-called First Peoples, those populations who already had settled the Americas and preceded the mass migrations from other continents (Borneman 1995). If a similar precondition to inclusion were demanded of First Peoples today, it would mean to erase the genocide against the indigenous ("Indian") populations that preceded European settlement as well as to erase the entire Hispanic colonial past. There is among them a struggle between demands for erasure and demands for recognition of this past, and because many have intermarried, they are pulled by competing heritage claims of African, European, and Asian descent. In any case, if the American people as a collective have a relation to the sacred in the United States, it is not as an amalgam of pasts but as the possibility of becoming American through an exchange of pasts for the future.

Given this collective demand for exchange, the decision to withhold something sacred for the collective therefore becomes understood ideologically not as a matter of affirming a principle integral to group cohesion but as a matter of mere expediency—attributed to individual choice. According to this doctrine, anything, in principle, is not only exchangeable, but exchange itself is understood as the very condition of the survival and betterment of the group. To be constituted only with respect to exchange makes it difficult to see any limits to one's self; the entire world and everything in it is seen as a potential extension of the collective self. Any self is a potential other, any other a potential (American) self.

In the field of foreign policy, this creed of naturalized exchange has often been translated into "free trade" and the "freedom to intervene" in the affairs of other states, and it dates back at least to the 1840s, and the Jacksonian Democrat doctrine of "Manifest Destiny." Initially used to justify war with Mexico and then annexation of much of what is now the Western United States, it was discredited as it got caught up in the slavery debate and was largely discredited by 1855, then again revived in the 1890s by Republicans to justify expansion outside North America. Today the idea of "free exchange" as well as "free choice" is naturalized to the extent that even the taking of U.S. territory by foreigners—buying American land or buildings—provokes protest only when the buyers are Arabs or Muslims, the groups designated now as America's most dangerous enemies.

The Gift: Democracy for Oil, Military Bases, Peace with Israel?

Consider, then, democratization as one of the gifts the United States wants to bestow on the world—since 9/11 on Iraq and the Middle East in particular—

a possession central to its own identity but nonetheless universally translatable and of sufficient value to warrant an obligatory, future-oriented exchange. Such a gift demands a response, and the receiver, as Mauss writes, in order to avoid weakness or indebtedness, must usually give something of equal or greater value back. "Gift," in its Sanskrit-Germanic etymology, means both an offering and a poison. Leave aside, for the moment, the status of stated intent—what President Bush and the neocons meant by invoking democracy, whether they were sincere or merely used democracy as a ruse to get at Middle East oil or to secure Israel—for the predicament of the Iraqis, from their perspective, was in fact structural, independent of the actual intent of the Americans. Iraqis had to choose: either adopt democratic form as the Americans define it and give the Americans something extra in return (the expectation of possible return gifts was clear: peace with Israel on Israeli terms, a permanent base from which to exercise political influence on the Middle East, and secure access to their oil); or refuse the debt, refuse the demands of the giver, refuse obligatory reciprocal return—in other words, resist the terms of the occupation.

It is important to keep in mind that to enter into gift exchange, however initially asymmetric or coercive it is, is to enter into a relationship with a future in mind that is bound to change both parties over time. The giver may initially determine the conditions of exchange but is not left unaffected by the relationship. This boomerang effect always becomes apparent over time. And in the process of exchange, the problems in U.S. democracy then become increasingly exposed (though, through mechanisms of repression, not brought to consciousness). More precisely, as the United States tried to export its political form, the limitations (and hypocrisy) of its intent were exposed. The examples are many: the U.S. government cut back on investments in education and health in the United States while paying many Iraqis not to work and securing their social welfare system; it fought for unrestricted gun ownership and use as a basic right in the territorial United States while arbitrarily confiscating guns in the personal possession of Iraqis; it pushed to expand the influence of religion in the American political sphere while calling for secularism in Iraq; it privatized energy production in the United States while guaranteeing the collective ownership of oil fields in Iraq; it gerrymandered districts and worked for making permanent single-party dominance in U.S. elections while encouraging multiple parties and free and fair elections in Iraq.

Perhaps most noteworthy, in this very period the United States encouraged democratic elections in the Middle East but then refused to recognize the electoral success of Hamas in Palestine, Hezbollah in Lebanon, and the Muslim Brotherhood in Egypt—all Islamic-based parties (see chapter 10). Middle East actors, especially because of new Arab televisual media, were thoroughly aware of all of these American hypocrisies, thus leading to a further distrust and resistance to the gift. Such an exchange of ideas and ideologies contains within it a Trojan horse kind of danger, for each exchange inevitably reflects back on and illuminates the giver, with the risk of unintended revelations and consequences for both parties.

Moreover, ideas must be translated into foreign contexts, where they germinate and are often transformed so as to radically subvert the initial intent behind the idea. Witness the transformation of the German Romantic idea of *Volksgemeinschaft*—intended in its original context to resist French colonial rule—into an endogamous and militaristic Zionism in Israel. Or witness the transformation of European "nationalism" when joined with the fourteenth-century concept *asabiyya* (Arab blood solidarity) into the peculiar authoritarian mixes of Syrian and Iraqi Baathism. But the refusal to exchange poses an even greater threat, that of endemic warfare and the violence of resistance, which in fact characterized the Cold War.

Democratic Form, the Double, and Its Exchange Value

What, exactly, happens to the exchange value of this political form—democracy—when it is exported through military intervention and occupation? While one should take seriously the Bush administration's stated intentions about democratization in Iraq, one cannot trust that its spokespeople mean what they say. Even if members of the administration spoke sincerely and in good faith, it would be foolish to assume that their language choice reveals their intentions, or that their intentions are transparent, even to themselves.

Moreover, the lack of a consistent definition of democracy, by the administration and scholars alike, leads to skepticism about actual intent when praising the institution. Attempts by scholars to arrive at a universal definition of democratization have proven futile. The political scientist Philippe Schmitter (1998, 33), for example, concludes that "no single set of institutions and rules—and, above all, no single institution or rule—defines political democracy. Not even such fundamental characteristics as majority rule, territorial representation, competitive elections, parliamentary sovereignty, a popularly elected executive, or a 'responsible party system' can be taken as its distinctive hallmark." Hence, it should be expected that most of the Iraqis initially active in importing democracy—leaders Massoud Barzani and Jalal Talabani of the Kurdish minority; the Shia businessman Ahmad Chalabi; the formerly exiled Sunni businessman A'yad Allawi, the administration's early favorite; as well as Shia clerics Muqtada al-Sadr and Abdel-Aziz al-Hakim—employed different understandings at different times.

Despite the disagreement among scholars about the *content* of democracy and its exportability, there seems to be consensus among them that democracy as a form is still superior to other forms of governance, especially with regard to the accountability of ruler to ruled—that is, to some version of Abraham Lincoln's "government of the people, by the people, for the people." And although most rulers in the Middle East may not be equally enthusiastic about democratic form, large majorities of the people in those countries, presumably including in Iraq, if we are to believe polling data, would seem to agree with the political scientists.[9] (Under the weight of failed expectations and the transparency of American hype, this pro-democracy consensus has been very fragile, although the democracy's logic and its multiple definitions can appeal for different reasons to different audiences at different times.)

An explication of the exchange value entailed in democratic form should, then, begin with an understanding of why the central concept of "the People" and the doctrine of "popular sovereignty" are difficult to define but nonetheless find such general resonance in both the United States and the Middle East. It is often remarked that, in a Euro-American chronology, democracy effects a transformation of authority by replacing a single God with the People. The People become a formally secularized site of a sacred source of power, the basis on which and for which is developed a theology without theodicy (an explanation of goodness in the face of evil) and without soteriology (a doctrine of salvation or redemption through suffering). Like belief in God, belief in the People is full of ambivalence and intrinsically riven—by age, culture, ethnicity, class, gender, and religion—with division and unpredictability. To deal with this ambivalence and division, the doctrine of popular sovereignty claims to overcome or constrain division by representing the People as united and one.[10] And much as the monotheistic Semitic versions of God cannot be exchanged for another God, the People cannot be exchanged for another people.[11]

But to create democracy as a universal equivalent, the United States must admit the substitutability of the People, which in principle is the very thing that defines it. It must make replicas elsewhere of the People, perhaps the only object which, for Americans, should theoretically be regarded as sacred and withheld from exchange. That is why enthusiasm for the project of exporting democracy is tempered by a latent fear, often expressed in a fear of new emigrants in democracies, for there is the risk that the copies will extract something from the original in the process of exchange, eviscerating and diluting the sovereign power of the People (cf. Taussig 1992).

The export gift of democracy—the People and their sovereignty—generates, for Americans, a series of doubles, copies of themselves, other People in whom they can recognize themselves but who are nonetheless different. A "double," writes Freud (1953, 219–53), "was originally an insurance against the destruction of the ego, an 'energetic denial of the power of death.'" That is, the initial identification with the double is a reassurance of existence, an affirmation of self through reproduction in the copy. "But," continues Freud, "when this stage has been surmounted, the 'double' reverses its aspect. From having been an assurance of immortality, it becomes the uncanny (*unheimliche*) harbinger of death. . . . The 'double' has become a thing of terror, just as, after the collapse of their religion the gods turned into demons." Following this logic, the attempt to generate replicas of American political form, to create fellow popular sovereigns through a global democratic revolution, yields only a fleeting sense of importance and satisfaction, if not of immortality. The double soon becomes an uncanny "thing of terror"—a demon.

For Americans, then, the People in Iraq appeared as a prospective double, but this appearance yields only a very brief sense of satisfaction. The familiarity with Iraqi People is uncanny in the sense that it uncovers, as Freud writes, "what is hidden (anxiety) and by doing so, effects a disturbing transformation of the familiar into the unfamiliar." The People, a site of the sacred and the bedrock of American collective beliefs, are similar in form to Americans but strange in a way that elided United States' nation-building efforts in Iraq.

In evoking the global democratic revolution, from the very start of the Bush administration the world of reality is left behind and a magical system of belief is adopted: the turn to the conspiratorial philosophy of Leo Strauss,[12] the assumption of secret powers and belief in the omnipotence of one's own thoughts, a denial of costs for future generations of an extravagant defense budget, the Faustian sense that an American-led "liberation" of the Iraqi People—or Muslims generally, from Damascus to Teheran—can produce democratic form. These wishes become especially problematic when ambivalence about their realization is denied in favor of total certainty and the abolition of doubt.

Such was the case in the lead-up to the Iraqi war, when skeptical media reporting largely disappeared and the truth claims of government leaders were taken at face value. Dissimulation was necessary to create this gullible public, where doubts about actions were replaced with assertions of self-certainty. That logic was evident in Secretary of Defense Donald Rumsfeld's clever spin on the Iraqi invasion and war: "As we know, there are known knowns. There are things we know we know. We also know there are known unknowns. That is to say, we know there are some things we do not know. But there are also unknown unknowns, the ones we don't know we don't know."[13]

The initial presentation of Bush administration spokespeople that assured the People of an easy victory was indeed a cover for the great uncertainty behind the occupation: the search for "known knowns" and "unknown unknowns," the turn to cabbalistic, inner-circle plotting and animistic beliefs to motivate a global democratic revolution. While the imperial plot of the "unitary presidency," not to mention the quieting of the press, the occupation of Mideast oilfields, or the overthrow of Saddam Hussein, had long gestations, the public event of 9/11 presented a propitious opportunity to realize these visions. The uncertainty provoked by 9/11 contained unusual emotional force, however, especially as the massacre in New York was subsequently framed around questions of "our vulnerability," fears normally associated with the extreme vulnerability of childhood. This emotional force was prey to the reemphasis on defense and security of the "homeland" and the representation of terror as a permanent threat to the collective. The so-called War on Terror became a never-ending fight against omnipresent and omnipotent animistic devils intent on destroying the West.

Until 2005, Attorney General John Ashcroft was the initial member of the Bush administration most in charge of bringing these threats into the symbolic order. On December 6, 2001, he informed the Senate Judiciary Committee of steps needed to "save innocent lives from terrorists." He went on to say, "My day begins with a review of the threats to Americans and American interests that were received in the previous 24 hours. If ever there were proof of the existence of evil in the world, it is in the pages of these reports. They are a chilling daily chronicle of hatred of America by fanatics who seek to extinguish freedom, enslave women, corrupt education and to kill Americans wherever and whenever they can. The terrorist enemy that threatens civilization today is unlike any we have ever known. It slaughters thousands of innocents—a crime of war and a crime against humanity. It seeks weapons of mass destruction and threatens their use against America. No one should doubt the intent, nor the depth, of its consuming, destructive hatred. Terrorist operatives infiltrate our communities—plotting, planning and waiting to kill again . . . To those who scare peace-loving people with phantoms of lost liberty . . . your tactics only aid terrorists, for they erode our national unity and . . . give ammunition to America's enemies." By defining any opposition to counter-terror strategies as itself terrorist, Ashcroft effectively eliminated the possibility of opposition—all in the name of saving democracy.

This "chronicle of daily hatred" leads one to see a proliferation of terrorists and escalation of terrorism—"drug," "environmental," "biological," "strikers," "teachers"—each to be fought with increasing sophistication and ruthlessness. The creation of a new Department of Homeland Security was a collective response to these threats, supported by Democrats and Republicans alike.[14] But protection from this uncanny threat to the home can come only from the mother, who for the child represents *das Heimliche,* and for the modern adult is connected to being part of an organic whole, such as being a member of the People. Indeed, our most powerful experiences of the uncanny are those that bring repressed memories of our mothers to the fore—in this case, of the love, wholeness, and security she provides or fails to provide. The horror and threat of terror recalls this time before separation when every wish was fulfilled and the imagined was the real.

An anxiety that the export of democracy as a universal equivalent will be unsuccessful is evident in the ubiquitous discourse around the question "Why do they hate us?" used to explain 9/11 and all forms of subsequent opposition to U.S. policy. The flip side of this refrain is "They no longer love us." The copies—other popular, democratic sovereigns—should love the United States, the mother of democracy, but they do not. Moreover, the expectation that democracies are fundamentally alike and peaceful, less likely to war with other democracies, was easily translated into the American idiom of "They love us." Even European opposition to American policy appears to many Americans, from the perspective of love, as rationally incomprehensible.[15] It is not surprising, therefore, that the perceived withdrawal of this love is experienced as hate.

The War on Terror inflected the newly proclaimed "global mission" of democratization, in that its success or failure served as a barometer for whether other democracies love us. Democracy thus is not primarily about political organization but is an anti-terror tool needed to make the United States invulnerable again (cf. Butler 2004).[16] In the name of defense of the homeland, violence was deployed ruthlessly, using the most lethal weapons available, bending legal constructs to justify the outsourcing of torture to other states, and permanently incarcerating suspected enemies. The inability to create reassuring replicas in response to the destruction of 9/11, to master this export of democracy, led not to the search for alternative ways of securing the collective but instead to a cycle of aggressive expenditure similar to the Kwakiutl Potlatch first described by Franz Boas (1920). In the face of the destruction of the late-nineteenth-century colonial encounter, the Kwakiutl, a northwest Indian community decimated by losses to disease and military conquest, organized ever-greater sacrifices in which they expended everything, including their most valuable possessions. No destructive excess was too great in trying to control the destruction that had been unleashed on them.

Similarly, the Bush administration tried to control the power of destruction through excessive expenditure, following in a long line of American attempts to install democracy through war, irrespective of outcome. One repeats something in order to master it, but if mastery is impossible, the repetition becomes obsessive, driven by a *Bemächtigungszwang*, a compulsion to empowerment through appropriation. The pattern repeats itself over time in places as diverse as postwar

Europe, Iran, Guatemala, South Vietnam, Afghanistan, and Iraq.[17] Exporting the form of democracy in these coercive exchanges produced only one predictable outcome: guerilla wars of resistance.

The Right's Rejection of the Rule of Law

Thus far, my argument has been that the United States offered to Iraq democratization through military intervention, a gift of the maternal register: the People and popular sovereignty. Law, conversely, is traditionally associated with the Father, with language and the symbolic order—and in the United States with the Republican Party. However, as I suggested at the beginning of this chapter, we have to revise our traditional ways of seeing the traditional Right. The Berkeley linguist George Lakoff, writing in 1995, states the conventional view of political ideology clearly: "The conservative worldview and the constellation of conservative positions is best explained by the Strict Father model of the family, the moral system it induces, and the common Nation-as-Family metaphor that imposes a family-based morality on politics." The liberal worldview, on the other hand, relies on a "Nurturant Parent model of the family." Differences between conservative and liberal aside, both agree, then, on at least one point: the nation as family—indivisible, one. But is the Right, despite its muscular and radically interventionist foreign policy and its domestic policy initiatives intending to "starve the Beast" (in other words, the social welfare functions of the state), still a Strict Father? Or rather, should we ask whether the Right is no longer conservative at all but regressive and boldly transgressive at the same time? Does it still favor the stability of tradition over change, or instead dream of eliminating any progressive changes and returning to an imagined prelapsarian past?

The entire exchange with Iraq, beginning with the invasion in 2003, would seem to demonstrate a fundamental dismissal of the significance of the rule of law. Disregard for the advice of legal experts at the State Department and elsewhere about the lack of preparation for the war's immediate aftermath initially resulted in well-publicized and widespread looting, arson, and grand larceny at the Religious Endowment Library, the Central Library of Baghdad University, and eighteen galleries of the National Museum. That was quickly followed by an ongoing, widespread campaign of assassination of civil servants and a violent insurgency and civil war that delayed, if not destroyed, the possibility of any functioning civil society, much less democracy, for decades.

At a news conference at the start of the occupation, Rumsfeld insisted that the looting was not as bad as some television and newspaper reports indicated: "Freedom's untidy, and free people are free to make mistakes and commit crimes and do bad things. . . . They're also free to live their lives and do wonderful things. And that's what's going to happen here. . . . Stuff happens" (cited in Loughlin 2003). Stuff does happen, of course, but some stuff happens predictably. The old conservative idea that legal order may be a precondition of democracy, that "principles of accountability are necessary to a democracy in a way they are not to other political forms," is a point not wholly original that I elaborated in 1997 in the context of an analysis of Central European democracies. These principles "set the minimal conditions necessary to secure the democratic state's monopoly on the legitimate use of violence" (Borneman 1997, 3). Following 9/11, the American Right inverted these values, exporting democracy with the gun, with nearly total disregard for law, tradition, and the symbolic register.[18] We should not, then, misrecognize the aggressive "alpha male" posture of the American Right as action in the register of the Father. It is because of perceived vulnerability at home, domestic insecurity, that the Right remains ambivalent about strict adherence to the rule of law, instead imagining return to an organic unity and peace in the image of the mother-child dyad. Only the threat of unexpected disorder to the home, I would suggest, introduces a discordant note of uncertainty into its present. In short, the evidence points not to Lakoff's "strict Father model" but to a rejection of the register of the Father, the symbolic, language, and the law.[19]

Certainly, this perspective, of the People as a site of an imaginary wholeness with the Mother, has not been lost on the local actors in Iraq or Afghanistan, all keen on democracy's promise of power through representation of the People. There is little imagination of legitimate opposition and of limits to the exercise of one's own power.[20] Instead, there is a continual reassertion of religio-tribal structural groupings similar to the Euro-American category of the ethnic or *Volk*, with each group alternately uniting and opposing each other based on local notions of familiarity and segmentary lineage.[21] This process one might call the construction of a "postcolonial tribal." It is a negation of the last two centuries of a colonial-induced refiguring of heterogeneous groups into artificial nations under one law. It is imagined not as an imposition of the Father but as a return to the Mother. Within this frame, conflict appears as a necessary fight between sovereign and competing unities. Internal opposition is therefore unacceptable, for opposition within any group is not seen as necessary and rational, not a struggle with difference and against the Father, but as a revolt of the children against their Mothers. In Iraq, for example, the American democracy project initially united the country's Shi'ite-identified groups into an electoral majority, and prior overlapping and shifting alliances and identifications are forced, literally at gunpoint, to give way to united representations of religio-tribal sovereignty, ultimately creating new collectives, not as constituent parts of, but as obstacles to, the Iraqi People. This dynamic of Iraqi nation building is not a return to prior group coherence but a negative symbiosis with the West, a parasitic relationship made possible only through the encounter with the colonial and continued exchange with an American gift that contains the poison as well as promise of such offers.

9 The External Ascription of Defeat and Collective Punishment

An important understudied phenomenon is the experience of a collective defeat in violent conflicts such as wars, cases in which all members of the defeated group are ascribed the same social state of having been defeated and deserving collective punishment. Most groups—ethnic or religious, national, clan, or tribe—think of themselves as good and worthy, and they tend to castigate their own members who might question these assumptions. Acknowledging defeat seems to call into question this essential goodness, so groups especially resist thinking of themselves as defeated, even when others see them this way. In an increasingly interconnected world, however, recognition of external ascription at various scales has become an important factor for the internal constitution of a group. Resistance to the recognition of how one is seen by outsiders is perhaps one of the largest obstacles to peacemaking generally. Such resistance breaks down, if at all, only over generations.

With respect to the consciousness of defeat, Americans are one collective who still see themselves as largely undefeated, if not "Number One" in all important domains of life. In the last half-century, for example, most Americans have refused to see Vietnam as a defeat (after having hastily abandoned Vietnam, in humiliation, in 1975), even though the rest of the world sees the United States as defeated in that war. That refusal, a common response across political party lines, is one of the reasons that the George W. Bush administration pursued a policy of hubris after 2002. In part intending to reverse a defeat it could not openly recognize as such, members of both political parties and a majority of the American public overwhelmingly welcomed, in 2001 and 2002, the opportunity to fight two wars against vague enemies (e.g., al Qaeda, the Afghan Taliban, Iraq) in faraway places that had nothing to do with the conflict (Vietnam) that led to original defeat. One conclusion I draw from this (and the hypothesis with which I am working) is that the refusal to acknowledge defeat will drive that experience deeper into the unconscious, making it more likely that the scene of defeat will be restaged in the future in an attempt to redo history as one wishes it had occurred originally.

This hypothesis could be explored by tracking the complex status of victory, defeat, and denial among four interrelated peoples—Americans, Germans, Israelis, Palestinians, and Lebanese. The immediate connection between these peoples is a sequence of historical encounters involving tragic losses: the German attempt to annihilate the Jews led to the founding of the Jewish state of Israel, which expedited the ongoing expulsion of Palestinians from their homeland in the Levant, which led to many Palestinians seeking refuge in Lebanon, where their presence then destabilized the already precarious Lebanese political structures, which was followed by a massacre of Palestinians on Lebanese soil by Lebanese, which resulted in an attempt to prosecute the complicitous Israeli military leaders who oversaw the massacre, as well as the Lebanese actors responsible for executing it, in a court in Belgium, which was successfully circumvented through hardball lobbying by American and Israeli authorities. All members of the above-mentioned groups have experienced collective defeat, and all, except the Americans, have experienced collective punishment.[1] But of these groups, only Germans have accepted and internalized this defeat.

This set of interconnections between countries reveals the complicated and shifting relations between internal and external boundaries as well as the flow of rebounding violence and its infection by the poison of denial as it circulates. My focus, however, will be more narrow. I would like to suggest that the German acceptance of defeat might inform the current Israeli-Palestinian conflict. More specifically, I ask how about the process whereby the external ascription of defeat becomes internalized. I will first explicate the issue of collective punishment theoretically, then restrict myself to a comparison of two experiments in collective punishment—by the Allies against Germany following World War II, and by Israelis against Palestinians in the present ongoing resistance to Israeli occupation.

Holding Individuals Responsible for Collective Defeat

There is general agreement among philosophers and legal scholars, if not among politicians, that only individuals can and should rightly be held accountable for crimes.[2] Collective punishment—punishing the group for injuries inflicted by particular individuals—is today widely condemned as inherently unjust, but its exercise (in the form, for example, of group lustration or purification rituals, reparations, disqualifications, or imprisonment) is quite common in relations between groups in all parts of the world. I will not discuss collective punishment's legitimacy here, but will focus solely on its effects on the consciousness of groups of punished people.

The experience of victory or defeat operates simultaneously in psychological and social registers, and within a political context. To represent oneself as victorious is always welcomed, and as defeated as something to avoid under all conditions. For individuals after victory, the experience is usually ambiguous and fundamentally ambivalent—one's own life is usually saved at the cost of the other's death, and one is left marked by guilt for the conflict, even in victory. After defeat, individuals and their groups usually labor to transform their story into one of overcoming defeat. Outside of admitting defeat when one is losing a conflict, groups have two equally unpalatable options: to insist that victory is at hand, despite the apparent defeat (and therefore to suffer even greater losses); or to negotiate a settlement on bad terms in order to avoid acknowledgment of defeat. The experience of individuals is, of course, highly variable, since there is a wide range of forms and degrees of participation in collective endeavors such as wars. Over time, however, ambivalent individual experience tends to yield to the clarity of the perception of the group in public representation, which is influenced by the external ascription—either denied or incorporated—of the "enemy." Individuals then tend to assimilate their diverse experiences into a single unambiguous collective representation of either victory or defeat.

Whereas a collective representation suggests that groups orient themselves around a single set of symbols or ideas, members of the group have different emotional investments in the collective and interpret its symbols in different ways; some may in fact dread the idea that their own group wins, while others dread the loss. Irrespective of whatever clarity or unity is obtained by the group representation, the ambivalence within any individual—about either collective victory or defeat—tends to linger in the unconscious and resurface in unexpected ways. Therefore, consciousness about defeat or victory is unstable and emerges unevenly over time. Conclusions reached from either an assumption of victory or defeat may always appear premature.

Reactions to the ascription of collective defeat range from resentment and conscious resistance to embracing the possibility of starting over or, at its most extreme, to finding defeat so unacceptable that thinking of this ascription by others is repressed, relegating any relevant conflicts to the unconscious and making the entire experience inaccessible except through the involuntary reappearance of symptoms. Regardless of the mode of dealing with defeat, no individual is able to escape the call of collective representations. In one way or another, each person internalizes external ascriptions of defeat, which can in turn become active as internal representations against which one must defend oneself. Nonetheless, the experience with them accumulates over time into a concrete memoro-politics, as group members in interaction with outsiders must deal with their humbling, if not humiliating, status, and as political leaders and cultural elites of all groups explain and shape the meaning of the loss to form competing public representations. As each person is interpellated by these collective representations, a loss in need of address is inscribed at the core of the individual.

My immediate concern in the next two sections is the process of internalization: in how this collective loss or defeat is incorporated individually, and in the specific role of collective punishment in the internalization of the ascription. I will compare German and Palestinian experiences of collective punishment, in which the former collective has accepted defeat, while the latter has resisted. To be sure, Germans resisted the ascription of defeat in World War II to varying degrees, even though the ultimately victorious Allies collectively punished them and even after their leadership had unconditionally surrendered. Over time, however, acceptance of defeat has become the norm in Germany. By contrast, most Palestinians today appear unwilling to accept defeat—hence, an omnipresent latent or active *intifada* (uprising)—and Israel continues to collectively punish the Palestinians for, among other things, this refusal.

Allied Collective Punishment of Germans

Germans experienced two devastating political and social defeats in quick succession in the first part of the twentieth century for which they were collectively punished, and the reactions and effects could not present more extreme contrasts. After leaders capitulated in 1918, German public discourse was dominated by narratives of victimization and myths of betrayal. Germans, it was claimed, had suffered a *Dolchstoss* (were stabbed in the back), but they remained "undefeated on the field of battle." People called for *Vergeltung* (revenge) against the French and demanded an end to the crippling sanctions of the Versailles Treaty. National Socialism capitalized on these myths of betrayal and used social discontent to come to power.

A bit more than two decades later, after the unconditional surrender ending World War II, Germans responded differently. It might be argued that they had little choice, given the terms of unconditional defeat and the occupation by four armies. In addition to deaths through fighting or hunger, Germans had suffered the firebombing of nearly all their major cities; huge population displacements, including some 12 to 15 million refugees from East-Central European countries; and the loss of the Eastern territories (*Ostgebiete*), which were ceded to other countries after the war. But in the subsequent half-century, in addition to the Allied efforts at re-education (*die Umerziehung*), they submitted to a number of measures, some self-imposed and some externally mandated, to redress the injuries they inflicted during the war, especially those resulting from German militarism and genocidal policies.

In short, there was a shift in the understanding and representation of the collective defeat: from an emphasis on unjust victimization and autochthony—*Wir sind das leidende Volk* (We are the suffering people)—to a relational narrative: Germans deserved the defeat; Germans are not self-defined but are embedded in relations with neighbors in a larger unit, Europe. There was, of course, resistance to this story line too, but this resistance has waned, and the outcome, for now, is clear: ultimate submission to a relational or intersubjective understanding of the collective and internalization of the ascription of collective responsibility for World War II and the Holocaust.

My point is that this acceptance of defeat, and the subsequent transformation of group identification, resulted at least in part, if not primarily, from forms of collective as well as individual punishment. France, the enemy in both world wars, is now Germany's closest partner in building a unified Europe; and Germany has done much to establish a more egalitarian basis for relations with Poland and the Czech Republic as well as with Russia, countries that it historically victimized. And Germany, which tried to annihilate European Jewry, is now Israel's leading European trading partner and its major advocate and defender within the European Union.

How was this collective narrative of defeat and punishment internalized by individuals? It is increasingly clear from studies of the aftermath of violent conflicts, such as postwar situations of occupation, that women bear a peculiar if not disproportionate burden as recipients of collective punishment—rape and sexual violence being very common—in the immediate aftermath. What I want to stress in the following account is the importance ascribed to women in bearing the stigma of the social and how, in this one exemplary case, one woman transformed this stigma by internalizing the experience of collective defeat.

Between April 20 and June 22, 1945, during the first two months of the Red Army's occupation of Berlin, a woman kept a daily diary of her experiences and those of other residents in her house and on her street. Under heavy bombardment and near the Eastern Front, more than half the residents of Berlin had left in the final years of the war, but 2 million nonetheless remained. We still know very little about this woman—her book calls her "Anonyma"—only that she was in her early 30s, came from a bourgeois family, and had once traveled to Russia and learned to speak elementary Russian. Her diary was first published in the fall of 1954 in New York, and the following year in Great Britain, but it took a full half-century for a German publisher to make the account available to Germans (Anonyma 2003).

Anonyma's descriptions are unflinchingly direct, lively, and breathtaking to read. She makes clear that no German could have remained oblivious to the anti-Soviet rhetoric of the Nazi propaganda machine, and all knew full well that those left behind—mostly women, children, and old men—would bear the brunt of any punishment for the many cruelties that their German sons, husbands, and fathers had inflicted not only on the Russians but on all Slavs.

Anonyma describes two major struggles in the immediate occupation: one with hunger, the other with rape—and they preoccupy her in that order of importance. After being raped several times, her priority becomes to find a high-ranking officer of the Red Army, in what becomes a succession of officers, and she offers herself to them in return for protection from other men. *"Ja,"* she writes, *"die Mädel sind allmählich verknappte Ware. Man kennt jetzt die Zeiten und Stunden, in denen die Männer auf die Weibsjagd gehen . . . Wir sind Anatols privater Hirschpark."* (Okay, the girls are gradually a commodity in short supply. One knows now the times and hours in which men go women hunting. . . . We are Anatol's [the Soviet general in charge in this neighborhood, ed.] private harem) (2003, 108–109). But being a member of Anatol's harem protects her only when Anatol is around; when he leaves, even temporarily, she is hunted and forced to make accommodations with her hunters.

From our current perspective, of course, what Anonyma experienced is a war crime, a clear violation of human rights that could be prosecuted in the International Criminal Court in The Hague. This human rights norm did not exist at the time of her victimization, however, though she surely considered the Soviet behavior unjust. The surprising aspect of her experience to which I want to draw attention is how the violence she suffered leads her neither to dehumanize the Russians as a group nor to feel singled out individually. Instead, she writes of her location within the collective, "German," and gives us a highly differentiated account of ethnic types, of their attractiveness or repulsion, of how kind or sensitive or crude they are in bed, of their patterns of speech, their knowledge of current and historical events. That is, she humanizes them without identifying with them.

Anonyma repeatedly uses the word *"Gemütlich"*—homely, comfortably—to describe scenes when the Soviet soldiers, in their hunt for women, find their way into some apartment or another. They bring along war booty—vodka, schnapps, caviar, marmalade, preserves, canned meat—some of it taken from captured German men, which they then share not only with German women but also with older men in the apartment. They sit on a bed or around a table and drink and talk—frequently discussing difficult theoretical issues, like who is civilized, what happened to German culture, why the Germans became Nazis—and they sometimes stay overnight, in which case Anonyma is usually expected to sleep with the highest-ranking soldier. She does this reluctantly, and each experience is different; but she adjusts, motivated all along, as she explains, by a sense of collective defeat: *"Keins der Opfer kann das Erlittene gleich einer Dornenkrone tragen. Ich wenigstens hatte das Gefühl, daß mir da etwas geschah, was eine Rechnung ausglich"* (2003, 288). "None of the victims can carry the suffering as if carrying a crown of thorns. I, at least, had the feeling that something happened to me similar to the paying of a debt."

Anonyma invokes Jesus' crown of thorns in order to disavow an identification with his sacrifice. She resists the temptation of assuming her suffering is like that of Jesus at the hands of the Romans. The punishment is unjust to her as an individual, but a different logic of deserved punishment pertains to her membership in a collective. On the surface, the demand that she provide sexual services to the invading army appears comparable to Jesus' sacrifice for the collective, but instead Anonyma senses that the more accurate meaning of her punishment is the repayment of a debt. She is part of the repayment for what had been done in the name of Germans. The collective debt is separate from her individual fate, and that debt will remain even after she is individually punished. Simply as part of the group, of a defeated group, she recognizes the necessary, though individually unfair, work of redress. In this acknowledgment, she becomes more fully conscious of the significance of defeat, which initiates the process of internalization of the external ascription, even without yet grasping the enormity of the crimes Germans engaged in and the extent of the debt still to be repaid.

Israeli Collective Punishment of Palestinians

Two unconditional surrenders of the nineteenth and twentieth centuries produced models that informed each other: the American Civil War and the unconditional surrender of the South, and the "total war" that characterized the two world wars and reached its apogee in both German genocide and eventual unconditional surrender. These experiences inform the logic of the current aggression of Israel against Palestinians, which intends to produce a similar defeat. The Israeli social historian Baruch Kimmerling (2003, 4) interpreted the Israeli policies as "politicide . . . whose goal is to destroy the national existence of a whole community and thus deny it the possibility of self-determination. Murders, localized massacres, the elimination of leadership and elite groups, the physical destruction of public institutions and infrastructure, land colonization, starvation, social and political isolation, re-education, and partial ethnic cleansing are the major tools used to achieve this goal." Politicide is consistent with the goal of modern defeat, aiming for an unconditional surrender. As Schivelbusch (2003, 28) writes, it is "to liquidate the losing side as a legal entity."[3] Politicide stops short of the physical annihilation of the group, however, and in this respect it harks back to the strategy of the American Civil War, not to kill all individuals but merely to dissolve the "enemy" collective and the possibility of a collective identification.

While a genocidal total war and politicide differ as to their ultimate goals, the former wanting annihilation of all individuals, the latter merely dissolution of the collective, they resemble each other as well as civil war in the tactics to be employed to bring about defeat: collective humiliation and punishment. As described by General William T. Sherman, the father of the "scorched-earth policy" in the American Civil War, "The proper strategy consists in . . . causing the inhabitants so much suffering that they must long for peace, and force the government to demand it. The people must be left nothing but their eyes to weep with over the war" (cited in Schivelbusch 2003, 39). Speaking to the press on March 5, 2002, then Prime Minister Ariel Sharon explained Israeli policy in nearly identical terms: "The Palestinians must be hit and it must be very painful. We must cause them losses, victims, so that they feel the heavy price."

Indeed, the world knows the very heavy price for all of the Palestinians, as well as for some Israelis. But suffering itself is not very relevant here, certainly not comparative suffering. The degree of suffering alone will not lead to the acknowledgment of defeat. In fact, inflicted suffering can often strengthen a group's resolve to resist. This was certainly the effect of Allied-inflicted suffering on the German civilian population during World War II: instead of rebelling against their leaders, it increased their resolve and made it more difficult for individuals within the collective to resist Nazi leadership. Rather, the initial German defeat was largely a military one, the defeat of one military by a larger (Allied) coalition. But the acceptance of this defeat was a cultural reckoning whose recognition took time and required shifts in generational authority. Still today, Germans do not have a single, unambiguous relation to their own defeat—but the point is, they do have a relationship.

The hopelessness of the current Israeli-Palestinian conflict, where both sides engage in asymmetrical collective punishment of different sorts with different means, rests on the seeming impossibility of either side to impose the kind of victory it desires or to admit the kind of defeat the other wants of it. Israelis, whose dramatic occupation of the Palestinian people began with a victory in the 1967 war, are by far the more powerful of the two adversaries, and they want a defeat of the most modern of types: unconditional surrender. But today, given the instruments and modes of violence available for resistance, such unconditional surrenders are difficult to achieve with neighbors. Groups in violent conflict with states rarely find any sort of resolution outside some kind of international or external group mediation. Appeals to human rights, as empty as they may seem in a place like Darfur, tend to slow or punctuate the business of killing the opponent. The United Nations is the most prominent of the many supra-national organizations that enter conflicts as a third party to prevent the most egregious abuses by powerful states. Israel, however, repeatedly rejects the mediation of others, including the UN. It has steadfastly refused to recognize the judgment of the UN Security Council, of Resolution 242 following the 1967 war, which called for a withdrawal of Israeli armed forces from territories it then occupied and a termination of all claims or states of belligerency. The presence of an external mediator like the United Nations also strengthens the resolve of the Palestinians, since it makes it unlikely that the "victor," in this case Israel, can ever claim an unconditional defeat and unilaterally impose conditions on the vanquished party.

If increased suffering on either side will not lead to sensitivity to loss or to recognition of an external ascription, then what, in fact, will? Of historical significance for Israelis and Palestinians, in comparison with Germans, is that the refusal to accept a defeat enables Israeli Jews and Palestinians to elide the question of how they are defined through relations with their Arab and Jewish neighbors. In the last half-century, these neighbors often ascribe defeats to the Palestinians and Israelis, respectively: the Jews being driven from Europe and the Holocaust; the mass Palestinian expulsions of 1948; Arab, including Palestinian, losses in the 1967 War and in many subsequent conflicts not classified as war; Israeli withdrawal from southern Lebanon in 2000 or Gaza in 2005.[4] It is difficult to sustain a picture of any victor in the Palestinian intifadas or Israeli occupations. Yet because each of these defeats is publicly denied, the actual experience of loss is banned from the conscious and only works in the unconscious. Much of the desire for humiliation of the other is a symptom of the repression of this loss (see Rose 2007). As the long-term violence of an occupation continues, the majority of Israelis, in particular, cannot envision what engulfs them as a tragedy that by definition has evolved into a reversal of roles.

Given the military power differential between the two, a scenario of Palestinian victory and Israeli defeat is unthinkable. And given Israel's intent on an unconditional surrender by the Palestinians, it is difficult to imagine an alternative to endemic warfare. Yet if anything from the German case is applicable here, it is that the acceptance of a collective defeat sends the group in a trajectory opposite to those caught up in endemic warfare. This acceptance stabilizes the group by recognizing the other's suffering and interiorizing the ascription of guilt. The opposite of the interiorization of guilt is exteriorization: the projection of fault onto the other—which precisely characterizes the inter-group dynamic at present. The German historian Reinhart Koselleck goes even further, writing, "There is something to the hypothesis that being forced to draw new and difficult lessons from history yields insights of longer validity and thus greater explanatory power. History may in the short term be made by the victors, but historical wisdom is in the long run enriched more by the vanquished. . . . Being defeated appears to be an inexhaustible wellspring of intellectual progress" (cited in Schivelbusch 2003, 4).

It is important to acknowledge that a collective defeat did not dissolve the Germans as a group but simply forced them into a relational self-definition. By contrast, the Palestinians, who have suffered individual losses that they refuse to internalize as collective, resist an unconditional surrender and an ascription of defeat because they fear such a surrender might mean the death of the group itself. As they hold on against impossible odds, they hope for the possibility of another reversal of roles. In a penetrating analysis, Tony Judt (2003) suggested the paradox of such a possibility: "Unless something changes, Israel in half a decade will be neither Jewish nor democratic." The only alternative to politicide and ethnic cleansing, he concludes, is a "binational state," which then is no longer Jewish. Such a binational state would, in one sense, be a kind of collective defeat for both Palestinians and Israelis, forcing them to give up dreams for autochthonous, self-determining collectives. The condition for continued existence would be the recognition of each other's eventuality.

PART 3 An Anthropology of Democratic Authority

Part Three focuses on the mechanisms and operation of democratic authority in Europe and North America. Chapter 10 analyzes the meaning of election rituals in terms of the tension between the demands for participation and representation on the one hand, and those of the sacrificial logic without which elections lack the transformative function of ritual on the other. Chapter 11 analyzes the development of Berlin's (and Europe's) largest ritual, the Love Parade, over the course of the 1990s. This ritual poses questions about the changing nature of the political and about new forms of participation in a democratic Germany specifically, but also in Europe as a whole, since the collapse of the Cold War ideological binary of communism/capitalism. The Love Parade flourished in the decade after the Cold War and indexed two processes: first, the dissolution of the inherited nineteenth-century political structure in which democratic political parties either set the ideological filters in which the political was to be imagined or appropriated the schisms of the everyday for their own purposes; and second, the development of nascent forms of authority and ritual identification under the aegis of an emergent acephalic political authority. Chapter 12 argues that categories such as "the West," "the Occident," and "Euro-American" have lost much of their salience because the United States and Europe have been following different social trajectories. In fact, the United States has become Europe's Other. New self-definitions and sociopolitical demarcations are crystallizing in part, it argues, because of the very different ways in which Europe and the United States have internalized Middle Eastern identities and oppositions.

10 What Do Election Rituals Mean? Representation, Sacrifice, and Cynical Reason

Elections as Technology of Political Legitimation

Elections are a political technology of selecting leaders, or representatives, in rituals used to renew or remake collectives. Although certainly not the only means to select representatives, they are today employed in some capacity in nearly all contemporary groups, both religious and secular. Formally, they perform delegation by staging an orderly mode of what anthropologists in the past took up as "succession to high office."[1] In collectives that tend toward authoritarian rule, delegation works without surprise. Power is transferred as if the outcome of the ritual process is known in advance. Elections in authoritarian systems legitimate a fait accompli. In more democratically inclined forms of rule, however, the key to the efficacy of elections is unpredictability, that the outcome of the process of selection of delegates is unknown and ambiguous.

To produce this element of surprise, elections must stage a liminal moment for the social, briefly dissolving "the People." In this liminal moment, where people are reduced to isolated voting monads ostensibly independent of group affiliation, there is always the possibility that the ruling majority and its representatives lose, in which case they must cede power to and exchange place with their opponents. When in fact a new delegate assumes office and representation changes, we can speak of the orchestration of a sacrifice—someone must lose and accept the loss. But orchestrated losers do not always easily accept defeat. Because of the ambiguity of this critical moment of transfer of power, violence and the threat of social dissolution tend to increase as elections near. Moreover, if the person or group that loses questions the legitimacy of the outcome, or the winner seeks not merely victory but the annihilation of the opponent, the violence that threatens the social before elections does not subside after the ritual is performed. Hence, many ritual elections successfully stage succession to office but are nonetheless not efficacious in reducing the resort to violence within the collective. That is, elections may lead to civil strife and social dissolution rather than social regeneration. The efficacy of elections, this essay argues, turns on the periodic constitution of an internal loss, requiring that success in representation be accompanied by sacrifice.

In what follows, I first analyze elections as rituals of representation and of sacrifice; second, I explore what happens to the violence within this ritual, in other words, when the ritual is efficacious in reconstituting the social such that violence is renounced and subsides; and third, I show, through an examination of a short election period in the Middle East, how cynical reasoning conjoined to electoral rituals vitiates the work of modern sacrifice and hence perverts the efficacy of this technology.

Elections as Sacrificial Ritual

Is a sacrificial logic inherent in or immanent to modern electoral rituals?[2] Nearly a decade ago, I argued that political elections in democracies, specifically, are the recurrence of an archaic form of sacrifice. This ancient form, first outlined by Sir James Frazer, entailed the sacrifice of declining kings, which I will call, following Frazer's major ethnographic inspiration, the Icelandic solution, where kings, who represent the entire social body, sacrificed themselves after nine years of rule.[3] Frazer plotted this archaic form in an evolutionary sequence: sacrifice of the king subsequently displaced into the sacrifice of the king's firstborn son, and finally displaced into the substitute sacrifice of marginal or alienable others (the scapegoat). While the idea of social evolution has been largely discredited, it may nonetheless be useful to think through these forms as substitutions in temporal sequences. How does the logic of each form of sacrifice relate to the others in any place over time?

In Germany, the trauma of the two world wars (the First World War was indeed called "the Great Sacrifice"), and the historical legacy of the Nazi regime of sacrifice (also the meaning of the word *holocaust*) largely delegitimated the utility of both the firstborn-son solution (the substitute sacrifice of sons in wars) and of the sacrifice of Jews or minority others (the scapegoat) as ways of constituting loss. Instead, following the two world wars in Germany (as in Europe as a whole) there has been a return, hesitantly and unevenly, to the archaic form of sacrifice. This is not to say that all elections prior to 1945 avoided taking on this ancient form of sacrifice, but that the social functions of sacrifice were realized in other action domains (e.g., wars, pogroms), and that the constitutive function of sacrifice today continues primarily in political elections.[4]

Modern democratic elections are performatively efficacious as a kind of ritual turn-taking of opposition and incumbent, which demands that the incumbent ultimately step down (lose an election) and willingly yield authority to an opponent. This is true of both parliamentary and presidential systems. To the extent that incumbents, or ruling parties, refuse to take turns, rule becomes more authoritarian, needing more violence to sustain itself; and demands intensify for sacrifices of sons or scapegoats, losses that reconstitute the social in place of the loss of the "king."[5] Contemporary analyses of sacrifice focus almost exclusively on the "son" and "scapegoat" forms of sacrifice. These two forms of loss may have indeed characterized pre–World War II Europe, but the Cold War and processes of decolonization changed many structures in the global landscape; especially, they encouraged an ideology of institutionalized elections in their democratically inclined form. Since the end of the Cold War and the period of decolonization, however, that framing of elections has also lost its compelling character. A proper historicizing of electoral rituals requires us to ask how this Icelandic solution to sacrifice increasingly gives way to a conjoining of the technology of delegation to cynical reason, threatening to vitiate the logic of modern elections which is efficacious precisely by reinstituting an archaic form of sacrifice.[6]

By *cynical reason,* I am following Peter Sloterdijk's characterization of the contemporary as an age of "enlightened false consciousness": "It is that modernized, unhappy consciousness, on which enlightenment has labored both successfully and in vain. . . . Well-off and miserable at the same time, this consciousness no longer feels affected by any critique of ideology; its falseness is already reflexively buffered" (1987, 5).

Sloterdijk's critique is aimed not at the Enlightenment itself but at the state of consciousness that has accompanied this tradition. Enlightened false consciousness is based on an attitude of cynicism. Cynicism undermines all absolute values, substituting, to use Weberian terms, means-ends rationality for any normative or principle-driven rationality. A cynic is therefore someone who acts in ways that belie his principles. Therein rests his unhappiness. The only way of knowing still available to a cynic is reason, but reason alone cannot ground or provide an ultimate rationale for action, and this is also why the cynic, though "well-off" (good at realizing his/her ends), remains "miserable."

This relation between being both miserable and well-off is the key to understanding why cynicism is so widespread, especially among elites, and not only in the West, and why an attitude of enlightened false consciousness increasingly frames elections. Leaders in nearly all authoritarian regimes hold regular elections, much as do the leaders of the more democratic countries of the world. Holding periodic elections seems to be a requirement of contemporary rule. Even where the outcome is not in doubt, they offer some measure of legitimacy for rule. But many elites no longer seem to believe in a *periodic* reversal of roles. Since the nineteenth century, this periodic reversal has been organized around political parties, but their loss of control over the process of delegation has accelerated since the end of the Cold War. Increasingly, delegates strive either for permanent incumbency—electoral success without efficacy—or they engage in more intense rivalry with the opposition. As they engage in a game of one-upmanship, roles are reversed at an accelerated pace such that stable systems of value and meaningful references are undermined in manic, ritualized sacrifices that are no longer periodic. This quick turn-over in representatives resembles the return to the scapegoat function of sacrifice within the political sphere, but it also encourages the increasing concentration of power by the well-off outside the political sphere—what I identify as a neo-authoritarian turn.

Power within the governmental sphere is then exercised by inexperienced and cynical (often puppet) representatives without the conditions that might be imposed by more accountable (because, in part, they are not always campaigning) political actors in a stable system of periodic turn-taking. In the spirit of enlightened false consciousness, elected representatives buy off the less well-off by participating with them in a ritual whose meaningfulness is reduced to its function of delegation. In other words, the misery of behaving solely on the basis of means-ends calculations is ameliorated, to some extent, by holding successful elections, which legitimate to some degree the delegation of author-ity and the assumption of representation—without, however, attention to ritual efficacy. That is, elections remain popular as periodically staged ceremonies to legitimate political delegation. Efficacy, however, means they would lead to the renunciation of violence and the regeneration of the social.

Success and Efficacy of Electoral Rituals

The distinction between successful staging and efficacious outcomes is key. Today even the most repressive political systems successfully stage ritual elec-tions, yet they do so only on the condition that their victory is assured. Such staging encourages a cynicism with a strong affinity to enlightened false con-sciousness. Knowledge of the subfield "American politics" in the disciplines of political science and law is essential to nourish this cynicism, both in the United States and abroad. Such knowledge is used to perfect elections as a set of techniques for representation, either to increase the power of incumbency or to support manic turn-taking, *and* to void the logic of the Icelandic solution to sacrifice.[7] The incumbent is either perpetually reelected or unceremoniously unseated through the manufacture of major voter "mood swings." Rather than risk sacrificing him/herself by losing, new victors are often under added pressure, to which they increasingly succumb, to act only as delegates of those particular interests that financed their campaigns in order to assure reelection. The tension between delegation and sacrifice at the heart of democratic elections is thereby displaced into one of successful staging of technology. Elections lose the character of a quasi-religious rite involving death, disaggregation, and reconstitution of a transcendent "People," and instead are reduced to their magical techniques of producing majority rule.[8]

Both political parties in the United States use this knowledge, but the George W. Bush administration carried the development and employment of these techniques to new cynical levels. Under the mentorship of Karl Rove, it attempted to transform the electoral ritual in the United States into a predictable, nonliminal event where the advantages of incumbency assured reelection; the same party always wins, sacrifice is unnecessary, and no inversion is possible.[9] But also, after it initiated the Iraqi war, the Bush administration, along with experts trained in political science, tried to export this model of the successful staging of elections as the desired form of political ritual to other countries, especially to the Middle and Far East.

American politicians and consultants are of course not solely responsible for creating this particular cynical mode of staging elections. A logic of pragmatism and manipulation is always a part of ritual, and certainly non-American actors preceded and accompanied the Americans in their mission to spread the electoral form. In their defense, it also true that these American experts are, in fact, responding to the heightened international demand for their technical expertise. That said, American electoral experts of all political ilk today have indeed been perfecting the art of staging elections, and that means creating the technical knowledge necessary to manipulate participation—the magical process that delegates authority and produces representatives.[10] In perfecting this technical knowledge, however, they have tried to obviate the logic of the Icelandic solution to sacrifice, leading the way, I will argue later, for the return to the use of the scapegoat, a substitute victim.

Success in staging elections makes them popular rites, functional and exportable to other countries as models for organizing the political—but successful staging does not make them efficacious. This distinction between rituals that are successful but not efficacious is similar to one Victor Turner (1977) draws between ceremony and what he called "pure ritual." Ceremony, he argues, lacks the possibility of transformation; it lacks the regenerative potential of ritual. The ceremonial part of elections pertains to the deploying of its machinery—campaigns, political oratory, gerrymandering, polling, secret ballots, vote counting. This merely introduces modern technologies, innovative modes of influencing the selection of delegates for political representation, into the process of delegation. Such ceremonies are made to conform to the constitutional orders of democratic states, and in this minimal requirement offer solace to the loser and lessen the threat of violence, especially the threat of serious revolution.

But ritual generally, while a constant struggle to maintain form over indeterminacy, as Moore and Myerhoff (1977) argue about its function, must nonetheless *sustain unpredictability* to be efficacious. The moment of social dissolution must not be seen as merely an act of engineering that results, hocus pocus, in a predictable outcome: the production of delegates and legitimate majority rule. The collective must risk a possible transformation, a comedic inversion of the social order; and that is the logic of the Icelandic solution to sacrifice, where the ruler, the incumbent, periodically risks losing and ultimately does in fact lose an election. This loss, and its threat, is, to draw again on this older distinction, the religious efficacy of ritual—and it distinguishes electoral efficacy from its more narrowly conceptualized magical component in that it ties meaning to something outside individual interest, to social regeneration.[11] I wish to explicate this with evidence from the Middle East, examples of a variety of cases that adumbrate a particular pattern.

Elections in the Middle East, the Last Decade

In the first decade of the twenty-first century, a number of noteworthy elections were staged in different parts of the world, but the most significant symbolically, those that played out the dramas of world political events, have been elections in Latin America and the Middle East. Both areas are of decided strategic interest to the United States, but since the end of the Cold War, the United States has had a declining ability to control either. The differences in outcome and in levels of American investment and participation in these two geographical areas are very revealing. Latin Americans, relatively neglected by the current U.S. regime, rejected incumbents and elected new leaders. However, in the Middle East, outside of Saddam Hussein in Iraq, leaders remained in office through electoral means.[12] That is, Latin American elections have become more open and democratic, while Middle Eastern elections have not. Permit me to narrow my analysis to elections in the Middle East in which the United States has claimed a direct strategic interest following the invasions of Afghanistan in October 2001, and Iraq in March 2003.[13]

The major rationale for these invasions at that time was only secondarily about democratization. In Afghanistan, the goal was to defeat Al-Qaeda and close its base for terrorist operations; the removal of the Taliban regime from power and creation of a democratic state were derivative ends. In Iraq, the explicit primary goal was not to democratize but to eliminate the nonexistent "weapons of mass destruction." Yet democratization was always present in some form in the overarching Middle East strategy put forth by President George W. Bush. In a speech on November 6, 2003, he argued that democracy and elections were to inaugurate an aggressive "forward strategy of freedom in the Middle East . . . from Damascus to Teheran."[14]

Especially in the Middle East at the time, political leaders were known to suspend their constitutions and the freedoms of their citizens on national security grounds, often invoking the specter of "Islamism" as the only alternative to their own rule, while some elements of their regimes unofficially bankrolled the very same terrorist groups behind the specter. That said, constitutions themselves cannot uphold the rights of citizens; additional mechanisms, such as ritual elections and independent judiciaries, are necessary to periodically check the leadership. Hence, Bush was correct when, in June 2004, on a five-day trip to Europe and Turkey, he called on Muslim nations to end "the cycle of dictatorship and extremism" and warned them that "suppressing dissent only increases radicalism" (Sachs 2004). But this moral exhortation was followed by a plan that emphasized technical solutions to staging elections to address problems of social disenfranchisement.

To their credit, after the Cold War the United States and Europe had increased their financial support for democratization efforts worldwide, albeit with a narrowly instrumental understanding of what part elections might play in such a mission. The assumption was that elections were a prelude to democratic institutions and would initiate processes such as parliamentary rule, civilian control of the military, independent judiciaries, fair taxes, stable and just property rights, respect for minorities, and the creation of networks of trust. However, in most parts of the world these various democratizing processes might be better conceived as a precondition for open and fair elections. As better technical innovations in electoral manipulation assured results, the effect of this focus on elections often produced a perverse result, strengthening authoritarian regimes rather than bringing about more freedom.

An authoritarian turn was in fact part of a general Middle East narrative in this period, especially following the event of 9/11, in which electoral technology was conjoined with cynical reasoning. In Afghanistan, the occupiers encountered major problems by staging elections along the Euro-American model of delegation while also trying to incorporate indigenous models of representation such as the descent-based traditions of the council of leaders (*loya jirga*). A good case can be made that the elections of 2004, 2005, 2009, and 2010 have each successively become less democratic and more corrupt.

In Iraq, in 2005, the American occupiers, with the assistance of the United Nations and many INGOs, staged two national elections, one in January for an assembly to draft a constitution, and another in December, following ratification of the constitution, to elect a permanent 275-member Iraqi Council of Representatives.[15] The deposed (and subsequently executed) dictator Saddam Hussein had also staged periodic elections for a National Assembly, the last one in November 2000. His elections had indeed been successful in delegating authority to representatives of the diverse groups (men and women of all religious and ethnic groups, albeit of one political ilk), but there was no sacrifice, no loss, no turn-taking of authority, and in this respect they were not ritually efficacious. Because elections were staged to merely rubber-stamp the current social order, Hussein required sustained violence to keep that order.

The 2005 Iraqi elections intended to produce a new legitimacy tied to two key public variables: participation and turnout. Many people participated in the campaigns, and voter turnout was extremely high, much like under Hussein; but violence in the social did not lessen following the election. What was missing was the logic of sacrifice: the election was successfully staged but not efficacious as ritual for the simple reason that the participants were unwilling to accept the constitution of a loss. If everybody wins simply by participating and electing representatives, then who loses? Equally important, the winner must welcome an opposition, with the expectation there will be a moment in the future when the tables will turn. Instead, the jockeying for non-losing positions continues to this day.

Palestinian elections in 2006 unseated the long-ruling and corrupt Fatah Party. But the United States and Israel instead worked to foment a civil war between Fatah and the unexpectedly victorious Hamas Party. Instead of regenerating the social, then, the election marked an escalation of fragmentation and violence.

This same tension between representation and sacrifice, successful staging and ritual efficacy, is integral to understanding the complex function of elections in Lebanon. In chapter 1, I examined the more general case of accountability in Lebanon. Elections in Lebanon are staged to produce accurate representation, since each religious confession has an allotted number of seats in the parliament; the major offices (president, prime minister, speaker of parliament) are also allocated by confession. Hence, despite the Cedar Revolution in 2005 and attempts to open the system under the slogan "Freedom, Sovereignty, Independence," the political structure that guarantees sectarian representation based on religious-tribal affiliation also assures incumbency without accountability for some leaders; periodic turn-taking of elections is purposely elided in order to secure delegations of sectarian-affiliated blocks.

Finally, we might consider the role of elections in the last decade in Egypt, leading up to the current revolutionary moments. Hosni Mubarak assumed the presidency after the assassination of Anwar Sadat in 1981. For successive terms on prior occasions—in 1987, 1993, and 1999—he was re-elected president by majority votes in referendums. In each election, he first had himself nominated by a rubber-stamp parliament and then reconfirmed by popular vote. In February 2005, however, Mubarak amended the constitution to allow the first multi-candidate presidential elections in Egyptian history. This change was largely a response to international pressure, outlined most succinctly only after the fact, on June 20, 2005, by U.S. Secretary of State Condoleeza Rice: "For 60 years my country, the United States, pursued stability at the expense of democracy in this region, here in the Middle East, and we achieved neither. Now we are taking a different course. We are supporting the democratic aspirations of all people." She likely intended here to reiterate her warning to Egypt to follow the lead of Iraq and stage free elections.

Three rounds of elections later and Hosni Mubarak won the presidency again. Despite extremely widespread discontent with the corruption of and stagnation induced by his rule, and the relatively well-organized secular and religious opposition, on September 7, 2005, he was re-elected as expected with 88.6 percent of the vote.[16] The secular opposition, which at the time had coalesced around the Kifaya movement (meaning "Enough!"), was demoralized—surveilled, imprisoned, unpopular.

For our purposes, it is important to understand that changes at the time in political form—allowance of multiple parties, public debate, relaxation of censorship, and organized campaigns of opposition—were not prompted by a desire to institutionalize the essential features of modern democracies (most of these changes were in fact nullified after the election). Instead, Mubarak was motivated solely by a cynicism about how to maintain power. To do this, he used knowledge about election techniques in the person of Mohammad Kamal, Professor of Political Science at Cairo University, who organized around Mubarak's son what we call a "modern campaign."[17] Kamal had learned his skills in the United States, earning a doctorate at Johns Hopkins University while also employed as a congressional fellow. The three rounds of voting for the new parliament involved working the phones with the use of computers and detailed maps of voters, using the language of professional consultants, sophisticated polling, focus groups, television advertising, talking points about reform—and even an official campaign slogan: "Crossing to the Future."[18]

This sophisticated Americanization of the campaign was necessary but insufficient to guarantee the election of Mubarak. When the outcome appeared in doubt, approaching the liminal moment of the ritual, Mubarak turned to the police, the security apparatus, and the official state media to manipulate the election machinery and secure victory. Most of the prominent opposition candidates were ruled ineligible, and no international election monitors were permitted to oversee the voting. Candidates of the Muslim Brotherhood, officially still illegal at the time, had won most of the seats in parliament in the first round. So for the second round, the government's security forces stepped in to harass members of the opposition and to physically intimidate and block people from voting. When final tallies after the third elections were in, 44 percent of eligible voters had cast their ballots. The Brotherhood won 88 seats, five times the number they won in 2000, but still just a fraction of the 454-member parliament. The Tomorrow Party and other secular opponents were all but wiped out, winning no more than 10 seats.

The United States ultimately criticized the campaign for its "irregularities," but in March of 2006, Rice took back her earlier admonishment, saying, "We can't judge Egypt. We can't tell Egypt what its course can be or should be." One of the leading secular activists, Alaa Seif, who had been arrested and imprisoned on trumped-up charges—insulting the president, illegal assembly, and the most ridiculous charge for anyone knowing Cairo, obstructing traffic—commented, "Search for Egypt on YouTube, and all you'll find is tourism and torture." His pithy formulation points to how substantial interests of the West in Egypt are seen: the enlightened tourists of the West hold to principles of elections that they do not believe in, but they have in fact been actively using Egypt to "render" suspects in the "war on terror" to Egyptian authorities for torture.

The U.S. Secretary of State was no doubt sincere in wanting a democratization of Egypt through elections, but she was also fearful of the regenerative dimension of the ritual, meaning the possible replacement of Mubarak, who then used this ambivalence to secure his rule. Deprived of its ritual substance, the election's outcome resulted in a temporary freezing of violence with authoritarian means, dejection and disillusionment with the political process itself, and propagation of cynical reason.[19]

In January 2011, this frozen state of affairs began thawing quickly. A revolt in Tunisia proved contagious, spreading quickly to Egypt, Yemen, Bahrain, and elsewhere in the Arab world. As of this writing, only two leaders have stepped down (Tunisia and Egypt), and even in these places regime change is an ongoing project. It is important to note that elections did not bring about the changes, that instead in the years examined here they were used cynically, as a ruse for legitimacy, to strengthen authoritarian rule. Yet each of these revolts presents moments in which there is a breakthrough and an arrest of the social structural conditions examined above. These revolts are still unfolding, with the trajectory of change and the kind of electoral system to be installed dependent on ongoing struggles for representation and for sacrifice.

Elections and the Authoritarian Turn

The transformative potential of the Middle Eastern revolts makes it even more incumbent on us to rise to the challenge of resisting this new configuration of cynicism—enlightened false consciousness—that employs electoral technologies to produce disillusionment and an authoritarian turn in democracies. Anthropologists have largely ignored this recent turn and instead concentrated on a critique of liberalism in the West or on the impact of neo-liberalism inside and outside the West. To be sure, the unjust and often devastating effects of economic restructurings (included under the label "neo-liberalism") have provided the opportunity to milk poorer countries of their resources. Free trade agreements have been coercively enforced to the benefit of First World consumers, resulting in Third World reliance on the importation of basic foodstuffs (increasingly expensive due to rising energy costs), and on export-oriented farms that rely heavily on imported water-polluting agro-chemicals from the First World.

But the name "neo-liberalism"—more narrowly defined as limited government—is severely misleading and is a symptom of a more general problem of misidentification and critical distance. It deflects attention from the staging of elections, governmental power unchecked by democratic processes, illegal and unlimited detentions of individuals, arbitrary restrictions on freedom of movement, and corporations with limited liability—all of which entail weakened oppositions, weakened legislative bodies, and disregard for the principles of the rule of law.[20] And the question is not only how to democratize illiberal nations—as many constitutional scholars maintained in the 1990s—but also how to democratize liberal ones. One sign of this problem is the new alliance of the political class within the older Western democracies with refigured media conglomerates, the indebtedness to new super-rich classes in the unproductive financial sector, and the structural inability to make difficult decisions independent of the campaigning for short-term ends in temporally accelerated electoral cycles. In the United States, the corrupting influence of money and the new "power elite" symbiosis (of wealthy candidates and corporations) drives this authoritarian turn through electoral politics. Increased citizen surveillance, executive branch wiretapping, personal data mining, and the return to patronage and contract rule is not the result of liberalism or neo-liberalism, but it is authoritarianism made possible by staging elections as successful ceremonials about delegation rather than efficacious rituals about social regeneration.

Elections remain the key ritual technology for this turn within democratic form. My point is that it is precisely and only when elections function as a ritual of sacrifice along the lines of the Icelandic solution that they can contribute to the social regeneration we associate with the symbolic form we call "democracy." If political elections have become the ritual that promises to create and regenerate the social—replacing traditional marriage and seasonal festivals—then the functions of delegation and representation are secondary, technical solutions to problems of a quasi-religious nature.

Even when an election is "successfully staged," however, when the win is clean and the delegates are truly representative of majority and minority viewpoints, a legitimation crisis arises if there is no recognition of the loss and the importance of the loser's role in social regeneration. In the Icelandic solution, as Frazer reports it, the king sacrifices himself for the social, and this sacrifice is acknowledged by the society as necessary for its own vitality. His successor does not annihilate him, but rather endows him in death with the respect of the ancestor. While the sacrifice of the incumbent is necessary for ritual efficacy, its periodicity is of equal significance. The periodicity of electoral turn-taking can be perverted by other technologies, such as initiatives, referendums, and recall efforts, which bypass and destabilize the system of political representation. Such efforts can be important tools for accountability, but given the current dominance of cynical reasoning, they lead to demands for ever more ceremonial sacrifices in a return to the concept of substitute victim. Likewise, increased violence after elections tends to take the form of a substitute sacrifice or scapegoat and can be instigated by either the winner or loser.

One question for further research is why, given the world's diversity of cultural forms of delegation, a single technology has become so appealing, even modular for organizing political form (Anderson 1998). It may be that the universal appeal of elections has much less to do with its European origin than with the relation of sacrifice to another deeper myth: Freud's insight that the human order is first established through a death and an ambivalent usurpation of central authority. The myth he appeals to is the imagined primal sacrifice orchestrated by sons of their father, after which they collectively incorporate this loss (eating him in a totemic meal), which both satisfies their hatred of the authority to which they had submitted and leads to remorse for the murder and a resurgence of the affection for him that they had previously repressed. The guilt from this usurpation then reappears as "deferred obedience" in the creation of a collective totem, whose killing is now a taboo. Among Christians, this story—about how to install renunciation of violence after the violence of group formation—takes the form of the substitute sacrifice of Jesus-the-son, after which all believers, if they commit to proper worship and submit to this new deity, are absolved from guilt.

The electoral form in modern governments, I would argue, reenacts the myth of a violent sacrifice intended to legitimate the usurpation of authority through a renunciation of violence. But while an election is always a commemorative ceremony, it is not always an absolution that might enable humans to live with the ambivalence of their violent usurpation and resentful submission to authority. If the election is premised on the sacrifice of a substitute, such as the son by the father, then we have the mere appearance of absolution. The guilt remains and is perhaps even greater, driven deeper into the unconscious and requiring a high level of denial. Where authority remains in the hands of a despot, as in the Arab world during the period examined here, for example, elections do not result in absolution but instead seem to partake of this dynamic of substitute sacrifice, guilt, and denial. In the West, however, the decline in the authority of the father, and patriarchal authority generally, makes the idea of father-son sacrifice seem less compelling today. To sacrifice sons in wars or to identify social scapegoats is certainly possible, but it does not have any kind of automatic legitimacy or ritual efficacy. This of course may change if, given the death of the father, there is a waning of guilt generally, in which case a ritual that absolves one of the necessity to submit to authority appears less necessary. Self-interest and cynical reason, then, become two sides of the same coin, facilitating the neo-authoritarian turn. In that case, the notion that democratic elections are ritually efficacious only when they legitimate a renunciation of violence, one form of which is the deferral to the state of the "monopoly on the legitimate use of violence" that Weber theorized, may no longer be generally applicable.

Prioritizing periodic sacrifice over delegation in ritual elections is no guarantee, of course, of the production of the symbolic form of democracy. A stable political order that nonetheless stages rituals that risk change from within is a utopian possibility of non-repetition and regeneration that other political forms do not offer. That is, although the myth of deferred obedience to a collective totem persists, the efficacy of ritual elections must still be addressed within particular symbolic systems and under the increased dominance of cynical reasoning. My argument is that the cultural variability of forms of appropriation or resistance to the Icelandic solution of sacrifice can in part be explained by the further life of remorse for loss and the cultural specificity of grieving that elections stage.

11 Politics without a Head: Is the Love Parade a New Form of Political Identification?

Diese Geschichte wurde oft erzählt, und es war immer eine andere. . . . Wichtig: Der und der hat da und da so und so gespielt, und alle wären da gewesen. Ist ja geil. Dann wäre man später noch dorthin gegangen und da und da hingefahren, da wäre man schon so und so drauf gewesen, und die Musik so und so. Toll. Und man wäre dann irgendwo gelandet, mit dem und dem und der und der, und da hätte man dann noch das und das gemacht, bis dann und dann. Und erst dann und dann wäre man so und so verstrahlt, verpeilt, endfertig und hochgradig verstört daheim gewesen. Ein Wahnsinn.

This story was often told, and it was always different. Note: So and so played such and such like that and that, and everyone was there. Cool! Then later you went there again and drove there and there, where you were already so and so, and the music so and so. Excellent. And then you ended up somewhere, with him and him and her and her, and there you then again did that and that, until then and then. And only then and then were you at home so and so thoroughly cooked, spaced-out, wasted, and utterly out-of-it. Totally!

—Rainald Goetz, "Let the sun shine in your heart"

So and so, such and such, him and him, there and there, then and then, her and her, that and that, until then and then! This style of expression seeks to describe and evoke something of significance although it lacks an argument and makes no appeal to authority. It is a form of speech full of pronouns, demonstrative adjectives, and adverbs that reference no particular places, times, or persons because everything simulates everything else. It is the speech of Berlin's Love Parade, captured above by the poet Rainald Goetz in an article published a few days before the 1997 gathering, which ran under the slogan "Let the Sun

166

Shine in Your Heart." Begun in 1988, when 150 people came together on a weekend in mid-July to dance techno on the streets of Berlin, the Love Parade had become an annual ritual within a decade, with the participants numbering up to a million, nearly a thousand-fold increase in a decade.

Though it is dubbed pan-European, most of the participants are German, perhaps half under the age of twenty, most of whom are widely reported to come from small German towns to have their first big-city experience. Our own experience of the Love Parade was to accompany a few Berliners and their out-of-town guests, mostly in their thirties, and we always appeared to ourselves as elderly, though not the most elderly—but hardly anyone seems to notice.[1] The gathering has little to do with either "love" or "parades," conventionally understood. Less of an event than a happening, the Love Parade most closely resembles a machine, or a world of machine simulation, and participants take the metaphor of "machine experience" seriously. Over two days and nights the major experience is to alternate between silently standing and waiting, in no particular order, for nothing in particular, and "raving," a highly choreographed, robotic movement to the sound and super-accelerated beat of "techno music"—often supplemented with stimulants known as "designer drugs."

With no intention to communicate anything in particular, ravers seek a musical and kinesthetic experience in the Love Parade and hence place no emphasis on what language signifies and means. The name of the event, the "Love Parade," is never translated into German, for to put it in German— "*Liebesparade*"—sounds to the German ear funny (*komisch*) instead of kitschy, and somehow too meaningful. To leave the name in English but spoken in a German sentence empties the parade of its serious universalist or transcendent pretentions. Germans with *Bildung* sprinkle their sentences with English words much like their American counterparts use French, not to speak universally but to specify, to indicate cosmopolitan competence in cultural particularity. Hence, to juxtapose an English word like "love," which evokes deep, private emotions and has worldly pretensions, with "parade," which evokes a meaningful form of cultural politics, ironizes both terms when spoken in a German-language context. Moreover, it is important to emphasize that this irony is directed to oneself, that the naming is self-naming, self-description. In similar fashion, the slogans associated with each year's event have an empty yet universalist ring to them. They simultaneously parody and accurately describe the parade: "We Are One Family" (1996), "Peace on Earth" (1995), "One Love, One World," "Planet Love," and "Friede, Freude, Eierkuchen"—the only slogan in German, which, significantly, is recognizable as German kitsch but would sound to the German ear funny (*komisch*) in its English translation of "Peace, Joy, Pancakes."

But native exegesis is only one context in which to understand what is going on in the Love Parade, and our intention here is to situate these intentions and the phenomenological experience of the parade in an explanation of the happening.[2] Different native takes on the Love Parade might lead one to argue that it is a form of either religion or economics. Most participants claim to experience a kind of religiosity (although they do not call it that), a form of collective self-worship that established churches do not seem to be able to provide them. And many local critics point to the unusual tolerance shown by Berlin's political and economic authorities, to the fact that they now even promote the event openly because of the business and the reputation it brings to the city, as evidence of Berlin's economic and cultural significance. But the obvious religious and economic contextualization of the Love Parade does not adequately explain its importance as the largest regular mass event in Europe. We suggest that an explanation for this event is found in its relation to political identification in the (very) late-twentieth century.

This essay addresses the question of the nature of late twentieth-century political identification and its relation to religiosity. Our focus will be on Germany's Love Parade, with an ostensibly similar festival in the United States used only to set in relief the German example. We argue that certain processes in postwar Germany, such as the definition of "the people" and displacement of the site of "traditional politics," support a form of acephalic authority, elements of which can be found in other democracies, although in less extreme form. We suggest that these contemporary processes relegate "traditional politics" to a marginal role and reconstitute the political field in a new way.

Native Explanations

Most Berliners commonly explain the Love Parade with one of two radically opposed alternatives: either it is seen as a neo-fascist expression of populist self-worship, or it appears to lie outside the domain of formal politics and is an innocent and spontaneous celebration of universal peoplehood manipulated and sustained by the "market." Both of these alternatives are misleading. To interpret the Love Parade as an unfolding of the past in the present—a compulsive repetition of Nazi ritual—presumes a historical continuity in German character and an ineradicable Nazi essence. Evidence for the reappearance of Nazi ghosts and symbols in the Love Parade, as we make clear below, is remarkably thin. To interpret the Love Parade as an empty artifact of the global market, an expression of a narcissistic youth culture in an age of cyber-capitalism, is possible only by ignoring the action occurring during the event, what people actually do. We take seriously both the historical displacement of symbolic forms in processes of generational differentiation and the actual performances of participants during the Love Parade weekend. Although the Love Parade may appear to outsiders as depoliticized youthful consumerism, it is, we suggest, an emergent form of political identification, albeit one that situates itself as orthogonal to conventional politics and consumption. This thesis will become more plausible after we situate the Love Parade anthropologically within the social field of contemporary mass participatory events in Germany. Before doing this, however, we should address why we support an explanation that runs counter to most native explanations.

Participants with whom we have spoken, along with self-described public spokespeople for the event, tend to dismiss economic explanations in favor of a purely phenomenological description that in many ways approaches an explanation in terms of religiosity. Nonparticipants who nonetheless try to explain the event, including public media analysts, resort equally or alternatively to the two forms of explanations above. Both participants and nonparticipants tend to dismiss a political explanation for the event. They do so because the event does not correspond to standard formal definitions of politics. There are many concepts of the political, and the Love Parade corresponds to none of them. We might begin with Max Weber's classic essay "Class, Status, Party," where he attempts a theory of the orders of modern power. Participants in the Love Parade are certainly not members of a class, since they are not "represented exclusively by economic interests in the possession of goods and opportunities for income" (in Gerth and Mills 1946, 181, 180–85). They are also not a status group (concerned with the distribution of "honor"), and they refuse any connection to a party, to the legal-rational order. Consider the Love Parade in relation to the theorizing of three other German scholars: the Love Parade is orthogonally positioned to Carl Schmitt's code of "friend/foe"—it refuses to exclude; to Niklas Luhmann's notion of democracy as the code of government/opposition—it opposes nothing; and to Jürgen Habermas's utopian vision of a "communicative community" and of political identification as "constitutional patriotism"—it intends to communicate nothing. Foucault's concept of "disciplinary regimes" and a performative biopolitics perhaps comes closest to describing certain features of the Love Parade, but its ambivalences are also counter to Enlightenment concerns with truth, reason, and will, out of which modern disciplinary regimes developed. Specifically anthropological discourse on the political does not carry us much further. Consider, for example, Clifford Geertz's and Stanley Tambiah's attempts to capture the political as cosmological order, F. G. Bailey's or Abner Cohen's instrumentalist views, or Michael Taussig's concern with the relation of reification to domination. Cosmology, instrumental reason, domination—all three foci, as we will demonstrate below, are elided by the Love Parade. Hence, regardless of which concept of the political is used, the Love Parade stands as an exception. In what follows, we highlight shifts in the field of "the political" itself. Such shifts, as we make clear below, now situate the Love Parade as central to the field of politics.

Politics, Religiosity, and "the Market"

As an event of mass participation, the Love Parade belongs to the formal domains of either "politics" or "entertainment," fields that have become increasingly interconnected and subordinate to economic imperatives. Both politics and entertainment, moreover, are expressive of religiosity. Historically, within Europe, it was secular politics—political parties, governmental bureaucracies, elections—that initially took its cue from religion and developed ritual forms of group worship, crystallized in patterns of national belonging. As the Christian kings came to possess two bodies—one transcendent, one earthly—secular authorities generally encroached on religious authority's control over the definitions of transcendence, the bodies of subjects, and the institutionalization of their life courses. Despite the tendency toward functional differentiation and autonomy of the economic, political, and religious domains, a thesis long argued by such renowned scholars as Habermas and Luhmann, this differentiation never resulted in a clear delineation of the sources of authority. Those exercising power, whether secular or religious, derive their legitimacy from the same mechanisms of delegation and through appeals to the same symbolic forms. In other words, European authority derives from a necessary relation to religiosity (Gauchet 1997).

The fight to occupy and shape these symbolic forms has intensified in the twentieth century, partly due to the development and ubiquity of new technologies of communication. One result of this process has been the dispersion of the power over the control of religious expression that had been monopolized by the organized confessions. Since the end of World War II, however, traditional politics has not been the major beneficiary of this decline in the power of organized religious authority.[3] Instead, entertainment has emerged as the field dominating both the management of experiences of transcendence and of people's affective attachments and identifications. Could any contemporary politician fill a stadium with worshipful followers and rival the crowd-appeal of Madonna or Maradona, of Mick Jagger or Boris Becker? Mass participatory entertainment has further divided into sport (where "soccer" is the most important mass form) and music. The Love Parade would seem to belong to the category of music.[4]

Whereas the Love Parade is intimately related to stylistic and technological developments in popular music and the rock concert, it has had virtually no relation to the domain of conventional politics. The Love Parade does not fit readily into standard genres of mass events, which has made it extremely difficult for politicians to appropriate this happening for their causes. They have been unable to position themselves in relation to something that resists definition—What is it? A demonstration, a display, a celebration? What cause(s) does it support or oppose? Politicians have so far been unable to convert the Love Parade into an extension of political competition. What's more, the dramatic yearly increase in the number of "ravers" participating in the event has overwhelmed the city of Berlin, making it difficult for bureaucrats to plan for and regulate it as an event. Outside of licensing the parade and policing the parade route, city bureaucrats have been largely excluded from the planning stages. For the most part, private entrepreneurs and organizations have provided the food, drugs, music, dance clubs, and lodging enabling Berlin to host such a massive event.

The Love Parade is not, however, permeated by "the market." Neither corporate interests nor private entrepreneurs have been able to appropriate or subsume the Love Parade for their own purposes. It does provide millions of deutsche marks for Berlin's tourist industries, and small vendors also claim to profit immensely. But these relations between culturally differentiated spheres are symbiotic: while the Love Parade both provides for and requires Berlin's service industries, it also demands that they operate solely on the periphery of the event itself. Compared to the yearly North American Lollapalooza festival of "independent" and "alternative" rock music or to Grateful Dead concerts, the singularity of the Love Parade's symbiotic relation with the market becomes clear. North American festivals and concerts are fully permeated by, and indeed constitutive of, corporate and entrepreneurial enterprise. Grateful Dead concerts, for example, are marked by a rhetoric of communalism, but at the same time they are subsumed by the primacy of exchange—of music recordings, drugs, T-shirts—controlled by both corporate interests and private entrepreneurs. Moreover, unlike the Love Parade, American events embrace discursivity and political representation.[5]

Politics or Entertainment

As the Love Parade keeps growing in size and scale, and as it establishes itself as a major new ritual in the emergent German *Hauptstadt,* all forms of political and religious authority feel increasingly compelled to take a position on it—to comment on it, ban it, criticize it, lead it, or legitimate it. Love Parade participants, however, tend to deny all such links to authority. Most observers miss the political nature of the Love Parade because it does not express itself as traditional politics. This does not stop German officials from calling it political discourse.

In 1997, the categorical status of the Love Parade—as politics or entertainment—became a public issue when city officials and environmentalists tried to either block the parade or confine its march by forcing organizers to pay for the removal of the litter and trash left behind. Were the Love Parade merely entertainment, as the Social Democrats and the Green Party argued, participants would be responsible for their own garbage. Were it politics, however, as Berlin's Christian Democratic Mayor Eberhart Diepgen and his spokesmen argued, the Love Parade would be considered a "specific form of political argumentation" and thus entitled to public sanction and support. Berliners of our acquaintance, as well as the media, thought Diepgen's support was merely an instrumental attempt to gain leverage among the youth, who tend to be cynical about politics. The point is: no party made its support contingent on what the Love Parade does, that is, on its content. The opposition of the Left was based primarily on an assessment of effects, on environmental costs; the support of the Right, on a reaction to the Left's opposition. A German Administrative Court ultimately protected ravers from paying for their trash pickup by ruling against a last-minute complaint lodged by the *Piline Partsch von Bismarck* and the *Bund für Umwelt- und Naturschutz*. Legally, the court concluded, the Love Parade is not a party but a "political demonstration." What makes this legal definition so fascinating is that few outside the court actually believe it.

A Politics of Nonengagement

From the native's point of view, participants do not simply oppose political discourse but refuse discursivity altogether. They elide the moment in which expression is turned into discourse, when individual expressions take on patterns that can be represented in utterances that in turn make up a discursive field delineating an object. We dub this elision a *politics of nonengagement*. Expression in the Love Parade is visual, aural, and kinesthetic, rather than textual. To approach these expressions as if they were to be captured in the utterances of participants, or as if they were analogous to linguistic communication—talk—is to cognize a sensual and affective experience that itself purposely refuses to enter into a relation with official language. Hence, the experience of the Love Parade is not to be reflected upon, read about, or spoken of, but to be evoked, heard, seen, and felt. Later we will draw upon a distinction made by Senders (1998, chap. 1), between the "sensuous mimesis" of the Love Parade and the kind of "imitative mimesis" into which most scholars subsume all processes of identification. The Love Parade is a form of sensuous mimesis, and its relation to the political is solely at this level. Sensuous mimesis is a form of knowledge, as Michael Taussig (1992, 141) has written, "that functions like peripheral vision, not studied contemplation, a knowledge that is imageric and sensate rather than ideational." Before we discuss the relation of sensuous mimesis to political discourse and authority in the Love Parade, we first describe the experience of techno and rave in the Love Parade.

Raving to Techno in the Zone

The Love Parade is a collective happening, a machine experience that relies on techno music to encourage "raving." Techno music is the heart of this machine experience. Based on a pulse played at an overwhelming loudness, techno drowns out all speech. Linguistic communication is replaced by a highly choreographed transformation of collective waiting into relatively autistic dance movements that jerk, twitch, and shuffle the body. The Love Parade is about the magic of this transformation from collective waiting to emancipated, ecstatic dance, the Durkheimian "moment of prestidigitation." That dance is called raving, an experience that has become identified as a primarily northern European phenomenon.

Beginning in the early 1990s, techno music has become ubiquitous in contemporary German dance clubs. Indeed, young Germans claim that Germany is the world capital of techno music, a form that can draw its lineage back through "house" and "disco," but that in Germany is frequently traced to the synthetic and industrial sounds of Kraftwerk. Already in the 1970s Kraftwerk had developed a dehumanized, robotic sound that band member Ralf Hütter identified as essentially German: "We want the whole world to know we are from Germany, because the German mentality, which is more advanced, will always be part of our behavior. We create out of the German language, the mother [tongue], which is very mechanical, we use it as the basic structure of our music" (cited in Bussy 1993, 28). Hütter's point of reference was Nazi culture, and he, like many of those known as the *Achtundsechziger* ('68er generation), was making a critical statement about the machine-like precision with which Germans had engaged in mass murder, including the annihilation of the Jews in carrying out the "Final Solution." He positioned himself to Germany by means of an internalization and exaggerated display of his mechanical mother tongue, that which he considered stereotypical German. The techno scene consists of the next generation. Its techno may descend from the industrial sounds of Kraftwerk, but techno's ability to move people rests not on a relation to a pure German language and mentality but on the specific mix of music on any particular evening. Techno celebrates bastard form, appropriating anything and everything available for citation.

Techno differs fundamentally from most other musical forms in that it is neither sung nor composed in the conventional sense. Its sounds are samplings or digitally synthesized units that are then duplicated and arranged in sequences using computers. The completed "pieces" are not meant for listening. DJs, the on-site performers of techno, work this musical material by "mixing" and manipulating the recordings in the rave setting. The digital-to-digital process leaves no extra-musical traces and makes no appeal to an artistic aura, for mixed music is unconcerned with authenticity. It would be a pure example of Walter Benjamin's "mechanical reproduction," were it not for the necessity of the DJ to mix the samples. The DJs are not, however, new authority figures that produce original work. Although they regard their performance as self-expression, they are in a reciprocal relation with both the music and the public (Langlois 1992). In the words of Maximilian Lenz, alias Westbam, Germany's most successful DJ, "You don't mix only music, but rather you mix music with people. You take their reactions, the looks, the movements. It's a unique and magnificent ensemble" (interview in Assheuer 1997, 34). DJs, in other words, are seen as part of the "rave," and they move freely from the dancing audience to the DJ stage. For ravers, the origin of the music is clearly secondary to its sonic presence and illocutionary effect. Dancers may express their approval for a DJ, but that approval does not transform DJs into "stars." Even the names that DJs assume—DJ Noizer, DJ Uzi, DJ X-Ess, DJ Wax Weazle, DJ Wierdo, DJ Berry, or DJ Flanelli—downplay their individuality and accentuate their mutual replaceability. It is common during a rave for inexperienced DJs to take over for brief periods, learning their craft by merging their styles seamlessly into the mixes of more experienced DJs. Unlike rock stars and classical musicians, techno musicians do not go on tour. In short, the moment or act of production is truly alienated from the shamanic and charismatic magic of the musical performer.

When techno music works its magic—again, frequently aided by the effects of drugs—one enters a "zone." In this zone, one might experience an ecstatic sublime, a transcendence of the everyday comparable to experiences of possession in religious ritual. The feeling produced in the zone is primarily nonverbal, dependent on the illocutionary force of participating in the rave. As J. H. Austin (1962, 234), the inventor of speech-act theory, would say, there is no reliance on the propositional force of language, on meaning, because the intent is "not to report facts but to influence people." The primary influence, or work, of techno music, and what distinguishes this work from other contemporary musical forms, is accomplished through its rapid, mechanical pulse. The overwhelming effect of the pulse radically reduces the propositional content of raving. In most ritual, writes Maurice Bloch in an analysis of Merina circumcision ceremony, "syntactic and linguistic freedoms are reduced" through "stylized speech and singing" (1989, 20). Propositional content decreases as illocutionary content or performative force increases. On this basis, Bloch maintains that religious authority, because it does not intend to make sense but relies only on the performative force of formalized chanting, singing, and dancing, is an extreme form of political authority. In contrast to religious authority, the Love Parade includes virtually no formal speech. There is no "kick-off" with any leaders or DJs making announcements about what will happen. There is no chanting either, and because the music has no words or melodies, there is no participatory singing. Nonetheless, the entire event is characterized by the same reduction of syntactic and linguistic freedoms that Bloch says characterize religious authority. This reduction is managed through the gradual intensification of techno sounds over the course of the Parade. And the contrast between waiting and movement to these techno sounds constitutes the primary illocutionary content of the event.

Although the route of the Love Parade varies, the format has remained remarkably consistent. For the past several years, it began in Ernst Reuter Platz, and then proceeded to the *Siegessäule* monument at the center of the Tiergarten. In 1997, the parade began with 39 techno floats, each with a DJ mixing music, gathered in a semi-circle around Ernst Reuter Platz. As in previous years, each float blasted techno music with mammoth speakers driven by powerful, state-of-the-art amplifiers. The resultant aural and spatial effect is one of thickening and isolation; the crowd becomes ever more densely packed, and the possibility of everyday speech is eliminated. But as the DJ Westbam states, "What does isolation mean here? Everyone is dancing with everyone" (in Assheuer 1997, 34). In the condensed mass of sound and bodies it is nearly impossible to hear the speech of a person standing next to you, and the range of bodily movements available for dance is greatly restricted. As this slow and cumulative jumble continues for nine hours, participants lose track of time.

The frenetic, mechanical beat of techno might be understood as a denial of time and its irreversibility, as an expression of a fear or phobia that time will become meaningful, will vary, become irregular, stand still, or cause something to fade or disappear. To simulate a machine experience, as in the Love Parade, is at base an attempt to remove oneself from human time, to escape from the bio-temporal limits of life and death. Machines, of course, can also stop, but no discernable and necessary temporal frame governs them. Techno provides the sensation of going on forever, an experience of the sublime requiring the annihilation of any concrete past. To enter such an atemporal zone, participants combine techno with drugs, including marijuana, cocaine, and a wide variety of designer drugs such as "ecstasy," but rarely alcohol. The combined effect, as Bloch (1989, 44) argues for religious ritual generally, is to "transform reality into a timeless, placeless zone in which everybody is in his right place." Here one might, echoing Adorno (1970 [1956]), add *so that everybody is in the same place,* for the ideology of this affluent middle-class youth culture is radically equalizing rather than hierarchical. "Right" translates into "same." And given the metaphor of machine experience, participants, when in the zone, participate as cogs in a non-producing machine, each universally substitutable and all doing the same thing, endlessly. This zone experience, writes Goetz, is the "first successful total integration of world history" (cited in Assheuer 1997, 34).

Choreographing the Zone and Identification with the *Volk*

Compared to most dance forms, techno dancing seems less formalized and rule-governed, yet in practice the range of gestures used is extremely limited. Above all, the tightly packed space tends to restrict dance movement. The abbreviation of bodily motion is, however, a chosen choreographic style and not simply an artifact of physical space constraints; even when more space is available, ravers do not use it. Movement tends to be in-place, often consisting of little more than a swivel or a rock back and forth. Few dancers use flowing movements, and most of their motion is below the belt.

These dance movements do not, of course, constitute something totally new but are both a further development of certain contemporary forms and a differentiation from others.

A quickening of the musical pulse and an abbreviation of bodily movements, for example, marked the transformation of "disco" into "house" music. Techno has taken that quickening and accelerated it dramatically. One result of techno's super-tempo is an anti-sexualization of the dance movement and an increased inward orientation of the body, two features that were already characteristic of "house music" (Langlois 1992, 238). While dancing to rock music depended on an objective sexualization of the body and its direct response to the music, dancing to techno responds to subjective patterns derived from the dense layering of beats. The effect is one of a kinesthetic bricolage, or to use Hebdige's (1987) term, a "mosaic" patterning of danced rhythms articulated against the wash of the music.

Ravers also avoid bodily contact with each other. Their controlled and autistic movements stand in sharp contrast to the slam dancing of the 1980s, for example, in which dancers literally threw their bodies at each other in a celebration of physicality. Techno dancing also entails little in the way of gender differentiation, although men appear to be more avid and engaged ravers than do women. The marked reduction of sexualized and specifically gender-coded movements characteristic of techno contributes to a decentering of the heterosexual couple, something we will discuss later on. In short, the experience of long hours of alternate waiting and raving encourages entering a zone. Once in the zone, participants experience a sense of autonomy along with an identification with a nonproductive machine—or a group such as a *Volk*, in this case, a *Weltvolk*.

To understand the nature of this group or *Volk* feeling, contrast the simultaneously individuating and unifying effect of the rave to the dyadic identifications entailed in classical ballroom dance. Whereas ravers dance alone-together ("Everyone is dancing with everyone"), virtually all ballroom dancers move as heterosexual dyads. Rave does not spell the end of the couple, however, for couples—mostly hetero, but some homo and also some transgendered—abound. Yet the dancing itself is a monadic experience; couples may attend the rave together, but they do not dance together. The man no longer leads; the woman no longer follows. While techno is not unique in this choreographic division of labor—solipsistic styles of dancing in the 1960s and 70s were often accused of undermining the heterosexual couple—only with rave has it become an act of simultaneous mass participation. Only with rave is group identification being purposely reconstituted.

Another revealing contrast is that between movements characteristic of rave and those accompanying the major musical evocations of *Volk* on contemporary German television. Early evening German variety shows, called "family programs" in the United States, are typically situated in Bavarian-type beer gardens. The beer gardens are dreamscapes—spaces disconnected from real geographies and existing in a static and prior time. Small groups of people in traditional folk costumes sit on benches in rows facing each other, and they sway gently from side-to-side, occasionally singing along with the band. Germans collectively perform the same swaying movement at street-festivals, rock concerts, and leftist candlelight demonstrations. This movement has a lulling effect and supports a feeling of belonging to a people. In the United States, the most comparable form of television variety program would be something like the *Lawrence Welk Show,* periodic cable TV reruns of which are still popular, or the song-and-dance "Holiday Specials" that return like ghosts every Christmas season. Welk also staged sing-alongs, but the most common performances were solos and man-woman couples dancing and singing duets. Much like the German early evening variety show, Welk's music and dance foster a sense of communal bliss and affective identification. In the United States, however, communal bliss rarely extends beyond the heterosexual couple and the family. In Germany, by contrast, there is a much stronger sense of the coherence of the *Volk* and the priority of the collective.

In raving to techno at the Love Parade, the evocation of the group always has transcendent pretension, including in its embrace, for example, "humankind," "earthlings," or "world unity and peace." Techno itself, we have been told, is effective because of its ties to African Ur-rhythms, to something pre-cultural or natural and unbounded. Captured in parodic slogans such as "One Love, One World" or "Planet Love," such transcendent pretensions are too grand and sweeping, too emptied of content (mythical speech, as Roland Barthes would put it) to be meaningful without the assistance of drugs or dance or the accompaniment of the techno pulse. But these slogans are neither meant to be cognized nor to move people to any direct political engagement. They are effective only at the sensual level: as linguistic mirrors of both being in the unbounded zone and the "empathogenic" effect of "ecstasy" and other designer drugs used by ravers. The Love Parade differs in this respect from conventional mass musical events. Woodstock, for example, called for "three days of peace, love, and music," a time-bound slogan that directly engaged the dominant political discourse of the 1960s. Love Parade slogans are never time-bound but are universalistic, and they sidestep direct engagement or confrontation. In addition, unlike Woodstock, which quickly became a rallying symbol for "Woodstock Nation," the Love Parade effectively elides intermediate forms of belonging. Such intermediate forms—including national, ethnic, or religious identification—are particularistic and rely on coercive measures to enforce imagined and cognitive distinctions between insiders and outsiders. The Love Parade seeks instead a romantic unity without hierarchy, without conflict, and without politics. To have a politics would require that one position oneself within cultural, historical, and political boundaries and would create an outside (Koselleck 1985). To rave at the Love Parade is to be nowhere and everywhere, alone and together, all the time and at no time, for nothing and against nothing.

Being unlocatable is a position usually associated with the classic bourgeoisie, who in a move characteristic of phallocentric authority refuse naming and placement while insisting on remaining the measure of value for all others. By contrast, ravers reject phallic measures of authority. For instance, phallic authority tends to be associated with a serious masculinity, with the stance of a "macho" or a "gentleman," but most male participants in the Love Parade take a playful and ironic stance to masculinity. One of the few exclusively male activities is to climb the streetlamps in Ernst-Reuter-Platz and along the route in Tiergarten. To discourage this practice, police put barbed wire on top of the poles and grease them. Nonetheless, some of the poles can be and are successfully scaled. Participants watch and cheer as virtuoso men display their climbing skills. The hitch is that the taller poles, which attract the most spectators, become thinner at the top, making it impossible to reach the pinnacle. Men climb, stop, and slide back down the poles in a display of failed masculinity—in which very little is at stake. The stakes are low because the parody does not rely for its authority on a display of masculine assurance, on confirmation of a central norm that sorts participants into successful and failed men. Rather, since they are all doomed to fail at this norm, the parody is directed toward the very attempt to approximate and uphold it. The ethos is neither bourgeois nor anti-bourgeois, but supremely middle-class in its equalizing, and post-*Achtundsechsziger* in its anti-anti-sentiment. Young middle-class German and European participants can afford this display of failed authority because their security is so great and official (adult) authority so weak that they have no need to mobilize or represent or defend themselves to secure their dominance. Hence, the Love Parade plays with phallic authority, creating in its stead a space that simulates irony, horizontality, and equality.

Participants in a rave report that it takes time to enter the zone, and rave parties last for hours and sometimes for days. In the zone one feels autochthonous, self-sufficient, yet fully connected to the "the world." The "world" functions here as a substitution for the *Volk,* which has had primarily pejorative connotations in Germany since the end of Nazi rule. The economic and cultural difficulties experienced following German political unification in 1990 have further called into question the appropriateness of unity and oneness, of *Volk*-feeling. Nonetheless, since secular peoplehood continues to be mythologized as the major form of religiosity available in Europe, Germans search for its equivalents outside the nation. The Love Parade is a happening that offers the experience of one such equivalent.

Sartre's distinction between seriality and group-in-fusion may be helpful here. The individual waiting in a line for a bus is serial, standing with other people but not part of a group. To form a group, the separate individuals must be fused by a political will. The Love Parade achieves precisely such a transformation—from waiting to raving, from seriality to group-in-fusion—without reliance on political will. Participants attribute group effects to themselves and their bodies, not to any outside authority or to any narrative of the future. Although ravers deny the distinction between friend and foe, and thus reject Schmitt's definition of the political, they rely on alternative notions of authority and sovereignty (1996 [1932]). The somatic, sensual experience of rave movement ultimately encourages a feeling that authority—the control of the pulse and the movement—comes from within one's own body rather than from without. This internalizing logic is not a rejection but a reconfiguration and relocation of sovereignty. The passage into dance and the zone is the result of a decision to enter a realm of experience disconnected from the everyday. Yet in the rave "the decision" is unvoiced and without apparent origin; dancers appear to themselves as passive recipients of the rave.

Ravers reject the distinction between *collective will* in the abstract and *individual willing* as a political act. Rather than join together behind a political platform or ideology, they merge ecstatically with "the universe." In the rave, music is seen in Schopenhauerian terms as an "image of the will itself" that usurps the place of the political.[6] Raving unites individual dancers directly and subjectively with the *will* itself, and in so doing brings ravers together in ways that traditional politics cannot. This unification takes place without benefit of charismatic mediation or authority—and without representation. Participants create the fetish of a total inside, a total inclusivity embodying will itself, beginning with their own bodies, in which there exist no divisions—no outside, no inside, no head. They invoke an affective politics in place of an effective one. It is as if they have, as a group, extended the "rule of the domestic sphere" to recreate personal space wherever they are, including in the street.

The extension of the domestic sphere's rule entails a denial of traditional (male) political voice and a reconfiguration of the political field around an ideology of "nonengagement." Such a politics without utopian ambition escapes both conservative Hegelian communitarian and revolutionary Marxist understandings. It looks neither to the past nor the future. When Marx wrote, in his XI Thesis on Feuerbach, "The philosophers have only interpreted the world, in various ways; the point, however, is to change it," he claimed to have overturned Hegel's politics and epistemology of understanding. Yet neither understanding nor praxis drives the apolitical politics of the Love Parade. By refusing to deal with worldly categories, its participants can make no heretical break with the status quo. It was this refusal that Pierre Bourdieu had in mind when he wrote, "Political subversion presupposes cognitive subversion, a conversion of the vision of the world" (1991, 128–29). Participants may in fact be responding to an objective crisis in European political authority, but they spurn any critical discourse that might disrupt existing power structures. But does the refusal of discursivity limit the effects of this *happening* to a reinforcement of existing political authority?

The Refusal of Discursivity

We have said that ravers refuse discursivity, but that is not to say that they do not talk or communicate. The Love Parade is a gathering in which *something happens,* but that happening is structured through postponement. Ravers wait. They wait in cars, busses, trains, and planes while coming to Berlin. They wait to use the toilet, for the parade to begin, for the float of "*dem letzten Schrei*" DJ to arrive, for the next U- or S-Bahn that isn't full to bursting, for entrance into the next techno club. And while ravers wait, they have occasion to talk—rave talk. With reference to neither a definite past nor possible future, rave talk creates a constricted chronology of the present; devoid of locutionary force, it intends neither meaning nor significance.

A slightly longer description of the scene created by Rainald Goetz (1997), cited at the beginning of this article, captures the sense of rave talk:

> *Aber die ganz normale echte wirklichkeit, lustigerweise ja eben wirklich eine Wirklichkeit für alle—war eh längst woanders. Sie hatten sich einen anderen Antwort gesucht, um zu reagieren auf die neue Lage. Sie nannten es: Techno.*

But the completely normal reality, strangely enough really a reality for everyone—had been somewhere else for a long time anyway. They looked for another answer in response to the new situation. They named it: Techno.

Diese Geschichte wurde oft erzählt, und es war immer eine andere. Es war immer die Geschichte der letzten, gerade erlebten Nacht.

This story was often told, and it was always different. It was always the story of the last, the just-experienced night.

In unendlicher Variation wurde ein ums andere mal neu mit Worten dem irgendwie unfassbar Erlebten hinterher geredet.

In endless variations one or the other, sometimes new, was subsequently told, with words of the somehow incredible experience.

Dabei war es zunächst gar nicht so sehr wichtig, ob das nun so wahnsinnig treffend gelang. Es war mehr ein gemeinsames Lallen, eine Art Wortmusik, der Party selbst nachgemacht.

With that it wasn't so important for the time being whether it in fact wildly succeeded in getting the point. It was more a common babble, a kind of music of words, which recapitulated the party itself.

Wichtig: Der und der hat da und da so und so gespielt, und alle wären da gewesen.
Ist ja geil.
Dann wäre man später noch dorthin gegangen und da und da hingefahren, da wäre man schon so und so drauf gewesen, und die Musik so und so.
Toll.

Note: So and so played such and such like that and that, and everyone was there.

Cool!

Then later you went there again and drove there and there, where you were already so and so, and the music so and so.

Excellent.

Und man wäre dann irgendwo gelandet, mit dem und dem und der und der, und da hätte man dann noch das und das gemacht, bis dann und dann. Und erst dann und dann wäre man so und so verstrahlt, verpeilt, endfertig und hochgradig verstört daheim gewesen.

And then you ended up somewhere, with him and him and her and her, and there you then again did that and that, until then and then. And only then and then were you at home so and so thoroughly cooked, spaced-out, wasted, and utterly out-of-it.

Ein Wahnsinn.

Totally!

Jede Nacht ging es auf genau diese Art irgendwie um alles, nicht zuletzt um Auslöschung.

Every night it went exactly like this, somehow about everything, ultimately about dissolution.

Auslöschung von Erinnerung, Bewußtsein, Reflexion, Vernichtung von Geschichte.

Dissolution of memory, consciousness, reflexion, annihilation of history.

[...]

An den Rändern standen die Passanten, sahen uns und lachten.

Passersby stood on the corners, saw us, and smiled.

Und wir lachten auch, weil wir uns gegenseitig sahen und erkannten. Kann das sein?

And we smiled also, because we saw each other and recognized each other. Can it be so?

So vielen fremden Menschen sich so nahe zu fühlen plötzlich, das war doch Irrsinn.

Suddenly to feel so many strange people so near, it was really crazy.

Das brachte eine Qualität der Madness ins Spiel.

That brought a quality of madness into play.

This linguistic style of communication is characterized by an avoidance of particularity, of reference to authority, and of recognition of a public sphere differentiated from the domestic. Such a lack of engagement is more, however, than a sign of the absence of utopias. It is also a means of avoiding discipline and *of not doing anything wrong*. This is the orthogonal position of the Love Parade to politics. But it is orthogonal to a particular politics: Love Parade participants have displaced engagement with the *dunkle Vergangenheit* (the dark past). It is clearly a cheap shot for Americans to continually reduce German problems to confrontations with the Nazi past, and we do not mean to do that here. Certainly, difficulties encountered in reckoning with that past, as well as the recent dissolution of "real existing socialism," have contributed to a widespread German skepticism for metanarratives. But this skepticism is intergenerational and was already present in the 1950s and noted by the sociologist Helmut Schelsky (1954). Hence, the politics of nonengagement today unites several generations in Germany, enabling members of an older generation to distance themselves from the *dunkle Vergangenheit,* and those of a new one to distance themselves from the radicalism of their parents: the *Achtundsechsziger.* The universalist discourse of love is not a direct reaction to the "Holocaust" or "Auschwitz"—symbols of the dark past—but to representations displaced by and embodied in a politics of generational differentiation. Love Paraders appear to be identifying with their grandparents, not their parents, and acting out, through the mechanism of displacement, a return not so much of the repressed as of repression itself.

Participants' apolitical politics of return can be seen more clearly when contrasted with the speech and politics of their newly formed opposition: participants in the Hate Parade. In 1997, some 2000 people gathered during the Love Parade to celebrate a Hate Parade (in 1998, some called it the "Fuck Parade")—again the terms were left in English. The Hate Parade was inspired both as opposition to the universalism of the Love Parade and partly as a continuation and extension of the violence of the small (100 participants) but highly publicized "Chaos Tage," which had taken place in Hannover the previous year. "Who cares about Hannover?" asked the fliers, "This year it's happening in Berlin." Although the mélange of punks, skinheads, dissidents, and *Autonome* who took part in the Chaos Days and Hate Parade seemed to claim the same formal goal of just wanting "a party," they differentiated themselves fundamentally in content from Love Paraders. The punks and skinheads of the Hate Parade embraced traditional phallic tropes of masculinity—anger, strength, and violence—while Love Paraders invoked these only in parody, if at all. Participants in the Hate Parade wore mostly black and tried to look tough or nasty, whereas the Love Paraders appeared in various degrees of undress, and some, especially the males, dressed in drag and wore wigs and colorful clothes. The Hate Parade created a space of overt opposition and confrontation, and virtually all discourse surrounding it concentrated on the potential for violence and damage. By contrast, the Love Parade recreated Berlin as a harmonious domestic site, a *Kinderspielplatz* without violence, and any negative discourse surrounding it focused on the problem of dealing with the 200 tons of garbage left behind.

The Feminization of Public Space and Poetic Politics

In sum, the Love Parade creates for itself a symbolically *feminized* political space achieved through the extension of the domestic sphere to encompass the public sphere and through the parodic enactment of phallic authority. This *feminization* means neither more participation by women nor more significance for them. It is rather the inverse of modern feminism's goal. Feminism's move was to make the private political, to infuse the private sphere with politics that was anti-hierarchical and all-inclusive. The Love Parade turns that move on its head, first, by emptying the public sphere of its symbolically masculine politics; and second, by domesticating that public sphere through the use of a traditional feminine symbolic. The issue is not, then, as Habermas (1989) would have it, an "uncoupling from," or "colonization" of, "lifeworld" by "system." Rather, a defining characteristic of late twentieth-century social life may in fact be *the domestication of the public sphere,* the implications of which remain unclear.

One manifestation of this domestication in Germany takes the form of a politics of nonengagement. In the Love Parade the turn to a politics of nonengagement echoes the foreign policy of the participants' West German grandfathers. That foreign policy was formulated in opposition to the active engagement of the French and Americans—and predicated on the absence of that generation's political voice. The one exception was with regard to the GDR, where West German foreign policy was very active and oppositional, but that opposition was justified as an *innerdeutsche Angelegenheit"* (internal German affair). Today, it is as if the public sphere has been domesticated and occupied—on the street and in the demo—by the interiorizing force of the Love Parade. A major effect of this occupation is not, as many feminists had hoped, to inoculate the public sphere against market-driven forces and values and to replace them with an "ethics of care." Rather, the logic of the market, as in the Love Parade, operates unimpeded, without being subjected to political direction. The individualized universalism of the Love Parade reflects the realities of post-Fordist economics as well as new non-nationalist security configurations in Europe. States, nations, and classes no longer appear as self-evident categories of identification, and political parties are no longer looked upon to organize group activity. Identification, such as that made available in the Love Parade, is with a "universal person" (or simply, "the world") that does not work through imitation and representation.

The Love Parade, then, does not follow any Hegelian trajectory of *Volksgeist* entailing the realization a particular spirit in the form of a polity such as a state. Rather, *Volksgeist* is realized in the form of a personal and subjective entry into an impersonal "zone." The zone constitutes a political chronotope in which the subject merges with the *Volk* through a dispersed and nondiscursive authority. This authority, located at the intersection of techno and rave, is both charismatic and internal to its own subject. The sensual mimesis of techno music and rave effects a magical, ecstatic transformation through an inner conversion—*Ekstase der Befreiung,* or "ecstasy of emancipation" (Lenz, cited in Assheuer 1997, 33)—

of each individual subject from a waiting individual to a communal raver. Yet one waits, not for a leader, directive, or utopian narrative as in a Weberian charismatic authority, but for a romantic transformation that comes unbidden.

Is this the return of poetry? Unlike prose, poetry requires no narrativization; it refuses the domination of syntax and relies for its authority on the uniqueness and authenticity of voice and on the tension created in the play of anticipated meaning against the structure of the line, in *enjambement* (Agamben 1995, 40–41). Plato identified poetry as a mere (and detrimental) imitation of the pre-philosophical life (see Fink 1960; Spariosu 1984). To turn to a poetic authority means inverting the Platonic hierarchy and reevaluating poetry as both more real and more important than philosophy, narrative, or traditional politics. The Love Parade enacts precisely such an inversion through a domestication of the public sphere. Those outside oneself—hence, the conflictual domain of politics generally—become indistinguishable from oneself. My mother, myself. Other places and people can be represented in substitutable and nonreferential adverbs and adjectives. *"Wichtig: Der und der hat da und da so und so gespielt, und alle wären da gewesen."*

Politics without a Head: The Politics of Sensuous Mimesis

The refusal of formal ties to traditional political and religious actors and institutions situates the Love Parade uniquely within the political field of the Federal Republic of Germany (FRG). Republican in form, the government of the FRG is a representative system, based on the delegation of authority through ritualized elections. When citizens vote for representatives, they place themselves in a mimetic relation to their leaders that does two things: they dispossess themselves of direct power to decide and participate in decision-making, and they endow their delegates with the power of a fetish. This self-dispossession and delegation constitutes two fantasies, one original—the necessary fiction of "the people" created through the act of individual dispossession—and one secondary—the necessary activity of representative "politics." Thereafter, delegates face the temptation, as Pierre Bourdieu (1991, 205) has explained, of becoming fetishes. "Political fetishes," he writes, paraphrasing Marx, "are people, things, beings, which seem to owe to themselves alone an existence that social agents have given to them; those who create the delegate adore their own creature. The *ministerium* appears as a *mysterium*." The ministry appears as a mystery. The danger therein is the likelihood that politicians act, in turn, as if they can substitute themselves for the people.

Disillusionment in Germany with this democratic form of political fetishism led in the decade of the 1990s to the coinage and widespread use of the word

Politikverdrossenheit (politics as weary and morose). Participants in the Love Parade avoid the temptation to fetishize representation by refusing altogether the processes of dispossession and delegation. Because they do not seek to constitute themselves as a movement or a party, or even as a specific group of people with any particular project outside of the rave or machine experience, they do not avail themselves of the possibility or dangers of representation. This means that they also refuse articulation with a democratic political system structured by the "binary code of government/opposition" (Luhmann 1990, 175, see 167–83). This binary code, we may remember, replaced the single, unchallengeable head arrangement of the kingship or feudal estate. Instead of *cephalic* structure of monarchs or despots, or the *bi-cephalic* head that characterizes democratic authority, Love Parade participants appeal to an *acephalic authority,* a politics without a head (see Borneman 2004b, 1–32).

What is this acephalous authority? It resembles superficially Bataille's (1985, 198–99) surrealist project of the "acephalic man [whose] identification with the headless man merges and melds with the identification with the superhuman, which *is* entirely 'the death of God.'" But Bataille's critique was directed at democracy's "neutralization of relatively free and weak antagonisms," and it was "committed to destruction [as well as] the formation of a new structure [as a] truly liberating act." In their rejection of representation, participants in the Love Parade prioritize magic, ecstasy, and the transcendence of sensuality over reason, criticism, and narrative. Through irony they circumvent the politicization of purposeful statements, movements, and experiences, and they elide the field of traditional politics and any notion of commitment. Instead of an imitative mimesis, which is the basis of all representative politics, they practice a sensual one based solely on the participatory act of gathering to rave.

As a mode of interaction, sensuous mimesis acts out a quasi-erotic union, a form of knowing Adorno referred to as *anschmiegen,* snuggling-up-to (Horkheimer and Adorno 1972 [1944]; see also Cahn 1984, 63 n. 44; Früchtl 1986). Instead of using reason or understanding—what one could call "textual means"—to form a "group," participants in the Love Parade use sensual means—kinesthetic, visual, and aural. Hence, onlookers or passersby, such as policemen or Japanese tourists, who might be expected to represent radical alterity to those in the Love Parade, are seen as nothing more than people in other uniforms. They too can participate and respond, but not with the assertion of difference through argument and representation; only with their bodies, by moving with the beat, can they answer the call of techno. Adorno argued that the fixation on imitative mimesis characteristic of enlightenment thought—and this includes formulations of democratic, representative politics—proceeded only by virtue of the repression of sensuous mimesis. This repression resulted in the instantiation of a "mimetic taboo," a delegitimation of non-imitative mimesis, and its wholesale replacement by imitation. "Rationality in general," maintained Adorno (1970, 148), "is the demythologization of modes of mimetic behavior." But Adorno's own demythologization through ironic and rational distancing from his object of study is not recapitulated by participants in the Love Parade. The Love Parade represents a re-mythologization of mimesis—but mimesis without fetish. Hence, participants merely enact the "acephalic character of existence," its polymorphous expression, without any distancing by means of actual destruction and reformation. Through a nondiscursive and sensual participation, the Love Parade offers a magical incorporation of Otherness, or any Other, into the group.

It should now be clear why the Love Parade tends to escape understanding or comprehension as a political event. It is not fascist, for it aestheticizes only aesthetics and makes no claims on government or representational politics. It is not phallic but ironic, equalizing, and horizontal in its employment of power. Participants refuse to dispossess themselves of power, and they delegate no one to speak for the group. They are not suffering through a Great Depression, and they do not espouse any exclusions or imperialist intentions. They share no racial, religious, or sexual ideologies or utopian projects. In fact, they are prosperous and secure, members of a dominant country and continent with no need to mobilize as a people. The Love Parade itself is neither a carnival nor a liminal event, for it has no intent to invert or subvert anything, and it does not attempt to ritualize any specific content or mark the bodies of its participants through scarification.[7] Even the gender play is mild and unchallenging when compared to the hetero-oriented celebration of Fasching or the homo Christopher Street Day Parade. Techno music does tend to install uniformity rather than heterogeneity, but coercive uniformity is confined to the beat and movement in raving. Moreover, even as we write this, techno music and the scene around it is changing and diversifying. The Love Parade is a new kind of identification that both refuses to engage in the fetishisms of delegation and representation, something about which Taussig (1992) has written eloquently, and attempts to re-enchant group participation. Certainly this "challenges practically all critical practice," as Taussig (1992, 141) argues, but exactly how it challenges traditional politics is another matter.

Although participants in the Love Parade have no need for politicians and bureaucrats, the inverse is not true: politicians and bureaucrats do need the participants in the Love Parade. These participants are the next generation of voters, and politicians must appeal to them in the electoral game so they can claim a mandate to rule, where they promise certain goods or policies and pledge support for certain causes. Their legitimation rests on proving that they are delegated to wield power in the name of Love Parade participants. The only thing the ravers need from government is the license to proceed. Due, however, to the way in which representational authority is structured in the field of liberal-democratic politics, participants in the Love Parade, like all actors in the fields of entertainment and sports, must be brought into a relation with politics. This will likely occur by virtue of the routinization of the charismatic participation of the Love Parade. In fact, as the Love Parade imitates itself over time, it is becoming ritualized. In 1998, the Love Parade made its first lengthy appearance on German cable TV networks, with FAB (*Fernsehen aus Berlin*) devoting nearly a full day to the Parade. Such extended TV coverage dramatically changes the "happening," enabling an experiential distancing during its very occurrence. People now can "see" the Love Parade without going, or can split their time (which is what I [Borneman] did) between being there and watching on TV. The audience increases exponentially, while the intensity of actual participation frequently declines. Responding to the lack of temporal dynamism, TV coverage of the Love Parade in 1998 focused on repeated interviews with key DJs or random participants (who respond with the expected superlatives *"Toll! Super!"*) and on recurring shots of a bare-breasted Brazilian woman or several half-naked but body-painted muscle men dancing on floats. This yearly imitation makes the Love Parade representable, an icon of itself. Thereby it loses the capacity to bypass representational politics. The Parade's iconic body seeks to displace its sensual and experiential body. In this way, we suspect, the Love Parade will eventually (and probably very soon) be appropriated for the field of politics. Such a relocation within politics will likely effect, in turn, a shift in the definition of the political field.

What are the major tendencies in this emergent shift? All power is elided under the illusion of a refusal to engage. Political identification becomes the systematic elision of all that can be identified as authority. The new political field is marked by a politics of nonengagement and a re-mythologization of mimesis. Effective politics becomes affective politics, politics without a head.

We can now summarize the elements of this form of late twentieth-century political experience:

1. It rejects traditional politics without subverting or inverting any order.

2. It refuses discursivity and its own representation in speech.

3. It rejects cognition and imitative mimesis and instead strives for a purely sensual mimesis.

4. It refuses delegation of authority and locates authority in an inner religiosity.

5. It empties the public sphere of its traditional politics and domesticates that sphere through the use of a traditional feminine symbolic.

12 Is the United States Europe's Other?

The distance between European and U.S. self-understandings has recently widened, and in all likelihood the rift will become graver and deeper in the near future. In one sense, this distance was always there, as a cultural divide between what have long been called the Old and New Worlds. It was reinforced in the latter part of the twentieth century, especially by the Cold War, which sent European and U.S. societies on fundamentally different trajectories, including, most significantly, demilitarization of Europe and militarization of the United States, trends that the end of the Cold War only accelerated. The crucial reinforcing factor, though, was the Reagan project of the 1980s. At that time the United States embarked on (and is still undergoing) a revolutionary turn in its mission, away from a New Deal, more-or-less-egalitarian, internationalist consensus to a public policy of belligerent social Darwinism and class warfare—a path Europe never took. During the same period, Europe's welfare states not only retained their basic structures and motives but also expanded the application of their principles from a national to a continental vision of egalitarian, cosmopolitan democracies in an economic and legal union.

In another sense, however, the current Bush administration has transformed the distance between Europe and the United States into a political and societal rift that is fundamentally antagonistic, consequential, and perhaps enduring. I attribute the recent *widening* of this distance to two processes: *increasing depth and breadth of Europeanization,* and *increasing provincialism of Americanization.* The political rift is both popular and governmental, and it is reflected in differing strategies of capitalism (regulated vs. laissez-faire), penalization (minimal incarceration vs. the death penalty and three strikes, you're out"), military strength (strategically limited vs. total dominance), health care (preventive and access-for-all vs. palliative and limited access), and legality (embedded internationalism vs. national sovereignty). But the most volatile and "new" dimension of the growing U.S.–European divide concerns the shift in world power from Europe to the Middle East, as demonstrated by the recent U.S.-led war against Iraq. This war is not the divisive issue, however, but merely an occasion to express a more basic

189

disagreement over the Middle East and the Israeli–Palestinian conflict. In other words, the U.S.–European relation is no longer triangulated by Communism but by a new configuration of forces, by Europeanization, Americanization, and the Middle East.

How does the increasing depth and breadth of Europeanization and the increasing provincialism of Americanization relate to the topos "Middle East?" Let me develop this argument in three steps, discussing, first, the shift in world power from Europe to the Middle East; second, the post-1989 acceleration of Europeanization; and third, the provincialism of Americanization resulting from solidification of Reagan-era reforms and reactions to globalization.

Shift in World Power to the Middle East

After Yalta and the end of World War II, the epicenter of world power was clearly located within Europe—and this despite the exhaustion of Europe's moral authority and the end of much of Europe's colonial dominance of the rest of the world. NATO, along with the Allied occupation of Germany, guaranteed a U.S. presence within Europe. Although the United States approached Europe from the outside, it became internal to European development, especially to Europe's cultural (e.g., film, food, music) and military trajectories. Today, the Middle East has become the new epicenter of world power, and both Europe and the United States are external actors to its drama. Both have great strategic interests in the Middle East, including, of course, its oil resources; but neither is positioned, like the United States was within Europe during the Cold War or as Europe was within the Middle East during its colonial "mandate" period, as internal to Middle Eastern development. As a matter of fact, the inverse might be argued: Europe and the United States appear to have very little leverage on developments in the Middle East—who listens to them there? (This may change, or at least that was the intent of the Bush administration.) Instead, the Middle East is now actively internal to both European and U.S. development, to their self-definitions and visions of the future.

It is this internality, this interiorization of a foreign body, of Middle East people and things, while being excluded from any decisive influence in the Middle East that is a source of deep ambivalence and confusion, if not irrational action, for Americans and Europeans. The Middle East's internal presence in Europe and the United States goes well beyond the issue of oil dependence; it includes, more importantly, the presence of significant numbers of Arabs and Jews from Middle East countries. These peoples are active—Arabs and Jews in different ways, of course—in a kind of diasporic politics that is more reminiscent of the pre–World War I United States than of anything in the latter half of the twentieth century. Their integration—the ways in which they become or do not become European or American—as well as their close ties to and influence on the contemporary Middle East, give them very different locations in the New and Old Worlds.

Europeanization

How do developments internal to Europe and the United States—Europeanization and Americanization, respectively—relate to this global shift in the epicenter of power? The collapse of the Cold War, East–West division of Europe has resulted in a scramble among nations there for strategic positions and alliances, all of which increasingly take shape under pressures of Europeanization. In a 1997 *Annual Review of Anthropology* article, Nicholas Fowler and I introduced the concept "Europeanization" as an object of inquiry and began to lay out its terms and conditions. We argued that one should avoid swinging between pessimism and euphoria and instead acknowledge the European Union as a "continental political unit of a novel order." Europeanization should be understood "as a spirit, a vision, and a process" (Borneman and Fowler 1997, 510). We suggested five domains—language, money, tourism, sex, and sport—as particularly fruitful for ethnographic study to learn how different national peoples in Europe are becoming more "European." This new form of subjectivity, the "European," which looks more fragmented and incoherent the closer one gets to it, is nonetheless increasingly taking definition against the cultural practices of members of a particular other country, the United States.

To understand how Europeans have come to both resemble each other more and to differ from Americans, one might begin by looking at the institutionalization of their respective life courses. In an influential 1985 article, the German sociologist Martin Kohli argues that the life course (*Lebenslauf*) has its "own societal structural dimensions" (1985, 1), such that, much like "gender," it becomes institutionalized as a system of rules that orders life over time. Following the Cold War, a Europeanization of the national life course took place in European countries, driven largely by law and accelerated by the production of (and compliance with) EU norms. These norms regulate and make translatable intimate cultural practices—from eating and sex to marriage; from notions of equality and equity to rationalization of age grading and the treatment of minorities; from educational access to the issuance of occupational titles. One of the unusual aspects of this institutionalization has been that, although the EU norms are formulated within Western Europe, prospective EU members from the former Soviet bloc increasingly seek to comply with them in anticipation of membership. (Poland and Hungary were, to my knowledge, the first countries to fully adopt this strategy.) The national *Lebenslauf* about which Kohli wrote in 1985 is now in competition with a European one, a competition that often frames national and local elections and becomes discursive with regard to issues of immigration, national identity, and the future of welfare provisions.

What does this have to do with the Middle East? Let me approach this through the issue of migration. The European Union has struggled for at least a decade to establish uniform European immigration, police, and border policies, encountering a great deal of resistance among member nations—until the September 11, 2001 (9/11), massacre at the twin towers in New York's World Trade Center. Initially, these policies may have seemed oriented toward keeping "East" Europeans out of the West, but increasingly it is clear that their success depends on the cooperation of East Europeans, with the goal of regulating Muslim entry into and participation in Europe. Eight to twelve million Muslims live within the European Union, and if the union expands to the Balkans and southwestern Europe, that number will double. If Turkey is admitted, the face of Europe will change radically. The vast majority of present Muslim residents are the product of postcolonial economic and political migration, many arriving in the 1970s to work for failing industries or in low-skilled jobs. Most live on the margins of Europe; they are poorly integrated culturally, socially, and politically and are a potential source of unrest and illegality.

Although these Muslims come from many different countries, with corresponding differences in cultural and political orientations, they are treated as a relatively homogeneous group within Europe. In reaction, they increasingly unite around Islam, not as a religion but as a cultural identity. Analysts have only belatedly come to acknowledge, if at all, how the perpetrators of the 9/11 attacks were united in the European diaspora and how the new Europeanized Europe, as a place with advanced freedoms and opportunities derived from a specific institutionalized life course, was essential to solidifying their beliefs and alliances and to planning their attacks on the United States. This life course is the envy of much of the world, but that is also the problem: new immigrants and foreigners in Europe desire this life course, which is absolutely unachievable in their homelands and only partly achievable, if at all, in Europe itself. Europe does not have recourse to the U.S. model of multicultural and radically uneven integration, with its weak and diffuse norms, possibilities for continuous displacement and deferral of goals, geographical mobility, and self-imposed ghettoization. Europe is struggling to develop an alternative *Ausländlerpolitik,* a vision and a set of policies and practices that might satisfy both its native population and the desires of its new residents. My point is that a large Muslim and Arab population made up of peoples from ex-colonies, mainly low-skilled laborers, is now internal to European development, a fact of which European governments and societies are increasingly aware, making for new and more aggressive policies directed to the immigrants' internal placement and to their diasporic links.

Jews have a much longer and more prominent history within Europe than Muslims. They are fewer in number, less marginal, and more integrated into European social structures than Muslims, and the numbers of Jews now immigrating to Europe are very small compared with Muslims. It is not the number of Jews that is problematic, however, but how they are located; their representation and symbolic significance is the issue. The historical antagonism between Jews and Christians within Europe is most frequently read through the lens of the Holocaust, meaning that today Jews are generally understood as *the* symbolic victim group and, hence, deserving of some form of historical redress. Additionally, they form a fairly homogeneous status group; most are solidly middle class and generally considered less culturally oppositional than Muslims. One who publicly utters the particular conceptualization of Jews as fundamentally antagonistic to Christian Europeans is quickly censured, and an entire regime of guilt is brought to bear on him or her, leading to silence if not shame.[1] (The same censure does not occur when Islam is posited as radically alter.) Witness the recent stunted careers of Jean-Marie Le Pen in France, Jörg Haider in Austria, and Jürgen Möllemann in Germany, who in various ways pandered to anti-Semitic stereotypes. Muslims and Jews, then, are very differently positioned within Europe, and the extent to which they are considered a problem is directly linked to the issue of integration or separation and to the kind of ties they cultivate with the Middle East.

Their different positioning with respect to the Middle East is creating tensions between Jews and Muslims within Europe that carry over into domestic politics. Western European politicians, in particular, are increasingly sensitive not only to Israeli-identified Jews but also to Palestinian-identified Muslims, who increasingly provide a young workforce to support Europe's aging population. Although most European Jews are firmly European and do not consider themselves part of a diaspora, the Israeli government still considers them all potential returnees. The Knesset even recently passed a law claiming universal jurisdiction over the adjudication of harm done to a Jew anywhere in the world. And the Israeli government has been reacting hysterically to the indictment in Belgium of Ariel Sharon for responsibility for the 1984 massacre in the Sabra and Shatila refugee camps, not only breaking off diplomatic relations and threatening economic sanctions but also proposing an immediate airlift to remove all Jews from Belgium. Israeli politics of this sort implicates Europe's Jews in Likud's anti-Palestinian politics, and it positions them in potential opposition to Europe. Meanwhile, both European and U.S. media tend to give a great deal of weight to Jewish voices in Europe that speak with religious authority, hence, again interpellating Jews not as secular citizens but as somehow bound up with the Old Testament and a contemporary Israeli politics of revenge.

By contrast, although the European public increasingly recognizes the marginalization of its Muslims and the series of historical humiliations—up to the present Palestinian degradation—suffered by Arabs in the Middle East, often at the hands of European colonizers, European governments are less inclined to openly acknowledge or act on these perceptions. Instead, they, like many U.S. commentators, frequently blame Muslims for creating the conditions for their own victimization (i.e., Islamic so-called cultural backwardness is the cause of their political repression and stunted economic development; Palestinian suffering at the hands of Israelis is brought on by their own suicide bombers). Reacting to these narratives, many Arabs and Muslims are increasingly radicalized while living in the European diaspora. Some are active in the desecration of Jewish synagogues and graveyards in Europe, and many finance Islamicist political movements and parties in their countries of origin, from North Africa to the Middle and Far East.

Partly in response to the 9/11 attacks, European governments are engaged in a kind of measured aggressiveness against the Middle East diaspora of Muslims and Arabs. One should not dismiss this turn as mere xenophobia. The governments of France, Germany, England, Switzerland, Sweden, and Belgium are, as one might expect, especially ambivalent, if not fearful, of the effects of Middle Eastern immigrants' long-distance links—especially to Turkey, Algeria, Lebanon, Syria, Pakistan, or one of the Gulf States. This ambivalence is registered in contradictory policies that alternately encourage dual or single citizenship and in contradictory everyday practices that are alternately xenophobic or insist on social assimilation, encourage multicultural identifications or, as in France and Germany, learning a *Leitkultur*. It is stimulated both by what Benedict Anderson (1992) over a decade ago called "long-distance nationalism"—loyalties to the distant homeland where one no longer resides, which one no longer knows well, and to which one is not accountable—and by transnational terrorism, in which opportunities provided by European and U.S. science, telecommunications, and open financial markets—in short, global capitalism's goodies—directly enable the use of violence to foment widespread anxiety.

In many ways, these current ambivalences about Islam within Europe parallel the conundrum of the U.S. government and society in deciding whether to integrate or preserve the distinctions of what some today call *First Peoples*. U.S. ambivalence is revealed in the wild historical vacillation between policies of elimination, containment and preservation, or integration of the American Indians. I explored the relation of these policies to the development of U.S.

anthropology in an article published nearly a decade ago entitled "American Anthropology as Foreign Policy" (Borneman 1995). There is much ethnographic evidence for similar swings and reversals in policy and practice within Europe today. Observers might pay specific attention to areas of change in the model life course, such as the regulation of civil marriages. This regulation is of the utmost importance to religions such as Islam and Judaism, but it is no longer central to secularized Christian Europe, where marriage is increasingly deregulated and left to individual contract law. Observers might also pay attention to rituals of citizenship or civil status that require shedding or adding identifications: to language, education, and residence policies (that alternately encourage mono- or multilingualism); or to the integration or segregation of schools and residential neighborhoods.

Europe's domestic response to the presence of the Middle East within its own political and social body exists in uneasy tension with its foreign policy response to the territorial Middle East. Of course, Europe has no foreign policy; there are only national policies driven by national interests. Neither NATO nor the European Union has anything resembling a common foreign policy. Nonetheless, at the social level there is something resembling a consensus about European foreign policy, revealed in the European public's overwhelming rejection of the U.S.-led new war against Iraq. This public opposition to the U.S.-led war is also a response to the shift in the world epicenter to the Middle East and reflects an awareness that the most effective response to terror is not war against the enemy outside but finding a resolution to the Israeli–Palestinian conflict.

The public in Europe is also no longer merely a discursive referent or a utopian dream or an accumulation of national publics with their own corresponding projects. A European public does indeed exist and comes together (outside of and well beyond its current antiwar unity) with respect to a project of political globalization—some are calling it cosmopolitanism—that is shaped both by the awareness of nineteenth-century colonial and imperial failures and of twentieth-century nationalist (i.e., totalitarian, fascist) failures. It is also shaped by the experience of two world wars, leading to an awareness of the limitations of military solutions to political problems. One might claim that Europeans are merely cowardly, afraid of dying for their causes—and this may be true; but they have also become wise to the political instrumentalization of death cults, which only half a decade ago was a staple feature of national policies. Today, to be European is to be an internationalist without forsaking the benefits of local democratic control and to be unwilling to sacrifice society building for economic or military dominance.

My point here is that Europe is committed to a political-legal form that crystallized as a pan-European project in response to the collapse of East European state socialist regimes. This form is seemingly alien to present forms of governance in the Middle East and is also threatened by Europe's interiorization of the Middle East with its accompanying conflicts. Why then, given all this ambivalence about Islam and the Middle East, has the United States instead become Europe's Other?

Americanization

My argument about the United States will be shorter and merely suggestive of a line of analysis. U.S. provincialism is increasingly becoming the counter concept, and therefore the Other, for European self-understandings. By U.S. provincialism, I mean a reinforcement of U.S. particularities or "U.S. exceptionalism," a return to the same national boosterism, devotion not to a rustic but to an aggressively countrified vision. This is the voice of the United States as global moral project, the constantly invoked *we*, as in "we are the world," that has come to dominate the image of America within the United States and abroad.

The Columbia University historian Simon Schama, in an amusing and erudite article called "The Unloved American" (2003), attributes the distance between Europeans and Americans to the "national egocentricity" and "virtuous isolation(ism)" of the latter:

> Just as obnoxious is the fraud of Christian piety, a finger-jabbing rectitude incapable of asserting a policy without invoking the Deity as a co-sponsor. This hallelujah Republic was a bedlam of hymns and hosannas, but the only true church was the church of the Dollar Almighty.

These qualities posed no problem for Europe when the United States limited its exercise of power to its own continent, argues Schama, but they become threatening with present U.S. imperial policy and its global reach (Schama 2003, 334–39).

Schama does what anthropologists used to do and what many historians continue to do when they take up culture: he makes it constant and ahistorical. Schama's perspective—that U.S. culture is unvarying and can change only from without—vitiates the political thrust of his narrative. It would be more politically efficacious to historicize culture and this process of Americanization and to locate particular agents in the reproduction of U.S. national egocentricity. U.S. provincialism and exceptionalism in their current institutional forms date from the Reagan era, when, in the name of God-and-Country, a muscular rhetoric was employed to reinforce images of U.S. strength and national superiority—frequently set against a European foil of wimps, paceniks, and over-educated, over-cultivated cosmopolitans. It is a particular U.S. Republican vision of the world, naturalized by the active and powerful Republican media and think-tank propagandists and further radicalized by the Bush administration.

Since the end of World War II, Americanization has largely defined the conditions of globalization—the spread of ideologies, cultural values, and products, the idea of a "way of life"—for Europeans as well as for much of the rest of the world. But, at least since the end of the Cold War, the European continent departed from the U.S. trajectory, so that the old term *Westernization,* now used almost solely in a negative sense, no longer characterizes a Euro–American mission. If one asks, following Talcott Parsons, whether this divergence is driven by economic, political, or cultural factors, one must conclude that it is driven by all three equally. If one asks further whether there is a dominant system that serves both to integrate Europeans and Americans within their respective wholes and to drive them apart from each other, then, I want to argue, and this is my hypothesis here, that, through the first two decades after the formal end of the Cold War, the European *integrative revolution* (a term I take from an early critique of modernization theory by Clifford Geertz) has been dominated by a project of political globalization, whereas that of the United States is driven by economic globalization.

These two projects, of political and economic globalization, have been on a collision course, and they meet in the epicenter of the Middle East. One need only watch the evening news coverage of the Israeli–Palestinian conflict on any European television station and compare it with the U.S. news to realize the radical divergence in reporting.[2] And one need only compare the middle-class European life course, and its widespread distribution, with the more uneven, class-based life courses found in the United States, to understand why the two publics might find the different reporting styles appealing. Accordingly, the governments in Europe and the United States find themselves addressing publics with radically different domestic electoral agendas: a politics of security production for the middle classes in Europe and a politics of anxiety production for the middle classes in the United States.

Unlike American Muslims, American Jews are fully internalized within the cultural-economic scene (not to speak of the number of Israelis with U.S. passports). The way this internalization works is that no U.S. politician dares oppose Israeli foreign policy, a policy that is aggressively anti-Arab, even if Israeli actions run counter to U.S. national interests. And support for Israel's anti-Arab, anti-Muslim policies has nothing to do with how many Jews in the United States or Israel oppose or support Israeli nationalist positions. American politicians in both parties, despite constant assertions of fearlessness in the face of terror, are afraid to criticize Israeli policies. Given this configuration of ideology and power, it is not that difficult to convince Americans today that the territorial division of the world into an orient and an occident has given way to a deterritorialized mapping of virtue, the former associated with Islamic evil, the latter with Judeo–Christian good. An alternative U.S. imaginary that might call for a "Judeo–Christian–Muslim nation" is a notion that many Americans would find—well, un-American. The Obama presidency has done little to change this view, as Obama himself has been forced to reaffirm his Christian faith and to disavow any connection to Islam. Europe's advanced secularization of Christianity allows for a more consistent and more thinkable model of Jewish and Muslim integration, although in practice the integration of Muslims there too encounters much resistance.

Yet, although the mapping of assumptions of evil onto Muslims and Arabs is also prevalent within Europe, most European residents find the U.S. project of economic globalization (based on a social Darwinist model of the social) even more objectionable. U.S. economic imperialism threatens Europe's goals of a continuance of the welfare state and a globalization of their political-legal form. In this resistance to U.S. economic and military hegemony, Europeans find a nascent ally in many of the peoples of the Middle East. Whereas the United States may hope to assert itself over the Middle East through military might and through its alliance with Israel, the Europeans do not have the means or will to pursue this strategy, and instead must rely on the cunning seduction of their own modular life course.

My argument here is that the future of this relationship between the United States and Europe must be seen not only as a dyad but as a triangulation in dialectical development. The world financial crisis that began in 2007 has intensified the political and economic pressure to curtail the opportunities and benefits of this life course model. Citizen dissatisfaction with these modifications in expectations is often mobilized into anti-immigrant sentiment, which in turn translates, in many European countries, into anti-Arab or Anti-Muslim movements. Yet internal European labor needs and histories of migration patterns suggest that some substantial immigration of labor from northern Africa, Turkey, and the Middle East will continue. Internal xenophobic movements in Europe, which both deny these labor needs and place the blame for the curtailment of welfare benefits on immigrants, can, of course, bring about a reversal in the particular convergence of interest between Europeans and Middle Eastern Arabs that was noticeable around the turn of the millennium. Nonetheless, the rebellions in the Arab world against their own authoritarian regimes that began in 2011 were not only a response to a general crisis in political legitimacy but also a wish to partake in some of the imagined fruits of the European life course by creating the conditions for such lives in one's own country. In principle, the transformations of different kinds of regimes (e.g., monarchs, dictatorships, military rule) from Morocco to Yemen advances the European project of political-legal reform over and above the American one of economic globalization. The United States, given its energy needs and economic policies, appears much more dependent on Middle Eastern stability and authoritarianism, as well as politically on an alliance with Israel. The point is to remain analytically aware of the degrees of modes of internalization of the various conflicts.

Notes

1. Modes of Accountability

1. Most scholarly work today, especially in anthropology, is in fact focused on calculation (see Rose 1999, Strathern 2000). Strongly influenced by Max Weber's analysis of rationalization and Michel Foucault's of governmentality, and taking either "neoliberal" reforms or what Michael Power (1999) dubs "rituals of verification" in institutions as objects of inquiry, this research concentrates on social control, quantification, monitoring, and auditing.

2. I do not mean to endorse the argument that the Holocaust, an event that occurred more than half a century ago, *should* serve as a template for dealing with subsequent human rights violations in other contexts. Its use as a model for atrocities over time does have consequences, however, and it is with these consequences that I am concerned. Ratner and Abrams, for example, argue that international law is severely limited in dealing with many contemporary human rights violations, especially with the charge of "genocide," precisely because the "paradigm of the Holocaust . . . omitted protection for certain groups"—specifically, those defined as "political opposition" (1997, 41). Today's atrocities emerge in political contexts quite different than those before World War II.

3. The literature describing and attempting to explain this rupture is extensive and far beyond the scope of this essay. For the most recent work with extensive bibliographical references, see Jarausch (2010) on the history of the Federal Republic, and Langenbacher (2010) on debates on collective memory since unification.

4. Critics of "denazification" make the claim that it was extremely limited due to the growing Cold War threat and the U.S. need to quickly rebuild Western Europe as a bulwark against communism. In West Germany right after the war's end, an estimated 1,600 persons were convicted as "major offenders," and 150,000 Nazi party members were disqualified from holding public office (Vollnhals 1991, 227–36).

5. In 1948, Hannah Arendt, for one, harshly criticized the tendency by the Allies to abandon the distinction between Germans and Nazis, declaring these tactics "a victory for the Nazis." The "vast machine of administrative mass murder" worked to co-opt ordinary Germans, she wrote, and thus compelled them to be complicitous in its criminality. This totalitarianism of the everyday made it became impossible to distinguish between the innocent and those to be held responsible (1991, 274, 277).

6. Falk (2001, 9–10) argues that political elites strongly resisted an international human rights regime after World War II and that the "nominal regime" instituted came about only because of pressure from "civil society . . . reinforced by guilty consciences of governmental leaders about such official accommodations of the Hitler challenge as amicable participation in the Berlin Olympics of 1936, the diplomacy of appeasement,

the rejection of refugees, and the failure to bomb the railroad tracks leading to Auschwitz during the latter stages of the war."

7. By 1978, West German reparations totaled DM 56.5 billion, and since then have most likely doubled (Pross 1998, 40–41).

8. In her correspondence with Karl Jaspers, Arendt argues, "For these crimes, no punishment is severe enough. It may well be essential to hang Göering, but it is totally inadequate. That is, this guilt, in contrast to all criminal guilt, oversteps and shatters any and all legal systems" (cited in Kohler and Saner, eds. 1992, 121–22).

9. Jaspers distinguishes four kinds of guilt: criminal guilt (liability or "*Haftung*") refers to judgment and punishment in courts of justice; political guilt ("*Schuld*") applies to all citizens of a modern state insofar as they did not speak and act openly against that state's criminality; moral guilt concerns those actions and defaults of the German citizen that implied his support of the criminal regime; metaphysical guilt, the concept which has provoked the most debate, implies the failure of "solidarity among men as human beings that makes each co-responsible for every wrong and every injustice in the world, especially for crimes committed in his presence or with his knowledge" (1947, 32).

10. Drawing on the distinction between *Schuld* (guilt) and *Scham* (shame), it is often argued that legal guilt (*Haftung*) cannot be inherited, but shame can and usually is. *Schuld* (guilt) tends to be an external appellation projected onto Germans, whereas *Scham* (shame) tends to describe an inner psychological state. One says, "Ich habe Schuld" (I am guilty), or "Ich habe Schuldgefühl" (I feel guilty), but one speaks reflexively with shame: "Ich schäme mich" (I am ashamed of myself). Yet both shame and guilt share a problem inherent in representations: to what extent are they mere projections, or do they correspond to the internal states of the actors? Because *Schuld* in fact functions foremost as an external ascription, it is in this case more significant and durable, since it keeps being projected onto individual Germans, regardless of their inner reflexive states.

11. This second reckoning is sometimes even referred to colloquially as a "*zweiter Schuld*," meaning collective responsibility as the debt or guilt that remains after monetary restitution (see Giordano 1987).

12. Demand for apologies—national and international—continued after the end of the Cold War, with harms suffered by the East German regime now added to crimes of the National Socialists. Compared to the post–World War II period, the apologies were much more forthcoming and for many more kinds of injuries. For example, in 2001 the German foreign minister apologized for the German role in the transatlantic slave trade (Leicht 2001).

13. The movement of the capital and creation of the Berliner Republik, initially justified as *die Vollendung der Einheit Deutschlands* (completion of unity of Germany), is also about the cultural anxiety of having to experience the emptiness of the people. Proliferating memorials are intended, in part, to fill in that emptiness. For an interesting analysis that traces changes in commemoration of the Kristallnacht by Germans and Jews in Germany, see Bodemann 1996, 179–226.

14. The "Topography of Terror" was initially an unofficial museum and had to struggle to get public financing. Its exhibit of the Nazi regime's use of terror, the history of victims, and the methods of persecution did not single out any particular victim group. It was particularly impressive also due to its location, right on the Wall, off Wilhelm-strasse (the site of power in Germany for the last century), in a former Nazi bunker where opponents were tortured. It has been up-scaled and since 2010 is housed in a building

constructed by the Swiss architect Peter Zumthor. Some Berlin authorities speak of a balance between the three memorials: one to Jewish victims, one to Jewish history, and one to the subject of the perpetrator's society. Only the "Topography" mentions victims other than Jews, such as gypsies, homosexuals, the retarded, political opponents, victims of military justice, and POWs. Today it is not kosher to propose that the Holocaust Memorial include mention of other victim groups, though such a suggestion might have been taken up in the early 1990s when the memorial was first proposed.

15. The facts of the massacre are by now well established and incontrovertible: Lebanese Phalangist militias entered a Palestinian refugee camp shortly after 5 PM on September 16, 1982, and in the next 40 hours massacred, abducted, or disappeared hundreds or thousands (estimates range from 700 to 3,500) of unarmed civilians—butchered people in their homes, hacked off heads and limbs, slit throats, castrated men, slashed open pregnant women's bellies. Ariel Sharon was the minister of defense at the time and in charge of the occupation of that part of Lebanon, including the Palestinian camps. Upon hearing of the massacre, 400,000 Israelis took to the streets in protest. The United Nations General Assembly condemned the massacre on September 19 with Resolution 521, qualifying it as an "act of genocide" with a resolution on December 16. The Kahan Commission, charged by the Israeli Knesset (parliament) with investigating the event, concluded that Ariel Sharon bore "indirect" but also "personal responsibility" for the massacre (Borneman 2004c; Fisk 2002).

16. During the civil wars, Palestinians refugees, who number over 400,000, or 10 percent of the residents of Lebanon, were seen (and used) both as one source of the conflicts between local sects and also as one of the major victim groups of these conflicts. Although many factors internal to Lebanese social divisions were ultimately responsible for generating episodic violence, the Palestinian refugee crisis and the refuge that the Palestinian Liberation Organization found in Lebanon during its early years created a great deal of instability and resentment among the various Lebanese sects. While most Lebanese acknowledge the issue of Palestinian victimhood, many also resent that Israel and the international community have left Lebanon and Lebanese society to bear many of the costs of this victimization.

2. On Money and the Memory of Loss

This paper was initially presented at a conference, Gedächtnis und Restitution: Über historische Erinnerung und materielle Wiederherstellung in Europa, organized by Dan Diner and Gotthart Wunberg, Internationales Forschungszentrum der Kulturwissenschaften, June 21–23, 2001, in Vienna, Austria, and in the Department of German Studies at the University of Lisbon, Portugal.

1. Parties to both cases are of course not fully united in their resistance. The Argentinian group, for example, has worked in the spirit of "truth, justice, and memory," claiming that to accept money would invalidate truth and destroy memory. Nonetheless, the group has split into two, with one faction working with forensic anthropologists and DNA evidence to uncover the actual identities of victims, to confirm deaths, and to eventually "move beyond" the traumatic losses. The other faction has refused to cooperate in the search for such evidence since it would it would close the books on their losses and force them to admit their children or loved ones were actually dead. A group of mostly grandchildren of "disappeared," called "HUJOS" (combining history and justice), works to keep memories alive by performing mock kidnappings and murders at or near the

homes where they suspect the events had actually occurred and informing neighbors of who had done what (Billie Jean Isbell kindly provided me with this information).

2. *Wiedergutmachung* was initially used by Nazi ideologues to justify their entitlement to Jewish assets because of their alleged suffering at the hands of the Jews (Feldman 2001, 4).

3. Bazyler (2001, 3) quotes an interview with Holocaust survivor and head of the Anti-Defamation League, Abraham Foxman: "But there's another reason that we didn't deal with this issue for 50 years—because the trauma of the human tragedy was so tremendous, so enormous, so gargantuan, that nobody wanted to talk about material loss for fear that it will lessen the human tragedy. Because when you begin talking about property, then what about life?"

4. Essential reading on the history of life insurance is Zelizer (1979, 33), who argues that, while life insurance in early nineteenth-century United States was condemned as a sacrilegious, speculative venture, by the end of the century, it had become acceptable and widespread. She attributes this to a voluntaristic religious outlook that replaced the obligatory confessional standpoint and to the rise of a dominant entrepreneurial economic morality. In Europe, life insurance was banned in the sixteenth and seventeenth centuries—Belgium in 1570, Amsterdam in 1598, Rotterdam in 1604, Sweden in 1666, and France in 1681—and only fully legalized after 1860. In Japan, life insurance spread after 1881. Islamic law still prohibits "speculation on human life."

5. Coverage averaged less than $1,000 each, and heirs are now to receive ten times the amount stated on their policies. Interestingly, claims against European insurers remain unsettled because they have yet to produce a list of policyholders. See Joseph B. Treaster, "Insurer to Pay Armenian Massacre Claims," April 12, 2001 (www.nytimes.com/20001/04/12/national/12ARME.html).

6. On patterns of denial in reckoning with the Armenian genocide, see Hovannisian (1986).

7. Much of this narrative is initially developed in Borneman (1991, 1992).

8. For a balanced account of this process, see Maier (1997).

9. This argument is not premised, as is that of Finkelstein (2001), on the assumption of an "American-Jewish elite" debasing the Holocaust for financial gain. His general argument that the Holocaust is being instrumentalized, however, seems incontrovertible. My own research leads me to a more narrow conclusion: the part of the U.S. legal industry that has been most active in pursuing restitution cases is largely motivated by profit, much as Finkelstein might argue, while publicly representing this litigation as rectifying Jewish memory of loss from the Holocaust.

4. Reconciliation after Ethnic Cleansing

The first version of this article was presented in June 1999 at the conference on Potentials of (Dis)Order: Former Yugoslavia and Caucasus in Comparison, organized by Jan Köhler and Christian Zürcher at the Free University of Berlin. It was also presented in March 2000 as a keynote address at the annual meeting of the Swedish Anthropology Association in Uppsala, Sweden. I thank the organizers and participants for the opportunity to present these ideas. And I thank Billie Jean Isbell and Parvis Ghassem-Fachandi, the gifted listeners who helped me work through the ideas presented here.

1. In this essay, I seek to reveal something similar to Martin Heidegger's metaphor of the unthought as a clearing (*Lichtung*) in the forest. It is a matter of casting light on

an implicit opening, that of the unthought within the set of relations that structures reconciliation.

2. With regard to the questions addressed in this essay, Jews after the Holocaust are the only group that has been well studied. For diaspora Jews in North America, Switzerland, and South Africa, a noticeably declining birthrate, an increase in intermarriage, and an increase in divorce—all patterns that deviate from traditional Jewish cultural patterns and contemporary Jewish demographic patterns in Israel—have characterized the second generation after the Holocaust (DellaPergola 1992; Schmelz 1992).

3. Although survivor strategies among Jews varied tremendously, Yael Danieli, director of Israel's Group Project for Holocaust Survivors and Their Children, concludes that the primary strategy for coping was a quick "marriage of despair" that disregarded prewar socioeconomic and educational status. "The most tangible fulfillment of hope for the continuity and renewal of life was to bring a child into the world. Many survivors gave birth in displaced persons camps as soon as it was physically possible. Almost without exception, the newborn children were named after those who had perished" (1985, 298, 299). A 1983 study of Jewish reproduction in Israel by Eric Peritz and Mario Baras (1992) established that self-identified "religiosity" is by far the strongest predictor of a woman's desired and actual number of children. In a subsequent study, Israel Adler and Peritz (1997, 388) found that "self-assessed religiosity is a better predictor of fertility than religious observance."

4. The evidence for this impression of which I am aware is overwhelming, but it remains anecdotal and journalistic. For example, in 1997 the *Economist* reported that among Rwanda's Tutsi minority following the murder of 750,000 people in the 1994 genocide "procreation has become a public duty to replace numbers lost" (See "Rwanda be fruitful: Birth control in Rwanda," 1–7 February 1997: 43–44).

5. My gratitude to Stefania Pandolfo for this felicitous phrase as well as for the many insights I have gained from our conversations.

6. I am following Liisa Malkki's (1997, 94–96) lead here in suggesting the utility of witnessing as a mode of anthropological knowledge production, particularly in field situations where anthropologists are documenting violence or its aftermath. Similarly, my contrast of caring and retribution as two complementary institutional modes and processes needed for reconciliation roughly parallels her contrast of witnessing and investigation as two complementary "modalities of ethnographic authority." Where my analysis departs from hers is in my recovery of truth-telling and its relation to witnessing as opposed to confessing. Malkki makes a more limited claim, to refrain from "the extraction of truth for its own sake" (95).

7. I do not mean to imply that confessing and forgiveness have only negative effects but simply that they are not a substitute for witnessing and retribution. The philosophers Jeffrie G. Murphy and Jean Hampton (1988), working within an explicitly Christian framework, address the relationship of forgiveness to retribution in terms of a theory of channeling resentment. Of the two, Murphy (1988) takes the more radical position that resentment is appropriate "when forgiveness would be inconsistent with self-respect, respect for others, and for the moral order" (29) and that the "failure to resent moral injuries done to me is a failure to care about the moral value incarnate in my own person . . . and thus a failure to care about the very rules of morality" (18). Murphy seems to imply that forgiveness is therefore acceptable only when it is consistent with the rules of morality—when it is accompanied by redress of the wrong. Punishment of the wrong-

doer, on the other hand, is not merely vengeance or malice, since it is intended not to degrade the wrongdoer but merely to deny the gain accrued through the wrong and to vindicate the victim. A failure to punish, then, suggests a lack of respect for the value of the victim and a breakdown of the social, an inability to protect individuals from victimization.

8. For a very stimulating set of essays that analyze the relation of truth to justice theoretically, with a focus on South Africa, see the volume edited by Robert I. Rotberg and Dennis Thompson (2000).

9. This distinction between listening and observing was anticipated by Michel Foucault, who argued that "the subject in the discourse of eighteenth-century naturalists becomes exclusively a subject *looking* according to a grid of perceptions, and *noting* according to a code; it ceases to be a listening, interpreting, deciphering subject" (1991, 57).

10. Russian presence in the Caucasus offers an interesting example of the effect of the perception of active listening over political intervention. Initially, this presence destabilized relations among local communities, since it was perceived as a continuance of Soviet hegemony in the region. Later, the presence of Russian monitors helped stabilize the situation. My thanks to Gia Tarkhan-Mouravi for this insight.

11. To his critics, Archbishop Desmond Tutu, who headed South Africa's commission, responded that trials were not necessarily an effective way of establishing the truth or guilt, that they were too expensive, and that obtaining the necessary amount of evidence would have been impossible. Although the commission produced a public record of inestimable value for the future, the immediate response of most South Africans was most often skeptical or negative. The journalist Martin Meredith concludes: "For those whites hoping for a moment of catharsis, there was only bitter disappointment. For blacks, it was nothing more than they had expected" (1999, 320).

12. Schemes of distributive justice may also be integral to reconciliation, but here the policies of the old regime present a critical variable. Another key factor is the degree to which the aggrieved parties have attained social and political positions that enable them to extract redress or redistribution. East European and Soviet socialist regimes (unlike the South African apartheid regime or most recent Latin American dictatorships, to give rightist counterexamples) were initially motivated as redistributive responses to unjust distributions of wealth, which they tried to rectify by creating forms of public wealth. The demise of these regimes—along with the reintegration of their successor states into the capitalist world system—has generally meant a re-redistribution of public and private property and wealth from the historically less well off to the better off. The immediate legitimation of postsocialist states has appeared more contingent on the symbolic aspects of legal, democratic, and property reforms than on these new re-redistributive schemes.

13. The impossibility of being "external" was clearly revealed in the position of the U.S. Marines in Lebanon between 1982 and 1984, but one could just as well take the examples of peacekeeping operations in Somalia, Bosnia, or Kosovo.

5. The State of War Crimes following the Israeli-Hezbollah War

This essay was originally delivered as a paper at a conference, Justice in the Mirror: Law, Culture, and the Making of History, organized by Kamari Maxine Clarke and Mark Goodale at Yale University, December 8–9, 2006.

1. In this nomination, I am following many Lebanese scholars, in particular the legal scholar Chibli Mallat (2006), who first used the term in an August 4 *New York Times* editorial.

2. The following facts are based on these reports: UN Human Rights Council, *Report of the Commission of Inquiry on Lebanon,* UNHRC, 3d. Sess., UN Doc.A/HRC/3/2 (2006) [UN Human Rights Council, *Report*]; "Lebanon: UN de-miners hurt as agricultural damage from conflict hits $280 million," UN News Center (27 November 2006), online: www.un.org/apps/news/story.asp?destruction, or "'Collateral damage'? Israel attacks on civilian infrastructure," Amnesty International (23 August 2006), online: web.amnesty .org/library/index/engmde180072006. "Under fire: Hizbullah's attacks on northern Israel," Amnesty International (14 September 2006), online: web.amnesty.org/library/Index/ENGMDE020252006; "Timeline of the July War 2006" *The Daily Star* (10 November 2006), online: www.dailystar.com.lb/July_War06.asp; Reuven Erlich, "Hezbollah's use of Lebanese civilians as human shields," Intelligence and Terrorism Information Center for Special Studies American Jewish Congress (4 December 2006), online: www.ajcongress .org/site/PageServer?pagename=secret2.

3. I have not included the massive and professional attacks on the Lebanese civilian infrastructure, most of which are arguably not war crimes per se but are nonetheless important for my later argument of disproportionality. When the costs to the Lebanese economy for the entire bombardment are totaled, estimates go up to around $7 billion. The major issue here, as discussed later, is why Israel continued its devastating air campaign, especially the use of cluster munitions, for punitive reasons alone, after it had already deployed its army, and after which it was already clear that only its army could penetrate the labyrinth of tunnels and underground sites from which Hezbollah launched missiles. During the campaign, Israel's Air Force flew more than 12,000 combat missions. The Navy fired 2,500 shells, and the Army fired over 100,000 shells, destroying 400 miles of roads, 73 bridges, and 31 targets such as Beirut International Airport, ports, water and sewage treatment plants, electrical facilities, 25 fuel stations, and 900 commercial structures. As many as 350 schools, two hospitals, and approximately 15,000 homes were destroyed. Some 130,000 more homes were damaged. In an analysis along similar lines, Wesley Moore (2006) argues that the "facts," although generally agreed upon by many independent sources, are nonetheless not yet "evidence." Evidence, he argues, could only be established by an investigation of both sides for war crimes by an independent, high-level commission of inquiry with international experts on human rights law.

4. Nir Hasson and Meron Rapoport, "IDF admits targeting civilian areas in Lebanon with cluster bombs," *Haaretz,* (21 November 2006), online: www.Haaretz.com. The *Interim Report* of the Winograd Commission, released on April 30, 2007, charged with examining the "preparation and conduct of the political and the security levels" in the campaign, restricted its findings to the period leading up to the war and to the first six days: Israel, Ministry of Foreign Affairs, *The Interim Report of the Winograd Commission* (Ministry of Foreign Affairs, 2007), online: www.mfa.gov.il/MFA/Government Communiques/2007/Winograd+Inquiry+Commission+submits+Interim+Report+30 Apr-2007.htm [Winograd, *Report Interim*]. This limited focus relieved the commission of assessing responsibility for major violations—the excess violence on which this paper focuses—of conduct in the 33-day war, much of which occurred during the last two days of fighting.

5. The commission's mandate was limited to investigation of actions in Lebanon, though it recognized the importance of understanding "conduct . . . with reference to all of the belligerents." It was not authorized to investigate the actions by Hezbollah in Israel, though it does report damage done within Israel (UN Human Rights Council, *supra* note 2 at 16).

6. That said, Lebanese MP Ghassan Moukheiber, head of the Parliamentary Committee on Human Rights, is chairing a committee determined to sue Israel for war crimes. Several lawsuits have already been filed against Israel in Belgium, Germany, Canada and the U.S. On December 1, 2007, the UN Commission suggested that Israel be made to pay compensation for damages, especially losses incurred by civilians, by setting up an international compensation program similar to the one which has paid out billions of dollars to cover losses due to Iraq's 1990–91 invasion and occupation of Kuwait. As yet, Israel has paid nothing, though other countries have contributed what is called "aid."

7. Kofi Annan is cited in "Annan 'shocked' by Israeli attack on UN Lebanon post that killed at least 2," *UN News center* (25 June 2006) online: www.un.org/apps/news/story.asp?NewsID=19306&Cr=leban&Cr1. In the leaked testimony of Prime Minister Ehud Olmert before the Winograd Commission, Olmert admitted that the attack on Khiam was of major concern, and the commission, in turn, concluded that the prime minister's actions during the war "add up to a serious failure in exercising judgment, responsibility and prudence."

8. My analysis seeks to broaden the debate within both the legal-political and the anthropological discourses on human rights violations. Neither discourse takes up the issues presented in this paper. The legal-political discourse tends to focus on the politics of trying war crimes and not on their nature (see Bass 2001; Cassese 2003; Robertson 2003). Within anthropology, the focus has been either on war itself as a form of conflict or on human rights, without addressing human rights violations in the conduct of war. For recent work, see Kelley 2000; Wilson 1996.

9. For example, steady advancements in the regulation of war crimes are often followed by conflicts characterized by excessive cruelty and barbarity (e.g., the Crusades, the Thirty Years' War [1618–48], World War I, and World War II), and then again followed by periods of renewed attention to regulation.

10. Rome Statute of the International Criminal Court, 17 July 1998, A/Conf.183–9 (entered into force 1 July 2002).

11. Nasrallah's justifications for the abductions and the war that followed, like those of Israeli leaders, shifted over time. For a reliable source on the shifting legitimations on both sides, see Israel's leading English-language daily, *Haaretz,* online: www.haaretz.com/.

12. In specifying only the necessity of a cross-border conflict and not what kinds of actors are involved, Article 8 of the statute establishing the ICC does not restrict prosecution only to conflicts between states but includes any person or persons, military or civilian, involved in "armed conflict." Violations in internal conflicts for war crimes are typically limited to local (national) jurisdictions.

13. UN Human Rights Council, *supra* note 2 at 24–26. 14 ICC Statute, *supra* note 10 at Article 8.

14. ICC Statute, *supra* note 10 at Article 8.

15. See Horkheimer and Adorno 1972 [1944]; Conklin 1985.

16. The primary hope of Nuremberg was the prevention of war and not the regulation of its conduct. Still, there have been subsequent advances in regulating the conduct of war and in making excessive violence illegal, such as the Universal Declaration of Human Rights in 1948 and the Geneva Convention on the Laws and Customs of War in 1949, with its supplementary protocols in 1977. For arguments about the increased

brutality in modern war, see Falk, Gendzier, and Lifton 2006; Gutman and Rieff 1999; Kassimeris 2006; Neier 1998.

17. UN Human Rights Council *Report, supra* note 2 at 5. Because cluster bombs by nature explode indiscriminately and are therefore likely to harm civilians when used in densely populated areas, their use by Israel in the past has been controversial. Israel had (mis)used them in its 1982 invasion of Lebanon, after which the Reagan administration banned their export to Israel for six years.

18. For anthropological accounts, on Hezbollah, see Deeb 2006b; Norton 2007.

19. Yuval Yoaz, "IDF general leaving post over pre-war Hezbollah kidnappings," *Haaretz* (12 December 2006), online: www.haaretz.com/hasen/pages/ShArtVty.jhtml?sw =IDF+lebanon+discipine&itemNo=797160http://haaretz05/12/2006. Even before the end of the hostilities, on July 30, Kenneth Roth of Human Rights Watch had explicitly rejected this defense, "Just because the Israeli military warned the civilians of Qana to leave does not give it carte blanche to blindly attack. It still must make every possible effort to target only genuine combatants. Through its arguments, the Israeli military is suggesting that Palestinian militant groups might 'warn' all settlers to leave Israeli settlements and then be justified in targeting those who remained": "Israel Responsible for Qana Attack: Indiscriminate Bombing in Lebanon a War Crime," Human Rights Watch (30 July 2006), online: www.hrw.org/english/docs/2006/07/30/lebano13881.htm.

20. The Winograd *Interim Report, supra* note 4, while not referring specifically to these facts, does support this critical perspective, affirming that from the start the plans were "not set out clearly and carefully, [and the goals] over-ambitious and not feasible." Three weeks after the ceasefire ending the war, the Israeli Foreign Ministry set up a special legal team to provide protection for officers and officials involved in the conflict. Associated Press, Jerusalem, "Israel fears war crimes prosecution after Lebanon war," *The Associated Press* (4 September 2006), online: International Herald Tribune http://www .iht.com/articles/ap/2006/09/04/africa/ME_GEN_Israel_War_Crimes.php.

21. Human Rights Watch, which had issued a report during the conflict that criticized Israel for its indiscriminate use of violence against civilians, has been the object of particularly vicious attacks. See "Fatal Strikes: Israel's Indiscriminate Attacks Against Civilians in Lebanon," *Human Rights Watch* (3 August 2006) online: www.hrw.org/ reports/2006/lebanon0806/. Kenneth Roth, director of Human Rights Watch, was accused of everything from Jew-hating to "blood libel." See the defense of HRW by Aryeh Neier (2006), former heard of HRW.

22. Since forming in 1982, Hezbollah has attacked Israeli targets worldwide. The end of the Israeli occupation in 2000 did not stop its attacks on Israel. It then competed in elections, gaining 14 seats in parliament and two cabinet posts. Israel holds the Lebanese state responsible for Hezbollah's attacks (and the failure to disarm it, mandated by a United Nations resolution). UN Security Council Resolution 1559, issued on September 2, 2004, coauthored by France and the United States, called on all "foreign forces to withdraw from Lebanon" and "for the disbanding and disarmament of all Lebanese and non-Lebanese militias," including the military wing of Hezbollah. On January 23, 2006, the UN Security Council called on Lebanon to make more progress in controlling its territory and disbanding its militias. Hezbollah's relation with the Lebanese state—both a part of and a force subverting the state's authority—complicates its relations with other Lebanese parties and political organs and explains, in part, the inability of the Lebanese state to disarm it.

23. "Shooting without a Target," *Haaretz* (18 September 2006) online: www. haaretz .com/hasen/spages/762427.html.

24. The idea of the buffer zone as official Israeli policy dates back to the first occupation of south Lebanon. For a short history of this idea, see Joshua Mitnick, "A buffer zone in Lebanon? A flashback many Israelis don't like," *Christian Science Monitor* (7 August 2006), online: www.csmonitor.com/2006/0807/p10s01-wome.html.

25. A similar argument of equity is dismissed in the "Limaj Judgment." See Prosecutor v. Limaj, Bala, Musliu (2005), Case No. IT-03-66-T (International Tribunal for the Prosecution of Persons Responsible for Serious Violations of International Humanitarian Law Committed in the Territory of Former Yugoslavia since 1991). The tribunal argued that prosecution of members of the Kosovo Liberation Army was permissible for "crimes against humanity," despite the fact that both sides employed similar tactics (specifically, the targeting of civilians) in this international armed conflict.

26. The best research on the efficacy of prosecution for international human rights violations concerns Nazi Germany. Although most of these trials have been for genocide or crimes against humanity, not for war crimes, questions of their merit apply for all three kinds of violations. While such trials can and are evaluated from many perspectives, perhaps their most important and enduring legacy is the historical record established. See the excellent review of recent historical literature on Nazi trials and their impacts by Godu (2006).

For a comparative theoretical perspective on the place of legal trials in establishing accountability, see Borneman 1997.

27. The attempted politicization of such trials appears inevitable, yet as the international trials for Nazi crimes during the Cold War suggest, the effects of such politicization can be fought (and the spin counter-balanced). See the study by Weinke 2002.

28. A Lebanese public opinion poll conducted with Zogby International in November 2006 suggests that all sects agree that if anyone won the war it was Hezbollah, although Hezbollah's popularity immediately after the war increased only among the Shi'a population (see Telhami 2006). Telhami concludes that this war has increased sectarian polarization, which portends instability and is not in the interest of Israeli security.

29. See Detlev Mehlis, *Report of the International Independent Investigation Commission established pursuant to Security Council Resolution 1595 (2005)* UNICC (2005). Detlev Mehlis, of Germany, appointed in May of 2005 to head the UN Commission to investigate Hariri's murder, issued two reports before stepping down on December 15, 2005. A number of assassinations of Lebanese public figures critical of Syria occurred during his term. He was replaced, first, by Serge Brammertz of Belgium, and then by the Canadian Daniel Bellemare.

30. For example, it is difficult to construct an argument that the trial of Saddam Hussein has contributed to trust in the rule of law. In fact, his trial seems to have contributed to the general destabilization of Iraq. The attempted prosecution of Ariel Sharon in Belgium for the Sabra and Shatila massacre also seems to have had the immediate effect of strengthening support for him among Israeli Jews, while having little effect on creating any legal trust that might lead to resolving the conflict with Palestinians generally (see Borneman 2004c). This is not an argument against the prosecution of war crimes per se, however, but for a consideration of the many structural reasons why such prosecutions are so fraught with difficulty. These reasons include: (1) the rules of war

are partly laid down in written treaties between states for which there is no effective enforcement; (2) these rules consist partly of unwritten "international" customs subject to widely varying cultural interpretations (the problem of cultural/legal pluralism); and (3) the lack of agreement about the definition of war is exacerbated today by the problem of asymmetry between belligerents and the difficulty of defining them in contemporary conflicts. Many such conflicts are caused or perpetuated by the aggression of non-state actors in unstable groups who are not signatories to any treaties.

6. Terror, Compassion, and the Limits of Identification

1. J. M. Coetzee, *Disgrace* (New York: Penguin Books, 1999).

2. Much of my information on the military tribunals comes from defense lawyers. I especially thank George Assaf [jassaf@inco.lb] from the Human Rights division of the Lebanese Bar Association.

3. Lebanon has a history of opposition to the death penalty. Between 1972 and 1994, only one judicial execution was carried out. However, at least 13 people were executed after 1994, two of them publicly, justified as deterrence in the aftermath of the civil war. A moratorium was imposed in 1998 by Prime Minister Salim Hoss, who refused to sign any execution orders. In January 2004, however, executions resumed—three men, one by hanging, two by firing squad, convicted of murders.

4. See Major-General Franklin van Kappen, Report dated 1 May 1996 of the Secretary-General's Military Adviser concerning the shelling of the United Nations compound at Qana on 18 April 1996. A revised report issued by former UN Secretary General Boutros Ghali concluded that "while the possibility cannot be ruled out completely, it is unlikely that the shelling of the UNIFIL compound was the result of gross technical and/or procedural error." See also the eye-witness reporting by Robert Fisk, who was present the day after the killing (Fisk 2002, 673).

5. There is another possible understanding of the reference to Derrida in the dream, brought to my attention by Gregoire Mallard, whom I thank for the following interpretation. Since Ahmed is fluent in French, he may be following a set of linguistic associations and displacements in which he substitutes "Derrida" for *"se dérider,"* a verb that means to relax. When somebody disturbs you, or makes an offensive or threatening comment about you, you usually react by making an "angry face"; and in making that face, many wrinkles appear (wrinkles translates in French as *"rides"*). But when you realize that the comment was not meant to be threatening or offensive, you relax and your face "de-wrinkles" (literally translated, *"se dé-rider"*). Ahmed's invocation of Derrida may be about an attempt to relax in the face of the threat posed by the violent images of bodies in the film of a massacre. The other spectators in the screening are surprisingly nonplussed, but Ahmed may feel threatened by the violence resurfacing in light of my research on the topic, which I am asking him to witness. To make the images less offensive to me and alleviate my discomfort, *"Il se dérida"*: he relaxes.

6. Two years after Mohammed told me this story, this very same man was one of the three executed, in the first use of the death penalty in Lebanon in six years. See above, note 3.

7. Drawing boundaries around what to disclose in personal interactions in fieldwork encounters, one faces many of the same difficulties as does the therapist in the psychoanalytic relation between patient and therapist. An awareness of our roles in knowledge production and of the kind of knowledge to be produced will help us to be more honest

and to better assess, describe, and understand the meaning of experiences of terror as they are told. On processes of transference and counter-transference, see Freud 1912; Devereux 1967; Searles 1986; Borneman 2011).

7. Responsibility after Military Intervention

This paper was initially delivered at the workshop, "What Does Justice Demand after Military Intervention?" in the CES-Berlin Dialogues: Generations, Responsibilities, Obligations and Power series, sponsored by the Harvard Center for European Studies, November 2, 2002, Berlin, Germany.

1. Members of the Bush administration consistently refer to these two concepts, while redefining their meaning and relative weight in the light of what they see as a historic mission. For example, on August 4, 2002, in a widely reported speech from the family vacation home in Kennebunkport, Maine, President George W. Bush explained, "Our task and our responsibility to history is more than just an Al Qaeda network. We owe it to the future of civilization not to allow the world's worst leaders to develop and deploy, and therefore blackmail freedom-loving countries with the world's worst weapons." "I'm a patient man," he continued. "I've got a lot of tools at my disposal. But I can assure you, I understand history has called us into action. And this country will defend freedom no matter what the cost." For more detailed analyses of Bush's statements, see Lewis 2002; Merken 2002; and Milbank 2002.

2. For documentation of these lies, see the series of columns by the Nobel Prize–winning economist Paul Krugman in the *New York Times* over the past two years (www.nytimes.com).

3. The Bush administration points to a similar fact, that Saddam Hussein used such weapons "against his own people," to place Hussein in the "Axes of Evil." Although American and Iraqi government motives for such use were opposite—Hussein wanted to kill those citizens; the U.S. government wanted to test the effects of certain weapons so as to use them effectively later against its external enemies—the willingness to "use weapons of mass destruction" on one's own citizens, which is the purported issue, was in fact shared.

4. It is also important to consider the significance of the mode of the leader's death (suicide, hanging, execution, trial) as it relates to how a regime ends. See Borneman 2003.

5. For new historiographical emphasis on rupture, see Dower 1999 as well as Jarausch and Geyer 2003.

6. Perhaps the primary strategic worry of military intervention is that it will destabilize the entire Mideast. Some in the administration appear to want such destabilizing, at least in the short-term, for it may create the momentum for other regime changes in the region. The opposing view is that it will set off a chain of reactions—secession movements, religious wars, fights for control of resources—that, once started, create their own dynamic of rebounding violence.

7. Debates about human rights are very relevant to this argument, though I see the rule of law, not as equal to, but as prior to and necessary for, the functioning of a human rights regime. See Ignatieff 2001.

8. In his "What I learned in Bosnia," Paddy Ashdown writes, "In Bosnia we thought that democracy was the highest priority, and we measured it by the number of elections we could organize. The result . . . is that the people of Bosnia have grown weary of voting. . . . In hindsight, we should have put the establishment of the rule of law first,

for everything else depends on it: a functioning economy, a free and a fair political system, the development of civil society, public confidence in police and the courts."

9. Under the French Mandate, a census was done in 1932, after which a National Pact assigned power along sectarian lines: parliamentary seats were divided between Christians and Muslims on a six to five basis, with a Maronite (Christian) president, a Sunnite (Muslim) prime minister, a Shi'ite (Muslim) speaker of the house. Because of the fear of upsetting this "balance" (an increasingly smaller number of Christians and increasingly larger number of Shi'ites), the state has not risked a census since.

10. Following the Syrian-driven amendment of the constitution to allow Emile Lahoud to retain the presidency and the assassination of former Prime Minister Rafiq Harriri, Chibli Mallat declared his candidacy for president—a bold attempt to introduce nonsectarian principles (of individual candidacy) into the electoral system of representation. Mallat's campaign received much media attention in the Arab (and Western) world but had difficulty generating support among the different sects.

8. Does the United States Want Democratization in Iraq?

1. *Kulturkreislehre,* an ethnological concept developed by Leo Frobenius in 1898 and subsequently taken up as a research paradigm in German and Austrian schools, theorized that similar cultural traits in different sites likely came from the same source (*Urkultur:* original culture). In theorizing the export of political form in this chapter, I hope to avoid two of the most telling criticisms of this concept: that the diffusion of cultural traits is teleological and follows evolutionary developments, and that all diffusion follows from a single source rather than multiple sources that then converge in what appears to be a single process. My assumption here is that while democratic form has spread, its content varies radically. On the world distribution of political form and the diffusion of democracy between 1946 and 1995, see Gleditsch and Ward 1999, 2000.

2. Historians are quick to emphasize that the eighteenth-century European romance with and rediscovery of Athenian democracy often overlooked the fact that Athenians thought of democracy as a form specifically for themselves, not something to export, a form unsuited for organizing the polity of non-Greeks (so-called "barbarians"). For an overview of questions from political theory addressed to Athenian democracy, see Ober and Hedrick (1996). Sammons (2004) makes the argument that while Americans are deluded by an inaccurate image of Athens, American democracy in fact shares some of the same fundamental flaws, such as a religious-like obsession with voting and a tendency for elected officials to engage in demagoguery.

3. The title of this essay recalls Freud's famous comment: "The great question that has never been answered and which I have not yet been able to answer, despite my thirty years of research into the feminine soul, is 'What does a woman want?'" (cited in Ernst Jones, *Sigmund Freud: Life and Work* (1955), vol. 2, chap. 16). Both questions are, of course, unanswerable, permitting only a variety of interpretations of what "wanting" means, because the real question concerns the unstable trajectory of desire and the resulting configuration of identification and satisfaction.

4. In Wilson's famous speech before Congress, his primary reference was to the "sovereignty" of the "people" as a necessary condition for peace and freedom. He used the word "democracy" only once, with reference to the "Russian representatives [who] have insisted, very justly, very wisely, and in the true spirit of modern democracy . . ." Post–World War II foreign policy responses were, above all, framed by anticommunism.

Republican administrations were generally more selective in their support of democracy. The Eisenhower administration, for example, argued strongly for democracy in Germany but also channeled generous secret aid through the CIA to Japan, in support of a one-party democracy, enabling the National Liberal Party to rule without anything but token opposition from 1949 to 1993.

5. For a historical sketch of American anthropology's relation with the foreign, see Borneman 1995, 663–71.

6. See www.whitehouse.gov/news/releases/2003/11/20031106-2.html.

7. Ajami (2006), among others, has argued that regime change itself was the gift. L. Paul Bremer III, head of the ill-fated Coalition Provisional Authority, wrote in his memoir that Bush was seriously interested only in whether the leaders in the Iraqi governments to follow the CPA would publicly show their gratitude to the United States (cf. Bremer and McConnell 2006; Galbraith 2006).

8. For many on the Left and Right, this age of immigration is at an end; hence the goal of securing the borders and punishing those—largely Hispanics—who try to enter.

9. See the Public Opinion Poll conducted jointly by the Anwar Sadat Chair for Peace and Development at the University of Maryland and Zogby International, from May 2004, which surveys six Arab countries (www.bsos.umd.edu/SADAT/pub/Arab%20 Attitudes%20Towards%20Political%20and%20Social%20Issues,%20Foreign%20Policy %20and%20the%20Media.htm, accessed August 20, 2006); and the Pew Global Attitudes Project survey from June 22, 2006, which surveys Muslim attitudes worldwide rather than the Arabs or Middle East residents alone (http://pewglobal.org/reports/display .php?ReportID=253, accessed August 20, 2006).

10. Claude Lefort (1986, 215) identifies fears of incompleteness and lack of unity as the major threats to totalitarian orders, which, in response to the problem of intrinsic division in democracy, create the fiction of People-as-One. The bourgeois order in a democracy tries to solve this problem of division by institutionalizing an idea of the opposition as necessary, most specifically in the concepts "division of powers" and "parliamentary opposition" (Borneman 2002b). The Bush administration responded to the idea of the bourgeois order by claiming to represent the People-as-One at the same time as it identified all internal and external opposition as People who are incarnations of evil. When an opposition forms among the People, the former God—the People—turns into a devil and reappears in many guises.

11. The absurdity of exchanging the People was the point of Bertolt Brecht's satirical poem, "Die Lösung" (The Solution), published after his death, about the 1953 workers' uprising in East Berlin, "Wäre es da/Nicht doch einfacher, die Regierung/Löste das Volk auf und/Wählte ein anderes?" (Would it not be easier/In that case for the government/ To dissolve the People/And elect another?).

12. See Nicholas Lemann, "The Next World Order," *New Yorker,* April 1, 2002.

13. Feb. 12, 2002, Department of Defense news briefing (www.brainyquote.com/ quotes/quotes/d/donaldrums148142.html, accessed April 3, 2004).

14. On March 11, 2002, its director, Tom Ridge, introduced the Homeland Security Advisory, "to warn all levels of government, law enforcement and the general public about the risk of terrorist attacks in the United States. The system is a multi-colored five-level indicator of the current level of risk. Each level (called a Threat Condition) designates a set of suggested 'Protective Measures' that organizations are advised to take." Other government departments soon weighed in. In mid-July 2002, the Justice Department

proposed a Terrorism Information and Prevention System to recruit up to one in every 25 Americans as domestic informants (subsequently not approved). On February 23, 2004, Education Secretary Rod Page identified the National Education Association, the nation's largest teacher union, as a "terrorist organization (see www.pbs.org/newshour/terrorism/ata/ashcroft_12-6.html; www.smh.com.au/articles/2002/07/14/1026185141232.html; www.usatoday.com/news/washington/2004-02-23-paige-remarks_x.htm; www.cdi.org/terrorism/alerts.cfm).

15. To be sure, the position of Michael Doyle, who was most frequently cited on this, is more nuanced than those of many of his followers. In the very same essay where Doyle makes this claim about democracy's link to peace, he also argues that democracies tend to be belligerent to non-democracies (cf. Doyle 1983).

16. In some of the first in-depth interviews with the first large division of soldiers returning from Iraq one year after the invasion, only a few dared express serious doubts about the legitimacy and necessity of the war. Most expressed loyalty to the cause of "liberating a tortured nation." For example, the night before he left for Iraq, Pfc. Jesse Givens, who was killed in service, explained to his six-year-old son, "There's a bad guy over there and he hurts mommies and little kids and he has to be stopped" (Span 2004).

17. Of course, the effort to install democracy is and always has been strategic and selectively deployed. For example, there has been no such attempt in Pakistan or Egypt, both authoritarian police states heavily dependent on U.S. support, and in 2006 the administration supported Israeli demolition of Lebanese democracy.

18. Another way of understanding the distinctiveness of the American understanding of law is to point to the different commitments to procedures and substance. While Americans tend to consider procedures, anchored in the Constitution, as stable, they are flexible in attitudes toward issues of substance (I thank Lawrence Rosen for this insight). The administration's pragmatism about substance (that law belongs to whoever controls it, or controls the procedures), in other words, is expressed in its ambivalence about any legal principles that it considers obstacles to the War-on-Terror-without-End. That is, the Bush administration, and the American Right generally, has abandoned any commitment to the principles of the Rule of Law, which would set limits on the use of procedures to undermine the substance of any particular law and might therefore limit the exercise of executive authority.

19. The Bush administration has been breathtakingly skilled at ideological dissimulation and linguistic free play, saying one thing and doing the exact opposite—claiming to protect trees by clear-cutting forests, saving Medicaid by ending it as an entitlement program, promising to leave "no child behind" while slashing financial support for education, claiming to reduce smog and mercury emissions as well as to stop acid rain by delaying required emission and pollution control upgrades—not to speak of the twisted and misleading information—the imminent threat of a "mushroom cloud"—employed to justify the necessity of an invasion of Iraq to eliminate its weapons of mass destruction. Such consistent, purposeful misnaming has the Orwellian effect of making representation unaccountable and reducing language to babble.

20. To be sure, from the beginning of the occupation there were efforts within Iraq to use the register of law, for example, the 2004 international assistance from at least five countries to the Regime Crimes Adviser's Office to prepare for likely genocide trials against Saddam Hussein and his closest associates. But such efforts pale in the face of an occupation through a war begun on false pretenses that continued under conditions

without international and domestic solidarity. Above all, the privatization of security and granting of immunity from legal prosecution of private contractors (like the infamous Blackwater) construed the relationship to law as one of convenience in the hands of the occupiers. In this context, one could not expect the register of the Father, division, justice, and accountability, to serve as a balance or corrective to the People's giddy excess.

21. Within hours of signing the new constitution, on March 9, 2004, Abdel Aziz al-Hakim, leader of the Supreme Council for the Islamic Revolution in Iraq at the time, stated this most eloquently: "In this law, we can see that there is an absence of the people's will" (cited in Burns 2004). Indeed, where is the evidence, if not in a new constitution, of the people's will? Hakim would likely suggest in the separate leaderships of religio-tribal groupings. Not that the new Iraqi constitution by itself could ever create the conditions for the Rule of Law or "people's will," as anyone who worked in the East-Central Europe during the Cold War knows. Possible interpretations and means of enforcement are never contained within the document; they require framing and enforcement, and a kind of modeling that the United States, with its post–World War II tradition of civil and human rights and support for supranational legal-making bodies, could have provided.

9. The External Ascription of Defeat and Collective Punishment

1. I am indebted here to the pathbreaking work of Schivelbusch (2003), the only comparative history, to my knowledge, that focuses on collective defeat. This essay hopes to bring more into focus the importance of external ascription and the way collective punishment articulates with the acknowledgment of defeat.

2. The Nuremberg Trials occasioned a lively debate among philosophers about the nature of collective moral responsibility. Writing in 1948, the British scholar H. D. Lewis, perhaps the strongest opponent of this concept, argued that one should not merge individual moral responsibility with that of all other fellow group members, for this makes it unnecessary to consider the intentionality of the individual as the legitimate basis for moral blame. Failure to value what individual intentionally brings about undermines any sense we have of personal accountability (Lewis 1991).

3. Gawrych (2000) argues that the clear-cut and quick victory in the 1967 "Six Day War" left the Israelis unprepared for the war in 1973, which then followed the course of most serial wars, more protracted and with more casualties on both sides. His major point, however, is that the loser in 1967 (Egypt) had learned by 1973, and achieved a political victory (its leader even received a Nobel Peace Prize), knowing that military victory or defeat alone says little about its long-term meaning, that is, how to transform defeat or victory into political ends after the cessation of military conflict.

Jacqueline Rose (2007) has argued that it is the shame of the Holocaust that is repressed by contemporary Israeli Jews, then resurfaces as an enacted punishment of the Palestinians for this repressed shame. We might add to her formulation the critical role of the proclaimed victory of 1967, which precisely rereads the Israelis both as no longer victims but also as potential victims forever even in their new homes. Any cursory knowledge of Israel reveals a plethora of publications right after the 1967 war and continuing up to the present narrating the '67 war as a victory. A sample of titles from 1967 (including only those in English, not the larger group in Hebrew): *The Victory: the Six-Day War of 1967* (Zmora 1967), *Swift Sword: The Historical Record of Israel's Victory, June 1967* (Marshall 1967), *Mission Survival: The People of Israel's Story in Their*

Own Words, from the Threat of Annihilation to Miraculous Victory (Bondy 1968). Benny Morris (2001) and others have written critically about the crucial role of this war, that this victory made Israel into its present aggressor state: self-absorbed, convinced of its chosenness and invincibility.

4. The idea of a Palestinian collective is complicated by the larger Arab collective, to which Palestinians undoubtedly belong but which acts largely outside their control. Both the Israeli and Arab states frequently instrumentalize and even hijack the Palestinian cause for their own purposes. I thank Kirsten Idriss, who alerted me to this fact.

10. What Do Election Rituals Mean?

1. On succession to high office in anthropology, see Goody (1966). On elections as "a procedure for aggregating preferences," see the excellent entry by W. J. M. Mackenzie (1986, 1–6). Since he argues that elections are a modern means of conferring legitimacy, he is critical of their export to countries where they are used for purposes other than that. Hence he also makes the important distinction between election as a means to legitimate assignment of a person to an office of authority (the object of my analysis) and as procedures to vote on propositions (e.g., referendums), where the legitimacy of rule itself is not the issue.

2. The following argument draws from Borneman (2002b, 3–25; 2004a, 63–103).

3. By democracy, I am following the minimalist conception put forth by Joseph Schumpeter (1942) that designates democracies as systems in which rulers are selected by competitive elections. Robert Dahl (1971, 8) has argued that other conditions—such as the equal access of candidates to voters, time off to vote, minimal living standards, competitive candidates, independent judiciaries, the rule of law—may also be necessary in order to guarantee that elections are fair and competitive. In a volume edited by Shapiro and Hacker-Cordon (1999), the contributors explicate these other conditions and the tensions between democracy and justice, equality, efficiency, and freedom. Przeworski (1999, 51), in this same volume, argues that democracies are more likely to "survive in wealthy countries . . . when no single political force dominates," and "when voters can choose rulers through elections." The argument I develop here is that in the creation of the modern collective, the ideal, even if met only in a minimalist empirical form, has the potential to institutionalize a form of sacrifice, the self-sacrifice of the ruler, that replaces the two other forms of substitute sacrifice (of sons or scapegoats).

4. In fact, today it is highly contentious, if not impossible, to constitute the German *Volk* through a substitute sacrifice other than the archaic form, and when such sacrifices are occur—as in the periodic persecution and murder of immigrants—they provoke a questioning of the sense and purpose of the Germans as a people, a discussion on the legitimacy of a *Volksgemeinschaft* and about possible (post-national) alternatives to this form of community. In other words, such substitute sacrifice disintegrates the social instead of re-substantializing it. See Borneman 2002b, 3–25; 2003, 197–206.

5. Unlike a religious order in which "the elect" claim to be chosen by a god (to whom the elect have unique access), modern secular elections assume the People elect their leaders in a ritual, periodically repeated so that these leaders are subject to recall by the People. The key principle at stake in a *democratic* election is that the ruler or ruling party regularly risks being replaced; the longer the incumbent person or party remains in power, the less "democratic" a regime becomes. Systems theorist Niklas Luhmann (1990, 139) has explicated the regime particularity of the relation between

ruler and ruled, arguing that democracy distinguishes itself by a particular code, ruling party/opposition: "perhaps the most important invention [in avoiding the arbitrariness of rule and control and in delimiting the domain of politics] resides in the institution of parliamentary representation with allowable opposition as the basis of the choice of government." The ruling party remains legitimate only to the extent that it maintains itself as distinct from a viable opposition. If societal interests and issues become political, they are taken up through this code, of government and opposition, which cannot be questioned if the political form is to be nominated as "democratic."

Following the logic of this form, the governed, or "the People," are necessarily separated from the state during everyday life, but they must re-enter the life of the state through the process of delegation in ritual elections. They enter as disaggregated monads, individuals who can rethink—independent of enduring ties of alliance or affinity—the choice between ruling party and opposition. Democratic states, then, must hold in tension the notion that the People both precede the state (the state lives for them) and are empty (a void needing to be continually reconstituted as an intersubjective group). Elections perform the work of constitution ritually, much like Van Gennep (1960) talks about initiation rites generally, by dissolving the people in order to reconstitute them as the symbolic focus of democratic government (of, by, and for the people).

For a single day, the group dissolves itself as a unity into a display of signs of difference and social division, and individuals are reduced to their "atomistic selves" and freed, if only for a utopian moment, from the totalizing pressures of all social groups and identifications. As Claude Lefort (1986, 303) puts it in his masterly analysis of democratic revolution: "The body politic was decapitated" and "the corporeality of the social was dissolved." To extend his insight to election day: the head is put in limbo, if not removed and replaced, and the social body dissolved. Building on Lefort's analysis, Slavoj Zizek (1989, 147–49) argues that democratic elections distinguish themselves from those in totalitarian systems (what he calls "organized democracy") in that the latter excludes "the irruption of the Real," the moment of social dissolution that risks random, "irrational" outcomes and reveals "the People" as the Lacanian Real, an empty site that resists symbolization. My difference with Zizek is only to insist that, for democratic elections, the risk of randomness in outcome is not itself sufficient over time to prevent "organized democracy" unless it actually results in periodic sacrifice, that is, random turn-taking.

6. Following the election, the symbolic focus has been transformed from "the people as rulers" to the "delegates of the people" who now rule them. In an influential essay, Pierre Bourdieu (1991, 204) analyzes this function of political "delegation" as a universal process of dispossession: "Individuals . . . cannot constitute themselves (or be constituted) as a group, that is, a force capable of making itself heard, of speaking and being heard, unless they dispossess themselves in favor of a spokesperson." His point, true for all political forms except direct democracy, is that political groups such as parties obtain their power to represent the individual through an act of willed dispossession.

If we situate delegation within the specific electoral ritual process of different types of regimes, however, then the meaning of the operation of "dispossession" varies by political form. In all forms today, the dispossession of voters through delegation of their power to a representative occurs through periodic elections. But in democratic regimes, these elections initially dissolve the social into individual monads and thereby deliver back to the individual his or her authority, which means an opportunity to hold the delegate accountable. This is certainly a different and superior form of constructing representation to that in non-democratic regimes, where there are no accountability mechanisms other than to the ruler or ruling class. The major and perhaps most significant difference neglected by Bourdieu is that delegation in democracies articulates with principles of accountability that apply to the delegates. Bourdieu writes, "Consecration of an official marks a magical act of 'institution,' a transmission of political capital, 'investiture.' The institution invests in those who have invested in the institution, to which they owe everything. They were nothing outside the institution, now they cannot deny the institution without purely and simply denying themselves" (1991, 195). This description holds for delegates in a system where there is no institutionalized system of "recall" or accountability—no obligatory sacrifice or turn-taking. Formal principles of accountability have developed as the "rule of law," and they are embodied in codes that democratic political forms cannot do without (see Borneman 1997).

Many political scientists also understand elections as accountability mechanisms, but they tend to define accountability in terms of the functions of delegation and not sacrifice. For example, in an edited book by Manin, Przeworski, and Stokes (1999), the contributors examine the responsiveness or representativeness of the new rulers to the preferences of the voters by analyzing the connections between democratic institutions such as elections, and the way in which governments act. They ask whether governments are "responsive," "representative," or "accountable" to the preferences of an electorate after having won an election, and they assume that there should be a connection between "voter preferences" and the policy outcomes of the electoral victor—in other words, that voter preferences are based on rational and instrumental motives rather than the expression of motives not consciously unavailable to them. Despite obvious limitations to what elections do, preferences may often be structured on the satisfaction of sacrifice: either scapegoating or the promise to replace more conventional forms of substitute sacrifice. In those cases, the meaning and legitimating potential of elections to voters is not primarily indexed by the relation between voter preferences and actual policy.

7. The major question among post–World War II American political scientists has been to explain incumbency in the U.S. Congress, which is framed as an "advantage" that has increased from 3.4 percent in the 1950s to 8.0 percent in the 1980s. In the last two decades of the twentieth century, over 90 percent of all incumbents in the U.S. House of Representatives were reelected. The focus, then, is not turn-taking but on delegation: why people "choose"—rationally—the same delegates. One study found the major advantage to be the increased ability "to deter high-quality challengers" (see Levitt and Wolfram 1997, 45–46). Another study focused on how the "arrangements" or "voting methods," by which they mean how expressed "preferences"—the vote—for delegates are mathematically calculated (proportional or simple plurality, approval voting, etc.). The conclusion: that these methods do matter in determining "fair and coherent group choices" (see Schepsle and Bonchek 1997, 166).

Much effort has also gone into econometric analysis, on establishing that economic events affect voting behavior, not mono-causally but in contingently predictive ways (see Kramer 1971; Fair 1996). Another study concludes that most of the incumbency advantage is due to factors other than the "personal vote" (having already represented voters in the past), but that the personal vote nonetheless becomes more important as party strength declines. Also, incumbents "develop larger personal votes when they are most vulnerable electorally." Once elected, however, candidates are increasingly "unresponsive to changes in their districts' ideological preferences" (see Ansolabehere, Snyder, and Stewart 2000: 17–34). Based on ethnographic research, Fenno (1977) concludes that representatives do pay attention to their home districts and not merely to their congressional or party constituencies—a trend toward marginalization of party machines that has since accelerated. All of these studies elide the question of what elections mean, given the general absence of regularized turn-taking, the lack of a periodic sacrifice. Their findings about the United States, then, are consistent with my own on the Middle East, that elections as they are being employed foster cynicism and lend themselves to becoming a tool to legitimate a new authoritarianism, a "technique" used not to measure "preferences" but to manipulate choice and mislead voters.

The "Americanization" of campaign consultancy outside the United States is well documented, with most analysts citing Joseph Napolitano, founder of both the American Association of Political Consultants and the International Association of Political Consultants, as the first private U.S. consultant to work abroad (in the 1969 campaign of Ferdinand Marcos in the Philippines). Before that, in the 1950s, CIA director John Foster Dulles sent many of his operatives to run or influence election campaigns throughout the world. Although most of these early consultants may have been anti-democratic in political orientation, this is no longer the case. At the end of the Cold War, following the opening of the Berlin Wall in 1989, many progressive, pro-democratic activists, such as George Soros, financed the use of consultants abroad to influence the decisive transformation or reform of many "frozen" political systems (see Bonner 1987; Bowler and Farrell 2000, 153–74; Chua 2004).

The question that is not asked is whether this infusion of American experts into the electoral systems of other countries has insidiously spread the ideology of enlightened false consciousness. Many of the techniques used involve "spinning" a candidate's past so as to make it unrecognizable or even to invert the actual facts. For example, in the Ukraine in elections in September 2007, American strategists (who worked for all sides), led by Paul Manafort Jr., once a senior aide to prominent Republicans, slickly transformed Viktor Yanukovich, a former Kremlin pawn and major opponent of any system changes in 2004, into a pro-Western, anti-corruption reformer.

8. My understanding of and distinction between magic and religion owes much to others, especially to several conversations with Parvis Ghassem-Fachandi and Abdellah Hammoudi. To begin, I am relying on a formulation first made by E. B. Tylor (1970) and Sir James Frazer (1911) of the affinity of magic and science as against religion. Working with this assumption of magic as a "primitive science," Marcel Mauss (2001, 17) notes, "Magic gives every outward appearance of being a gigantic variation on the theme of the principle of causality." In other words, the staging of elections to produce delegates is a magical process that, with the contemporary contribution of knowledge from political science, leads to perfecting the causal techniques of delegation. It is solely oriented to empirical outcomes (producing a winner), rather than to reconstituting a transcendent (people).

Mauss is also concerned with how historically magic becomes "contaminated by religion—has borrowed figures of gods and demons from magic" (2001, 17). Along the same lines, Bronislaw Malinowski, who instead grouped magic together with religion, nonetheless made the distinction between magic as a practical, technical activity, and religious rites, which had to do with ultimate values such as Providence and Immortality. Finally, I take from Hubert and Mauss (1981, 13) their insistence that sacrifice is fundamentally "a religious act," if not constitutive of religion in the rite itself. The efficacy of sacrifice, they argue, lies in "the mediation of a victim"—which, in the case of political elections, is the ruler/ruling party—"that is, of a thing that in the course of the ceremony is destroyed" (1981, 97). Destroyed, and then, as Freud argued, re-incorporated into the social along with a renunciation of the initial violence. Political elections, in the sense that I am proposing here, as following the archaic or Icelandic solution to sacrifice, do not become expiatory sacrifices unless there is a turn back to, or incorporation of, the two subsequent forms of sacrifice (sons or scapegoats). See Tylor 1970 [1877]; Frazer 1911 [1890]; Mauss 2001 [1902]; Hubert and Mauss 1981 [1898]; Freud 1950.

9. Irregularities (and alleged illegalities) in procedure periodically surface in American electoral cycles, especially when the outcome is in doubt, in other words, when there is a real potential for turn-taking. Most recently, many Democrats claimed that the 2000 election—in which Al Gore won the popular vote but George W. Bush the electoral college—was stolen (and decided by the Supreme Court by stopping vote recounts in Florida). Three strategies of cynical manipulation were apparent: (1) pre-election voter disenfranchisement through denial and misprinting of ballots; (2) election-day voter intimidation through selective denial of voting rights, shifting precinct registrations, and shortage and malfunction of ballots or voting machines; and (3) post-election subversion of counting or recounting of ballots and computer fraud. Republicans tended to focus on issues of "voter fraud"—voting by people inappropriately registered or unregistered to vote (meaning, on the whole, minorities, recent immigrants, the poor, or elderly with improper documentation); Democrats, on issues of voter intimidation and disenfranchisement. After the election, the Bush administration dismissed or removed from office twelve U.S. attorneys, motivated, as documents published afterward suggested, by their unwillingness to vigorously pursue allegations of voter fraud that might be critical to Republican electoral success (Callahan and Minnite 2003; Eggen and Goldstein 2007; Johnston 2007; Urbina 2007). The technical manipulation of electoral procedures in order to engineer a specific outcome is evidence of what I am identifying as an authoritarian turn.

10. One of the paradoxical side effects of the professionalization of campaigning, apparent above all in the United States, is that the heavy "message-oriented" campaigns tend to "de-align" voters from their traditional loyalties, making the process of candidate selection seem more random and volatile. The process of reducing voters to isolated monads is expedited, which should in theory foster less predetermined outcomes. While campaign consultants may intend to produce a predictable outcome (a win for the incumbent), the effect of perfecting a "message" that appeals to both a loyal "base" and uncommitted voters ends up leaving all voters in doubt with no good reason to adhere to any particular candidate or party (see Artenton 1992). Needless to say, cynical reasoning is the easiest resolution of this doubt, with voters frequently choosing abstractly or based on emotional reactions to spun messages and misinformed on the issues, given the randomness of candidate differences in messages.

11. The instrumental conception of magic that I rely on here has since been complicated by many others, especially with regard to its performative aspects. Tambiah (1990, 71), for example, calls for an appreciation of magical practices within ritual orders, and he draws special attention to the power of language in these practices. Magical words and incantations, he argues, cannot be reduced to pragmatic effects, but instead we should seek to understand the "interlacing of magical and technical acts to form an amalgam." My concern has been to understand how this "amalgam" enters into a secular ritual with quasi-religious functions.

12. Unlike in the Middle East, the last several decades in Latin American have been witness to a series of incumbent defeats—electoral turn-taking that runs counter to a tradition of entrenched rule by parasitic elites. By the 1990s, many Latin American countries were already rejecting their military/authoritarian rulers and embracing a palette of democratic reforms. The first in this new wave, in December 1998 in Venezuela, was the landslide victory (56%) of the populist Hugo Chavez, elected largely on a promise to redistribute the country's oil wealth in social programs that benefit the poor. Then came the even larger victory (61%) of the left-wing candidate in Brazil's presidential election, Luiz Inacio Lula da Silva, in October 2002. Three years later, in December 2005, Bolivians, with a large majority (54%), elected Evo Morales, a former union executive and social activist, as the first indigenous head of state in Latin America since the Spanish Conquest. Then in November 2006, leftist economist Rafael Correa was elected Ecuador's president, with over 57 percent of the vote. The movement toward democratization of the political systems of the region seems incontrovertible, yet these trends are reversible unless a functional multi-party system is institutionalized. Already Hugo Chavez, who, with over 60 percent of the vote, was elected for a third term in December 2006, flirts with a party dictatorship. His continued success has much to do with the conjoining of cynical reason and elections on the Left.

13. The fact that, in the last four decades, elections have been used largely to support authoritarianism in the Middle East and are largely rigged to favor incumbents has little to do with either the nature of Islamic beliefs or the lack of receptivity to democratic institutions of Arab culture. Muslims and Arabs desire to vote and select delegates as much as do people of other faiths or atheists, and they want to be able to recall these delegates, even those who might claim religious authority. Rather, as many analysts have explained, the dominance of "rentier economies" makes ruling elites less dependent on the taxation of citizens than on external and international sources of wealth, such as the sale of oil, foreign aid, and tourism. Both these native ruling elites and the foreign elites with whom they exchange wealth have a strong interest in stability of rulership; periodic elections quiet whatever qualms the publics of the foreign elites have about the political legitimacy of their trading partners. Thus, on the one hand, citizen participation is blocked or limited because it endangers the elite's direct control over resources and their distribution; and on the other hand, citizens, who pay few taxes and tend to be punished for civic participation outside their families or tribal affiliations, are less motivated to seek resources through political participation (see Beblawi 1987; Mahdavi 1970; and Pripstein-Posusney and Angrist 2005).

14. www.whitehouse.gov/news/releases/2003/11/20031106-2.html.

15. See Scott Bobb 2000; Watani 2007.

16. This high percentage of support is suspicious in light of the dramatic drop in the percentage of people voting. Three months earlier, the government reported a 57 percent turnout in a constitutional referendum, while the official count in the much more important presidential election was 23 percent. With 6,000 domestic monitors and more than 200 foreign reporters, the government in fact did reduce its "cheating and lying margins," reported Saad Ibrahim (2005), but still we cannot account for 10 million fewer voters going to the polls.

17. Elections are also rituals of excess that involve ever-increasing expenditures of wealth and large armies of volunteers, hired spin-doctors, consultants, and pollsters to run a "campaign." Especially in the United States, each campaign season begins early

and is socially elaborated, requiring ever-greater public and private expenditures of time and resources. The empirical cost of elections is also largely driven by the need to employ new visual technologies in staging events. That the content of elections appears to be less significant than the form, with electoral rhetoric often becoming merely a series of repeated platitudes, corresponds to a tendency observed in much ritual: the emptying of meaning through the institutionalization of repetition. The repetition occurs at two levels: the incumbent staying in power, and the political oratory (the "vision thing") based on comfortable homilies, messages spun to minimize differences between candidates or, inversely, to represent a false and impossible clarity of position. Hence, while success is measured by winning, electoral efficacy and democratic legitimation may be denied unless the election is true to the form of the performance: a form that requires the production of both a leader or ruling party (winner) and an opposition (loser) who acknowledge that this ritual of excess has regenerated the social.

18. See also Hammer and Spolar 2005.

19. See Shadid 2007.

20. Needless to say, democracy is always an unstable form, reliant as it is on referencing the mysterious and necessarily empty collective, "the People." But the authoritarian turn within democratic form is a new configuration of power that emerged in all continents at approximately the same time: the United States' "unitary executive," China's party dictatorship, Berlusconi's media empire-driven populism in Italy, Chavez's single-party populist socialism in Venezuela, Russian state dictatorship. Even when this turn ebbs, it remains significant as a structural possibility within democracy.

11. Politics without a Head

1. The research for this article is based on the separate experiences of Borneman and Senders at the Love Parade and was undertaken in the context of fieldwork projects on other topics. Borneman attended festivities in 1989, 1992, 1995–98. Senders attended in 1995.

2. Situating native exegesis in explanation of ritual has a long history in anthropological analysis. See especially Victor Turner (1977, 93–113), who interpreted the symbolism of Ndembu ritual through the eyes, and exegesis, of a very talented native; and the sympathetic critique of his work by Hammoudi (1993, 99–107).

3. Church membership in Germany has been declining for decades, with a dramatic post-unification decline in the West. Since unification, the Evangelical Church, Germany's largest Protestant church, has been losing approximately 300,000 members yearly. The Roman Catholic Church has been losing around 160,000 members yearly. Even before unification, 70 percent of all East Germans did not belong to a denomination (Lazar and Karst 1997, 6).

4. Both postwar German states made clear distinctions between politics and entertainment because of the legacy of National Socialist abuse of entertainment for political purposes. Nonetheless, the domain of entertainment expanded immensely in West Germany after the war, largely drawn from the U.S. entertainment industry.

5. See websites for Lollapalooza: www.lollapalooza.com (March 15, 1998), and the Grateful Dead: www.grateful.dead.net (March 15, 1998).

6. Music, wrote Schopenhauer, "is . . . totally independent of the phenomenal world; it simply ignores the world, and it could in some sense continue to exist even if the world did not. . . . Music, in other words, is just as *immediate* an objectification and image of

the entire *will* as the world itself is. . . . Music is thus in no sense, like the other arts, the image of ideas, but [it is] the image of the *will itself* . . . and for this very reason the effect of music is far more powerful and penetrates far more deeply than that of the other arts; for they communicate only shadows, whereas it communicates the essence" (1994, 67).

7. See, for comparison, the work of Gluckman or Frazer. For Gluckman (1954), carnival entails the inversion or violation of ordinary rules, resulting in a catharsis that consolidates authority. Frazer (1911), in his discussion, emphasizes ancient dramas of murder and resurrection within agricultural cycles, where reproduction was taken as the goal. In the Love Parade, however, one does not find tropes of sacrifice or reproductive teleology, nor does one find invocation of God.

12. Is the United States Europe's Other?

This article was first delivered at a conference on Eutopia: Enlargement and the Politics of European Identities, sponsored by the Russian and East European Center, University of Illinois, Urbana–Champaign, April 11–12, 2003.

1. Academics are not immune to these processes either. Timothy Garton Ash recently pointed to "the escalation of the Israeli-Palestinian conflict . . . [as] source and catalyst of what threatens to become a downward spiral of burgeoning European anti-Americanism" (2003, 8). But he is quite aware of the dangers for himself in writing about this conflict in a U.S. publication: It is "difficult for a non-Jewish European to write about [this] without contributing to the malaise one is trying to analyze" (2003, 8).

2. William Safire, the former Nixon speechwriter and columnist for the *New York Times,* is by no means a typical reporter, but he is a leader in producing the "finger-jabbing rectitude" and bad-faith stereotypes about which Schama writes and that circulate in other media as stereotypes about the European Other. For example, in making a case for blaming "Franco–German dominance" for the failure of Bush's diplomacy in bringing about support for the Iraq War at the United Nations, Safire wrote, in an article entitled "Bad Herr Dye," that German Chancellor Gerhard Schröder "does not share the free speech values of the West" (2003a). A week later, Safire described Germany's chancellor as having a "vast intelligence system and diplomatic corps" (2003b). In other words, Schröder (and Germany) is both wimp (bad Herr dye) and Nazi (vast intelligence system).

Bibliography

Adler, Israel, and Eric Peritz. 1997. "Religious Observance and Desired Fertility among Jewish Women in Israel." In *Papers in Jewish Demography, 1993: In Memory of U. O. Schmelz,* edited by Sergio DellaPergola and Judith Even, 377–89. Jerusalem: Avraham Harman Institute of Contemporary Jewry, Hebrew University of Jerusalem.

Adorno, Theodor. 1970 [1956]. *Zur Metakritik der Erkenntnistheorie. Studien über Husserl und die phänomenologischen Antinomien.* Frankfurt am Main: Surkamp.

Agamben, Giorgio. 1995. *Idea of Prose.* Albany: SUNY Press.

Ajami, Fouad. 2006. *The Foreigner's Gift: The Americans, the Arabs, and the Iraqis in Iraq.* New York: Free Press.

Anderson, Benedict. 1992. "New World Disorder." *New Left Review* 193: 3–13.

——— 1998. "Replica, Aura, and Late Nationalist Imaginings." In *The Spectre of Comparisons: Nationalism, Southeast Asia and the World,* 46–57. London: Verso.

Anonyma. 2003. *Eine Frau in Berlin.* Frankfurt am Main: Eichborn.

Ansolabehere, Stephen, James Snyder Jr., and Charles Stewart III. 2000. "Old Voters, New Voters, and the Personal Vote: Using Redistricting to Measure the Incumbency Advantage." *American Journal of Political Science* 44 (1): 17–34.

Arendt, Hannah. 1991. "Organized Guilt and Universal Responsibility." In *Collective Responsibility: Five Decades of Debate in Theoretical and Applied Ethics,* edited by Larry May and Stacey Hoffman, 273–84. Savage, Md.: Rowman & Littlefield.

Artenton, Christopher. 1992. "The Persuasive Art in Politics: The Role of Paid Advertising in Presidential Campaigns." In *Under the Watchful Eye: Managing Presidential Campaigns in the Television Era,* edited by Matthew D. McCubbins, 83–126. Washington, D.C.: CQ Press.

Ash, Timothy Garton. 2003. "Anti-Europeanism in America." *New York Review of Books,* February 13. www.nybooks.com/articles/archives/2003/feb/13/anti-europeanism-in-america.

Ashdown, Paddy. 2002. "What I Learned in Bosnia." *New York Times,* October 28: A25.

Assheuer, Thomas. 1997. "Ekstase, Befreiung, Glück. Maximilian Lenz alias Westbam ist Deutschlands erfolgreichster DJ—und der Philosoph des Techno. Ein Gespräch über das Wesen und die Zukunft des grossen Bum-Bum." *Zeitmagazin* (October): 30–35.

Barkan, Elazar. 2000. *The Guilt of Nations.* New York: Norton.

Bass, Gary Jonathan. 2001. *Stay the Hand of Vengeance: The Politics of War Crimes Tribunals.* Princeton, N.J.: Princeton University Press.

Bataille, Georges. 1985. *Visions of Excess: Selected Writings, 1927–1939.* Minneapolis: University of Minnesota Press.

Bazyler, Michael. 2001. "Holocaust Restitution Litigation in the United States: A Triumph of American Justice." Presented at conference on Confronting the Past: Memory, Identity, and Society, UCLA Center for Jewish Studies, February 4–5.

Beblawi, Hazem. 1987. "The Rentier State in the Arab World." In *The Rentier State,* edited by Hazem Beblawi and Giacomo Luciani, 49–62. London: Croom Helm.

Bloch, Maurice. 1989. "Symbol, Song, Dance, and Features of Articulation: Is Religion an Extreme Form of Traditional Authority?" In *Ritual, History and Power,* 19–45. London: Athlone Press.

———. 1992. *Prey into Hunter: The Politics of Religious Experience.* Cambridge: Cambridge University Press.

Boas, Franz. 1920. "The Social Organization of the Kwakiutl." *American Anthropologist* 22 (2): 111–26.

———. 1955 [1927]. *Primitive Art.* New York: Dover Publications.

Bobb, Scott. 2000. "Iraqi Elections." *Voice of America* 2–260691, March 28.

Bodemann, Y. Michal. 1996. *Reconstructions of History: From Jewish Memory to Nationalized Commemoration of Kristallnacht in Germany.* Ann Arbor: University of Michigan Press.

Bondy, Ruth, ed. 1968. *Mission Survival: The People of Israel's Story in Their Own Words, from the Threat of Annihilation to Miraculous Victory.* New York: Sabra Books.

Bonner, Raymond. 1987. *Waltzing with a Dictator: The Marcoses and the Making of American Policy.* Toronto, Ont.: Random House.

Bookman, Milica. 1997. *The Demographic Struggle for Power: The Political Economy of Demographic Engineering in the Modern World.* London: Frank Cass.

Borneman, John. 1991. *After the Wall: East Meets West in the New Berlin.* New York: Basic Books.

———. 1992. *Belonging in the Two Berlins: Kin, State, Nation.* Cambridge: Cambridge University Press.

———. 1995. "Anthropology as Foreign Policy." *American Anthropologist* 97 (4): 663–71.

———. 1996. "Identity, Exile, and Division: Disjunctures of Culture, Nationality, and Citizenship in German-Jewish Selfhood in East and West Berlin." In *Jews, Germans, Memory: Reconstructions of Jewish Life in Germany,* edited by Y. Michal Bodemann, 131–59. Ann Arbor: University of Michigan Press.

———. 1997. *Settling Accounts: Violence, Justice, and Accountability in Postsocialist Europe.* Princeton, N.J.: Princeton University Press.

———. 1998a. "Der 'Standort Deutschland' und die Verlegung der Hauptstadt." *Berliner Blätter: Ethnographische und Ethnologische Beiträge* 17 (June): 61–71.

———. 1998b. "Toward a Theory of Ethnic Cleansing: Territorial Sovereignty, Heterosexuality, and Europe." In *Subversions of International Order: Studies in the Political Anthropology of Culture,* 273–317. Albany: SUNY Press.

———. 2001. "Caring and To Be Cared For: Displacing Marriage, Kinship, Gender, and Sexuality." In *The Ethics of Kinship,* edited by James Faubion, 29–46. Lanham, Md.: Rowman & Littlefield.

———. 2002a. "Deutschsein: Fiction und das Reale." In *Inspecting Germany,* edited by Thomas Hauschild and Bernd Jürgen Warneken, 173–94. Münster: Lit Verlag.

———. 2002b. "Introduction: German Sacrifice Today." In *Sacrifice and National Belonging in Twentieth-Century Germany,* edited by Greg Eghigian and Matthew P. Berg, 3–25. College Station: Texas A&M Press.

———. 2003. "Why Reconciliation? A Response to Critics (to Laura Nader, Richard Falk, Richard Wilson, and Seven Sampson)." *Public Culture* 15 (1): 197–206.

———. 2004a. Editor, *Death of the Father: An Anthropology of the End in Political Authority.* New York: Berghahn Press.

———. 2004b. "Gottvater, Landesvater, Familienvater: Identification and Authority in Germany." In *Death of the Father: An Anthropology of the End in Political Authority,* edited by John Borneman, 63–103. New York: Berghahn Books.

———. 2004c. "Introduction: The Case of Ariel Sharon and the Fate of Universal Jurisdiction." In *The Case of Ariel Sharon and the Fate of Universal Jurisdiction,* edited by John Borneman, 1–30. Princeton, N.J.: Princeton Institute for International and Regional Studies Monograph Series.

———. 2004d. "Introduction: Theorizing Regime Ends." In *Death of the Father: An Anthropology of the End in Political Authority,* edited by John Borneman, 1–32. New York: Berghahn Books.

———. 2011. "Daydreaming, Intimacy, and the Intersubjective Third in Fieldwork Encounters in Syria." *American Ethnologist* 38 (2): 234–48.

Borneman, John, and Heinz Bude. 1999. "Grundung durch Umzug. Die Hauptstadtwerdung Berlins." *Mittelweg* 36 (6/98): 25–35.

Borneman, John, and Nick Fowler. 1997. "Europeanization." *Annual Review of Anthropology* 26: 487–514.

Borneman, John, and Jeffrey Peck. 1995. *Sojourners: The Return of German-Jews and the Question of Identity.* Lincoln: University of Nebraska Press.

Bourdieu, Pierre. 1991. *Language and Symbolic Power.* Cambridge, Mass.: Harvard University Press.

Bowler, Shaun, and David M. Farrell. 2000. "The Internationalization of Campaign Consultancy." In *Campaign Warriors: Political Consultants in Elections,* edited by James Thurber and Candice Nelson, 153–74. Washington, D.C.: Brookings Institution Press.

Brandt, Willy. 1994. *Erinnerungen: 'Mit den Notizen zum Fall G.'* Berlin: Ullstein.

Bremer, L. Paul III, and Malcolm McConnell. 2006. *My Year in Iraq: The Struggle to Build a Future of Hope.* New York: Simon and Shuster.

Bundestag, Deutscher. 1994a. *Bericht der Enquette-Kommission. Aufarbeitung von Geschichte und Folgen der SED-Diktatur in Deutschland* (Deutscher Bundestag, 1994a), 12. Wahlperiode Drucksache12/7820.

———. 1994b. *Beschlußempfehlung und Bericht des 1. Untersuchungsausschusses nach Artikel 44 des Grundgesetzes* (Deutscher Bundestag, 1994b), 12/7600.

Burns, John F. 2004. "Shiites May Demand Lifting of Limits on Their Power." *New York Times,* March 10: 1.

Bussy, Pascal. 1993. *Kraftwerk: Man, Machine and Music.* Middlesex: SAF Publishing.

Butler, Judith. 2004. *Precarious Life: The Powers of Mourning and Violence.* New York: Verso.

Cahn, Michael. 1984. "Subversive Mimesis: Theodore W. Adorno and the Modern Impasse of Critique." In *Mimesis in Contemporary Theory,* Vol. 1: *The Literary and Philosophical Debate,* edited by Mihai Spariosu, 27–64. Philadelphia: John Benjamins.

Callahan, David, and Lori Minnite. 2003. *Securing the Vote: An Analysis of Election Fraud.* New York: Demos. A Network for Ideas and Action: www.freepress.net.

Carrier, Peter. 2005. *Holocaust Monuments and National Memory Cultures in France and Germany since 1989.* New York: Berghahn Books.

Caruth, Cathy. 1996. *Unclaimed Experience: Trauma, Narrative, and History.* Baltimore, Md.: Johns Hopkins University Press.

Cassese, Antonio. 2003. *International Criminal Law.* Oxford: Oxford University Press.

Chua, Yvonne. 2004."With a Little Help from (U.S.) Friends." *The Campaign,* Special Election Issue, January–June.

Dahl, Robert. 1971. *Polyarchy: Participation and Opposition.* New Haven, Conn.: Yale University Press.

Danieli, Yael. 1985. "The Treatment and Prevention of Long-Term Effects and Inter-generational Transmission of Victimization: A Lesson from Holocaust Survivors and Their Children." In *Trauma and Its Wake: The Study of Treatment of Posttraumatic Stress Disorder,* edited by Charles Figley, 295–314. New York: Brunner/Mazel.

Deeb, Laura. 2006a. *An Enchanted Modern: Gender and Public Piety in Shi'i Lebanon.* Princeton, N.J.: Princeton University Press.

———. 2006b. "'Hizbullah Strongholds' and Civilian Life." *Anthropology News* 47 (7): 10–11.

DellaPergola, Sergio. 1992. "Recent Trends in Jewish Marriage." In *World Jewish Population: Trends and Policies,* edited by Sergio DellaPergola and Leah Cohen, 65–92. Jerusalem: Institute of Contemporary Jewry, Hebrew University of Jerusalem.

Devereux, Georges. 1967. "Elicited Countertransference: The Complementary Role." In *From Anxiety to Method in the Behavioral Sciences,* 234–51. The Hague: Mouton.

Diner, Dan. 1988. "Vorwort des Herausgebers." In *Zivilisationsbruch: Denken nach Auschwitz,* edited by Dan Diner, 7–13. Frankfurt: Fischer TB.

Dower, John. 1999. *Embracing Defeat: Japan in the Wake of World War II.* New York: New Press.

———. 2002. "Lessons from Japan about War's Aftermath." *New York Times,* October 27. www.nytimes.com/2002/10/27/opinon/27DOWE.html.

Doyle, Michael. 1983. "Kant, Liberal Legacies, and Foreign Affairs." *Philosophy and Public Affairs,* Part 1, 12 (3): 205–35, and Part 2, 12 (4): 323–53.

Durkheim, Emile. 1965 [1912]. *The Elementary Forms of Religious Life.* New York: Free Press.

Eggen, Dan, and Amy Goldstein. 2007. "Voter-Fraud Complaints by GOP Drove Dismissals." *Washington Post,* May 14: A04.

Egonsson, Dan. 1998. *Dimensions of Dignity: The Moral Importance of Being Human.* Boston, Mass.: Kluwer Academic Publishers.

Engholm, Bjoern. 1992. *Abschied: Dank an Willy Brandt.* Berlin: Schueren.

Enloe, Cynthia. 1993. *The Morning After: Sexual Politics at the End of the Cold War.* Berkeley: University of California Press.

Erlanger, Steven. 2005. "Why Democracy Defies the Urge to Implant It." Week in Review, *New York Times,* February 15: 1.

Evans-Pritchard, E. E. 1976. *Witchcraft, Oracles and Magic among the Azande.* Oxford: Oxford University Press.

Fair, Roy. 1996. "Econometrics and Presidential Elections." *Journal of Economic Perspectives* 10 (3): 89–102.

Falk, Richard. 2001. "The Holocaust and the Emergence of International Human Rights." Paper presented at conference on Confronting the Past: Memory, Identity, and Society, UCLA Center for Jewish Studies, February 4–5.

Falk, Richard, Irene Gendzier, and Robert Jay Lifton, eds. 2006. *Crimes of War: Iraq.* New York: Nation Books.

Feldman, Gerald. 2001. "Reparations, Restitution, and Compensation in the Aftermath of National Socialism, 1945–2000." Paper presented at conference on Confronting the Past: Memory, Identity, and Society, UCLA Center for Jewish Studies, February 4–5.

Fenno, Richard F., Jr. 1977. "U.S. House Members in their Constituencies: An Exploration." *American Political Science Review* 71 (3): 883–917.

Fink, Eugen. 1960. *Spiel als Weltsymbol.* Stuttgart: W. Kohlhammer.

Finkelstein, Norman. 2001. *The Holocaust Industry: Reflections on the Exploitation of Jewish Suffering.* New York: Verso Books.

Fisk, Robert. 2002. *Pity the Nation: The Abduction of Lebanon.* New York: Nation Books.

Foucault, Michel. 1977. *Discipline and Punish: The Birth of the Prison.* New York: Pantheon.

———. 1980. *Power/Knowledge: Selected Interviews and Other Writings, 1972–1977,* edited by Colin Gordon. New York: Pantheon.

———. 1991. "Politics and the Study of Discourse." In *The Foucault Effect: Studies in Governmentality,* edited by Graham Burchell, Colin Gordon, and Peter Miller, 53–72. Chicago: University of Chicago Press.

Frazer, Sir James. 1911 [1890]. *The Golden Bough. A Study in Magic,* Vol. 3: *The Dying God;* Vol. 9, *The Scapegoat.* London: MacMillan.

Freud, Sigmund. 1912. "Recommendations to Physicians Practicing Psychoanalysis." In *The Standard Edition of the Complete Psychological works of Sigmund Freud,* 12:123–44. London: Hogarth Press, 1958.

———. 1917. "Mourning and Melancholia." In *The Standard Edition of the Complete Psychological Works of Sigmund Freud,* 14:243–58. London: Hogarth Press.

———. 1923. "The Ego and the ID." In *The Standard Edition of the Complete Psychological Works of Sigmund Freud,* 19:12–66. London: Hogarth Press.

———. 1950. *Totem and Taboo: Some Points of Agreement between the Mental Lives of Savages and Neurotics.* New York: W.W. Norton.

———. 1953. "The Uncanny." In *The Standard Edition of the Complete Psychological Works of Sigmund Freud,* 17:219–52. London: Hogarth.

Friedlander, Saul. 1992. "Introduction." In *Probing the Limits of Representation: "Nazism" and the Final Solution,* edited by Saul Friedlander, 1–22. Cambridge, Mass.: Harvard University Press.

———. 1993. *Memory, History, and the Extermination of the Jews in Europe.* Bloomington: Indiana University Press.

Früchtl, Josef. 1986. *Mimesis: Konstellation eines Zentralbegriffs bei Adorno.* Würzburg: Königshausen & Newmann.

Fukuyama, Francis. 1995. *Trust: The Social Virtues and the Creation of Prosperity.* New York: Free Press.

Gadamer, Hans-Georg. 1975. *Truth and Method.* New York: Continuum.

Galbraith, Peter. 2006. "Mindless in Iraq." *New York Review of Books* 53, August 10, www.nybooks.com/articles/19197.

Gauchet, Marcel. 1997. *The Disenchantment of the World: A Political History of Religion.* Princeton, N.J.: Princeton University Press.

Gawrych, George. 2000. *The Albatross of Decisive Victory: War and Policy between Egypt and Israel in the 1967 and 1973 Arab-Israeli Wars.* Westport, Conn.: Greenwood.

Gerth, Hans, and C. Wright Mills, eds. 1946. *From Max Weber.* New York: Oxford University Press.

Giesen, Bernhard. 1993. *Die Intellektuellen und die Nation: Eine deutsche Achsenzeit.* Frankfurt am Main: Suhrkamp.

Gilsenan, Michael. 2003. *Lords of the Lebanese Marches: Violence and Narrative in an Arab Society.* London: I. B. Taurus.

Giordano, Ralph. 1987. *Die zweite Schuld oder Von der Last Deutscher zu sein.* Hamburg: Rasch and Röhring Verlag.

Gleditsch, Kristian, and Michael Ward. 1999. "Interstate System Members: A Revised List of Independent States since 1816." *International Interactions* 25: 393–413.

———. 2000. "War and Peace in Space and Time: The Role of Democratization." *International Studies Quarterly* 44 (1) (March): 1–29.

Gluckman, Max. 1954. *Rituals of Rebellion in South East Africa.* Manchester: Manchester University Press.

Godelier, Maurice. 1998. *The Enigma of the Gift.* Chicago: University of Chicago Press.

Godu, Norman J. W. 2006. "Law, Memory, and History in the Trials of Nazis." *International History Review* 28 (4): 798.

Goetz, Rainald. 1997. "Let the Sun Shine in Your Heart." *Die Zeit* 29, 11 July: 10.

Goffman, Erving. 1971. *Relations in Public: Microstudies of the Public Order.* New York: Basic Books.

Goody, Jack, ed. 1966. *Succession to High Office.* Cambridge Papers in Social Anthropology, 4. Cambridge: Cambridge University Press.

Gutman, Roy, and David Rieff, eds. 1999. *Crimes of War: What the Public Should Know.* New York: W.W. Norton.

Habermas, Jürgen. 1989. "The Uncoupling of System and Lifeworld." In Steven Seidman, ed., *Juergen Habermas on Society and Politics: A Reader,* 188–230. Boston, Mass.: Beacon Press.

Hacking, Ian. 1996. "Memory Sciences, Memory Politics." In *Tense Past: Cultural Essays in Trauma and Memory,* edited by Paul Antze and Michael Lambek, 67–88. New York: Routledge.

Hammer, Joshua, and Christine Spolar. 2005. "Ballot Initiative." *New Republic,* September 26: 16.

Hammoudi, Abdellah. 1993. *The Victim and Its Masks: An Essay on Sacrifice and Masquerade in the Maghreb.* Chicago: University of Chicago Press.

Hampton, Jean. 1992. "Correcting Harms Versus Righting Wrongs: The Goal of Retribution." *UCLA Law Review* 29: 1659–702.

Havel, Václav. 1986. *Living in Truth: Twenty-two Essays on the Occasion of the Award of the Erasmus Prize to Václav Havel.* London: Faber and Faber.

Havemann, Axel. 2002. *Geschichte und Geschichtsschreibung im Libanon des 19 und 20 Jahrhunderts.* Würzburg and Beirut: Ergon Verlag.

Hebdidge, Dick. 1987. *Cut 'N' Mix: Culture, Identity and Caribbean Music.* London: Methuen.

Heimer, Carol A. 1985. *Reactive Risk and Rational Action: Managing Moral Hazard in Insurance Contracts.* Berkeley: University of California Press.

Horkheimer, Max, and Theodor W. Adorno. 1972 [1944]. *Dialectic of Enlightenment.* Translated by John Cumming. New York: Continuum.

Hovannisian, Richard. 1986. "The Armenian Genocide and Patterns of Denial." In *The Armenian Genocide in Perspective,* edited by R. Hovannisian, 111–34. New Brunswick, N.J.: Transaction Books.

Hubert, Henri, and Marcel Mauss. 1981 [1898]. *Sacrifice: Its Nature and Functions.* Chicago: University of Chicago Press.

Ibrahim, Saad. 2005. "Promises to Keep in Egypt." *Washington Post,* September 24.

Ignatieff, Michael. 2001. *Human Rights as Politics and Idolatry.* Princeton, N.J.: Princeton University Press.

Irani, George Emile, ed. 1997. *Reconciliation Processes and the Displaced Communities in Post-War Lebanon.* Beirut: Lebanese American University.

Jameson, Fredric. 1984. "Postmodernism, or the Cultural Logic of Late Capitalism." *New Left Review* 146: 53–92.

Jarausch, Konrad. 2010. "The Federal Republic at Sixty: Popular Myths, Actual Accomplishments, and Competing Interpretations." *German Politics and Society* 28 (1) (Spring): 42–68.

Jarausch, Konrad, and Michael Geyer. 2003. *Shattered Past: Reconstructing German Histories.* Princeton, N.J.: Princeton University Press.

Jaspers, Karl. 1947 [1946]. *The Question of Guilt.* New York: Capricorn Books.

Johnston, Mark. 2007. "Voter Suppression." *ePluribus Media,* June 26. www.epluribusmedia .org/features/2007/20070621_supressing_the_vote_2004.html.

Judt, Tony. 2003. "Israel: The Alternative." *New York Review of Books* 50 (16), October 23, www.nybooks.com/articles/archives/2003/oct/23/israel-the-alternative.

Kassimeris, George, ed. 2006. *The Barbarization of Warfare.* London: Hurst.

Kelley, Raymond. 2000. *Warless Societies and the Origins of War.* Ann Arbor: University of Michigan Press.

Khalaf, Samir. 2004. *Civil and Uncivil Violence in Lebanon: A History of the Internationalization of Communal Conflict.* New York: Columbia University Press.

Kierkegaard, Søren. 1974. "Despair Is 'the Sickness unto Death.'" In *A Kierkegaard Anthology,* edited by Robert Bretall, 341–45. Princeton, N.J.: Princeton University Press.

Kimmerling, Baruch. 2003. *Politicide: Ariel Sharon's War against the Palestinians.* New York: Verso.

Klein, Melanie. 1940. "Mourning and Its Relation to Manic-depressive States." *International Journal of Psychoanalysis* 21: 125–53.

Kohler, Lotte, and Hans Saner, eds. 1992. *Correspondence, 1926–1969.* New York: Harcourt Brace.

Kohli, Martin. 1985. "Die Institutionalisierung des Lebenslaufs." *Kölner Zeitschrift für Soziologie und Sozialpsychologie* 37 (1): 1–24.

Koselleck, Reinhart. 1985. "The Historical-Political Semantics of Asymmetric Counterconcepts." In *Futures Past: On the Semantics of Historical Time,* 159–87. Cambridge: MIT Press.

Koselleck, Reinhart, and Michael Jeismann, eds. 1994. *Der Politische Totenkult: Kriegerdenkmäler in der Moderne.* München: Bild und Text.

Kramer, Gerald H. 1971. "Short-Term Fluctuations in U.S. Voting Behavior, 1896–1964." *American Political Science Review* 65: 131–43.

Kymlicka, Will. 1995. *Multicultural Citizenship: A Liberal Theory of Minority Rights.* Oxford: Oxford University Press.

Lakoff, George. 1995. "Metaphor, Morality, and Politics, Or, Why Conservatives Have Left Liberals in the Dust." www.wwcd.org/issues/Lakoff.html#STRICT. Accessed February 5, 2004.

Langenbacher, Eric. 2010. "The Mastered Past? Collective Memory Trends in Germany since Unification." *German Politics and Society* 28 (1) (Spring): 42–68.

Langlois, Tony. 1992. "Can You Feel It? DJs and House Music Culture in the UK." *Popular Music* 11/2: 229–38.

Laplanche, Jean. 1999. "Time and the Other." Translated by L. Thurston. In *Essays on Otherness*, edited by J. Fletcher, 234–59. London: Routledge.

Lazar, David, and Edward Karst, eds. 1997. "Cash Strapped Churches Increasingly Moved by Entrepreneurial Spirit." *Week in Germany* 7, October 10: 6. New York: German Information Center.

Leclaire, Serge. 1998. *A Child Is Being Killed: On Primary Narcissism and the Death Drive.* Stanford, Calif.: Stanford University Press.

Lefort, Claude. 1986. "The Image of the Body and Totalitarianism." In *The Political Forms of Modern Society*, 292–306. Cambridge, Mass.: MIT Press.

Leicht, Robert. 2001. "After Joschka Fischers Entschuldigung für die Sklaverei: Kann und soll man sich für die Sünden der Väter verantworten?" *Die Zeit* 37: 1–2.

Levi-Strauss, Claude. 1966. *The Savage Mind.* Chicago: University of Chicago Press.

———. 1971. *The Elementary Structures of Kinship.* Boston: Beacon Press.

Levitt, Steven D., and Catherine D. Wolfram. 1997. "Decomposing the Sources of Incumbency: Advantage in the U.S. House." *Legislative Studies Quarterly* 22 (1): 45–60.

Lewis, Anthony. 2002. "Bush and Iraq." *New York Review of Books,* November 7: 7–13.

Lewis, H. D. 1991 "Collective Responsibility." In *Collective Responsibility: Five Decades of Debate in Theoretical and Applied Ethics*, edited by Larry May and Stacey Hoffman, 17–34. Savage, Md.: Rowman & Littlefield.

Lillteicher, Jürgen. 2006. "West Germany and Compensation for National Socialist Expropriation: The Restitution of Jewish Property, 1947–1964." In *Coping with the Nazi Past: West German Debates on Nazism and Generational Conflict, 1955–1975*, edited by Philipp Gassert and Alan Steinweis, 79–95. New York: Berghahn Books.

Loughlin, Sean. 2003. "Rumsfeld on Looting in Iraq. Administration Asking Countries for Help with Security." *CNN Washington Bureau,* April 12. Posted: 12:24 AM EDT.

Luhmann, Niklas. 1990. *Political Theory in the Welfare State.* New York: Walter de Gruyter.

Mackenzie, W. J. M. 1968. "Elections." In *International Encyclopedia of the Social Sciences*, Vol. 5, edited by David L. Sills, 1–6. New York: Macmillan and Free Press.

Mahdavi, Hossein. 1970. "Patterns and Problems of Economic Development in Rentier States: The Case of Iran." In *Studies in the History of the Middle East*, edited by Michael A. Cook: 428–67. Oxford: Oxford University Press.

Maier, Charles. 1988. *The Unmasterable Past: History, Holocaust, and German National Identity.* Cambridge, Mass.: Harvard University Press.

———. 1997 *Dissolution: The Crisis of Communism and the End of East Germany.* Princeton, N.J.: Princeton University Press.

Malkki, Liisa. 1997. "News and Culture: Transitory Phenomena and the Fieldwork Tradition." In *Anthropological Locations: Boundaries and Grounds of a Field Science*, edited by Akhil Gupta and James Ferguson, 86–191. Berkeley: University of California Press.

Mallat, Chibli. 2004. "Accountability in the Middle East: The Sharon Case Polysemy." In *The Case of Ariel Sharon and the Fate of Universal Jurisdiction*, edited by John

Borneman, 31–54. Princeton, N.J.: Princeton Institute for International and Regional Studies.

———. 2006. "Who Is Really at War? The Patterns So Far." *New York Times,* August 4.

———. 2007. *March 2221: Lebanon's Cedar Revolution. An Essay on Non-violence and Justice.* Beirut: Lir.

Manin, Bernard, Adam Przeworski, and Susan Stokes, eds. 1999. *Democracy, Accountability, and Representation.* Cambridge: Cambridge University Press.

Marshall, Samuel L.A. 1967. *Swift Sword: The Historical Record of Israel's Victory.* New York: American Heritage.

Mauss, Marcel. 2000. *The Gift: The Form and Reason for Exchange in Archaic Societies.* New York: Norton.

———. 2001 [1902]. *A General Theory of Magic.* New York: Routledge.

Meier, Horst. 1991. "Reigierungskriminalität im SED-Staat." *Merkur* 514: 75–78.

Meredith, Martin. 1999. *Coming to Terms: South Africa's Search for Truth.* New York: Public Affairs.

Merken, Daphne. 2002. "George Bush and the World." *New York Review of Books,* November 7.

Milbank, Dana. 2002. "For Bush, Facts Are Malleable." *Washington Post,* October 22: A01.

Miquel, Marc von. 2006. "Explanation, Dissociation, Apologia: The Debate over the Criminal Prosecution of Nazi Crimes in the 1960s." In *Coping with the Nazi Past: West German Debates on Nazism and Generational Conflict, 1955–1975,* edited by Philipp Gassert and Alan Steinweis, 50–61. New York: Berghahn Books.

Mintz, Sidney. 1986. *Sweetness and Power: The Place of Sugar in Modern History.* New York: Penguin.

Mitscherlich, Alexander, and Margarete Mitscherlich. 1975. *The Inability to Mourn: Principles of Collective Behavior.* New York: Grove Press.

Moore, Sally Falk. 1978. *Law as Process: An Anthropological Approach.* Boston: Routledge.

———. 1987. "Explaining the Present: Theoretical Dilemmas in Processual Ethnography." *American Ethnologist* 14: 727–36.

Moore, Sally Falk, and Barbara G. Myerhoff, eds. 1977. *Secular Ritual.* Amsterdam: Van Gorcum.

Moore, Wesley. 2006. "A War-Crimes Commission for the Hezbollah-Israel War?" *Middle East Policy* 13 (4): 61.

Morris, Benny. 2001. *Righteous Victims: A History of the Zionist-Arab Conflicts, 1881–1999.* New York: Knopf.

Müller, Ingo. 1991. *Hitler's Justice: The Courts of the Third Reich.* Cambridge, Mass.: Harvard University Press.

Murphy, Jeffrie G. 1988. "Forgiveness and Resentment." In *Forgiveness and Mercy,* by J. Murphy and Jean Hampton, 14–34. Cambridge: Cambridge University Press.

Nader, Laura. 1985. "Civilization and its Negotiations." In *Understanding Disputes: The Politics of Argument,* edited by Pat Caplan, 39–61. Providence, R.I.: Berg.

———. 1990. *Harmony Ideology: Justice and Control in a Zapotec Mountain Village.* Stanford, Calif.: Stanford University Press.

National Security Council. 2002. *National Security.* www.whitehouse.gov/nsc/nss.html. Accessed October 10, 2002.

Neier, Aryeh. 1998. *War Crimes: Brutality, Genocide, Terror, and the Struggle for Justice.* New York: Random House.

————. 2006. "The Attack on Human Rights Watch." *New Review of Books* 53 (17): November 2.

Niethammer, Lutz. 2007. "Converting Wrongs to Rights? Compensating Nazi Forced Labor as Paradigm." In *Restitution and Memory: Material Restoration in Europe,* edited by Dan Diner and Gotthart Wünberg, 83–104. New York: Berghahn.

Nora, Pierre, ed. 1996 [1992]. "General Introduction: Between Memory and History." In *Realms of Memory: Rethinking the French Past.* Vol. 1: *Conflicts and Divisions,* 1–23. Translated by Arthur Goldhammer. New York: Columbia University Press.

————. 1997 [1992]. *Realms of Memory: Rethinking the French Past:* Vol. 2: *Traditions.* Translated by Arthur Goldhammer. New York: Columbia University Press.

Norton, Augustus Richard. 2007. *Hezbollah: A Short History.* Princeton, N.J.: Princeton University Press.

Ober, Josiah, and Charles Hedrick, eds. 1996. *Demokratia.* Princeton, N.J.: Princeton University Press.

Offe, Claus. 1992. "Coming to Terms with Past Injustice." *Archives europeanne de sociologie* 32: 195–201.

Osiel, Mark. 1995. "Ever Again: Legal Remembrance of Administrative Massacre." *University of Pennsylvania Law Review* 144: 463–704.

Peritz, Eric, and Mario Baras, eds. 1992. *Studies in the Fertility of Israel.* Jerusalem: Institute of Contemporary Jewry, Hebrew University of Jerusalem.

Peteet, Julie. 2009. *Landscape of Hope and Despair.* Philadelphia: University of Pennsylvania Press.

Power, Michael. 1999. *The Audit Society: Rituals of Verification.* Oxford: Oxford University Press.

Pripstein-Posusney, Marsha, and Michelle Angrist, eds. 2005. *Authoritarianism in the Middle East: Regimes and Resistance.* Boulder, Colo.: Lynn Rienner Publishers.

Prittie, Terence. 1974. *Willy Brandt: Portrait of a Statesman.* London: Weidenfeld and Nicolson.

Pross, Christian. 1998. *Paying for the Past: The Struggle over Reparations for Surviving Victims of Nazi Terror.* Baltimore, Md.: Johns Hopkins University Press.

Przeworski, Adam. 1999. "Minimalist Conception of Democracy: A Defense." In *Democracy's Value,* edited by Ian Schapiro and Casioano Hacker-Cordon, 23–55. Cambridge: Cambridge University Press.

Putnam, Robert. 1995. "Bowling Alone: America's Declining Social Capital." *Journal of Democracy* 6: 65–78.

Rabinovich, Itamar. 1984. *The War for Lebanon, 1970–1985.* Ithaca, N.Y.: Cornell University Press.

Ratner, Steven, and Jason Abrams. 1997. *Accountability for Human Rights Atrocities in International Law: Beyond the Nuremberg Legacy.* New York: Oxford University Press.

Rautenberg, Eduardo Christoforo. 1994. "Täter-Opfer-Ausgleich im Land Brandenburg." *Neue Justiz* 7: 300–303.

Reporters without Borders, ed. 2003. *Israel/Palestine: The Black Book.* Sterling, Va.: Pluto Press.

Ricoeur, Paul. 1981. "The Model of the Text a Social Action." In *Hermeneutics and the Human Sciences:* 197–221. Cambridge, Mass.: MIT Press.

————. 2000. "The Concept of Responsibility." In *The Just,* 11–35. Chicago: University of Chicago Press.

Robertson, Geoffrey. 2003. *Crimes against Humanity: The Struggle for Justice.* New York: New Press.

Rorty, Richard. 2002. "Fighting Terrorism with Democracy." *The Nation* 275 (13), October 21: 11–14.

Rose, Jacqueline. 2007. *The Question of Zion.* Princeton, N.J.: Princeton University Press.

Rose, Nikolas. 1999. *Powers of Freedom: Reframing Political Thought.* New York: Cambridge University Press.

Rotberg, Robert I., and Dennis Thompson, eds. 2000. *Truth v. Justice: The Morality of Truth Commissions.* Princeton, N.J.: Princeton University Press.

Rumsfeld, Donald. 2002. "Transforming the Military." *Foreign Affairs* 81 (3): 20–32.

Rückerl, Adalbert. 1982. *NS-Verbrechen vor Gericht.* Heidelberg: Juristischer Verlag.

Ryback, Timothy. 1993. "Evidence of Evil." *New Yorker,* November 15: 68–81.

Sachs, Susan. 2004. "Bush Urges All Autocrats to Yield Now to Democracy." *New York Times,* June 30.

Safire, William. 2003a. "Bad Herr Dye." *New York Times,* February 10. www.nytimes .com/2003/02/03/opinion. Accessed February 3, 2003.

———. 2003b. "Surprising Germany." *New York Times,* February 10. www.nytimes .com/2003/02/10/opinion. Accessed February 10, 2003.

Salibi, Kamal. 1990. *A House of Many Mansions: The History of Modern Lebanon Reconsidered.* Berkeley: University of California Press.

Sammons, Loren J. 2004. *What's Wrong with Democracy: From Athenian Practice to American Worship.* Berkeley: University of California Press.

Schachter, Oscar. 1983. "Human Dignity as a Normative Concept." *American Journal of International Law* 77: 848–54.

Schaefgen, Christoph. 1994. "Die Strafverfolgung von Regierungskriminalität der DDR—Probleme, Ergebnisse, Perspektiven." *Recht und Politik* 3: 150–60.

Schama, Simon. 2003. "The Unloved American." *New Yorker,* March 10: 334–39.

Schelsky, Helmut. 1954. *Wandlungen der deutschen Familien in der Gegenwart.* Stuttgart: Ferdinand Enke.

Schepsle, Kenneth, and Mark Bonchek. 1997. *Analyzing Politics: Rationality, Behavior, and Institutions.* New York: W.W. Norton.

Schivelbusch, Wolfgang. 2003. *The Culture of Defeat: On National Trauma, Mourning, and Recovery.* New York: Metropolitan Books.

Schmelz, U. O. 1992. "World Jewish Population in the 1980s: A Short Outline." In *World Jewish Population: Trends and Policies,* edited by Sergio DellaPergola and Leah Cohen, 37–52. Jerusalem: Institute of Contemporary Jewry, Hebrew University of Jerusalem.

Schmitt, Carl. 1996 [1932]. *The Concept of the Political.* Chicago: University of Chicago Press.

Schmitter, Philippe C. 1998. "Some Basic Assumptions about the Consolidation of Democracy." In *The Changing Nature of Democracy,* edited by Takashi Inoguchi, Edward Newman, and John Keane, 33. Tokyo: United Nations University Press.

Schopenhauer, Arthur. 1994 [1819]. "Music—the Unique Art." In *The World as Will and Representation.* Translated by Peter Le Huray and James Day, 65–70. Excerpted in Jost Hermand and Michael Gilbert, eds. *German Essays on Music.* New York: Continuum.

Schröder, Michael. 1993. "Fahnenflucht als regelmäßiger Rehabilitierungsgrund?" *Neue Justiz* 8: 350–55.

Schuller, Konrad. 1996. "Erinnerungsort deutscher Geschichte. Haupstadt der Reue. Gedenkpolitik ist zu einer HauptdisziplIn geworden." *Frankfurter Allgemeine Zeitung* 18 (December): 13.

Schumpeter, Joseph. 1942. *Capitalism, Socialism, and Democracy.* New York: Harper & Brothers.

Searles, H. F. 1986. "Countertransference as a Path to Understanding and Helping the Patient." In *My Work with Borderline Patients,* 189–228. Northvale, N.J.: Jason Aronson Press.

Sebald, W. G. 1996. *The Emigrants.* New York: New Directions.

———. 2000. *Vertigo.* New York: New Directions, 2000.

———. 2002. *Austerlitz.* New York: Random House.

Segev, Tom 2000 *The Seventh Million: The Israelis and the Holocaust.* New York: Owl Books.

Senatsverwaltung für Justiz. 1996. *Aktueller Stand und Bewältigung der Regierungs- und Vereinigungskriminalität sowie des Justizunrechts—Jahresbericht,* 67 Konferenz der Justizministerinnen und -minister. Wiesbaden: Germany.

Senders, Stefan. 1998. "Jus Sanguinis or Jus Mimesis: Aussiedler Repatriation from an Anthropological Perspective." Ph.D. diss., Cornell University.

Shadid, Anthony. 2007. "Egypt Shuts the Door on Dissent as U.S. Officials Back Away." *Washington Post,* March 19.

Shapiro, Ian, and Casiano Hacker-Cordon, eds. 1999. *Democracy's Value.* Cambridge: Cambridge University Press.

Silberstein, Lawrence. 1999. *The Post Zionism Debates: Knowledge and Power in Israeli Culture.* New York: Routledge.

Simmel, Georg. 1990. *The Philosophy of Money,* edited by David Frisby. New York: Routlege.

Sloterdijk, Peter. 1987. *Critique of Cynical Reason.* Minneapolis: University of Minnesota Press.

Span, Paula. 2004. "Military Families vs. the War." *Washington Post,* March 11: A01.

Spariosu, Mihai. 1984. "Introduction." In Mihai Spariosu, ed. *Mimesis in Contemporary Theory,* Vol. 1: *The Literary and Philosophical Debate,* i–xxiv. Philadelphia: John Benjamins.

Spiliotis, Susanne-Sophia. 2006. "Corporate Responsibility and Historical Injustice." In *Civil Society: Berlin Perspectives,* edited by John Keane, 51–70. New York: Berghahn.

Strathern, Marilyn, ed. 2000. *Audit Cultures: Anthropological Studies in Accountability, Ethics and the Academy.* New York: Routledge.

Tambiah, Stanley. 1990. *Magic, Science, Religion, and the Scope of Rationality.* Cambridge: Cambridge University Press.

Taussig, Michael. 1991. *The Nervous System.* New York: Routledge.

———. 1992. *Mimesis and Alterity: A Particular History of the Senses.* New York: Routledge.

Tavuchis, Nicholas. 1991. *Mea Culpa: A Sociology of Apology and Reconciliation.* Stanford, Calif.: Stanford University Press.

Telhami, Shibley. 2006. "Lebanese Identity and Israeli Security in the Shadows of the 2006 War." *Current History* 21: 21–26.

Todorov, Tzvetan. 1996. *Facing the Extreme: Moral Life in the Concentration Camps.* New York: Metropolitan Books.

Traboulsi, Fawwaz. 2007. *A History of Modern Lebanon*. New York: Pluto Press.

Tronto, Joan. 1993. *Moral Boundaries: A Political Argument for an Ethic of Care*. New York: Routledge.

Turner, Victor. 1977. *The Forest of Symbols: Aspects of Ndembu Ritual*. Ithaca, N.Y.: Cornell University Press.

Tylor, E. B. 1970 [1877]. *Religion in Primitive Culture*, Vol. 2. Gloucester: Peter Smith.

Urbina, Ian. 2007. "Panel Said to Alter Finding on Voter Fraud." *New York Times*, April 11.

Van Gennep, Arnold. 1960. *Rites of Passage*. Chicago: University of Chicago.

Vollnhals, Clemens, ed. 1991. *Entnazifizierung: Politische Säuberung und Rehabilitierung in den vier Besatzungszonen, 1945–1949*. Munich: Deutscher Taschenbuch Verlag.

Watani, Majlis. 2007. "Elections held in 2000." *Iraq: Historical Archive of Parliamentary Election Results*. Accessed 9/18/07. http://www.ipu.org/parline-e/reports/arc/2151_00 .htm

Weber, Jürgen, and Michael Piazolo, eds. 1995. *Eine Diktatur vor Gericht*. Munich: Olzog Verlag.

Weber, Max. 1958. *The Protestant Ethic and the Spirit of Capitalism*. New York: Charles Scribner's Sons.

Weinke, Anette. 2002. *Die Verfolgung von NS-Tätern in geteilten Deutschland: Vergangenheits bewaeltigung 1949–1969: oder: Eine deutsche Beziehungsgeschichte im Kalten Krieg*. Paderhorn: Schöningh.

Wilson, Richard, ed. 1996. *Human Rights, Culture and Context: Anthropological Perspectives*. London: Pluto Press.

Winter, Jay. 1995. *Sites of Memory, Sites of Mourning: The Great War in European Cultural History*. Cambridge: Cambridge University Press.

Winter, Jay, and Emmanuel Sivan, eds. 1999. *War and Remembrance in the Twentieth Century*. Cambridge: Cambridge University Press.

Young, James E. 1994. *The Texture of Memory: Holocaust Memorials and Meaning*. New Haven, Conn.: Yale University Press.

———. 2002. *At Memory's Edge: After-Images of the Holocaust in Contemporary Art and Architecture*. New Haven, Conn.: Yale University Press.

Young, Michael. 2010. *The Ghosts of Martyrs Square: An Eyewitness Account of Lebanon's Life Struggle*. New York: Simon and Schuster.

Zelizer, Viviana. 1979. *Morals and Markets: The Development of Life Insurance in the United States*. New York: Columbia University Press.

———. 1989. "The Social Meaning of Money: 'Special Monies.'" *American Journal of Sociology* 95 (5): 342–77.

ZERV. 1993. Zentrale Ermittlungsstelle Regierungs- und Vereingigungskriminalität (ZERV), *Zentrale Ermittlungsstelle Regierungs- und Vereingigungskriminalität. Jahresbericht*. Berlin: Der Polizeipräsident in Berlin.

———. 1994. *Zentrale Ermittlungsstelle Regierungs- und Vereinigungskriminalität. Sachstandsbericht. Police Publication 147*. Berlin: Der Polizeipräsident in Berlin.

———. 1996. *ZERV Bulletin*. Berlin: Der Polizeipräsident in Berlin.

Zizek, Slavoj. 1989. *The Sublime Object of Ideology*. New York: Verso.

Zmora, Ohad, ed. 1967. *The Victory: The Six-Day War of 1967*. Tel Aviv: E. Lewin-Epstein.

Index

SERIES TITLE LIST

New Anthropologies of Europe
Daphne Berdahl, Matti Bunzl, and Michael Herzfeld, founding editors

Algeria in France: Transpolitics, Race, and Nation
Paul A. Silverstein

Locating Bourdieu
Deborah Reed-Danahay

Women's Health in Post-Soviet Russia: The Politics of Intervention
Michele Rivkin-Fish

Divided Cyprus: Modernity, History, and an Island in Conflict
Edited by Yiannis Papadakis, Nicos Peristianis, and Gisela Welz

Colonial Memory and Postcolonial Europe:
Maltese Settlers in Algeria and France
Andrea L. Smith

Empowering Women in Russia: Activism, Aid, and NGOs
Julie Hemment

Migrant Media: Turkish Broadcasting and Multicultural Politics in Berlin
Kira Kosnick

Getting By in Postsocialist Romania:
Labor, the Body, and Working-Class Culture
David A. Kideckel

Women's Social Activism in the New Ukraine:
Development and the Politics of Differentiation
Sarah D. Phillips

On the Social Life of Postsocialism: Memory, Consumption, Germany
Daphne Berdahl. Edited and with an introduction by Matti Bunzl

John Borneman is Professor of Anthropology at Princeton University. He has done fieldwork in Germany, Central Europe, Syria, and Lebanon and has published widely on issues of kinship, sexuality, nationality, justice, and political form. His books include *Belonging in the Two Berlins: Kin, State, Nation* and *Syrian Episodes: Sons, Fathers, and an Anthropologist in Aleppo.*